Rejoining the Common Reader

Also by Clara Claiborne Park

The Siege: The First Eight Years of an Autistic Child

You Are Not Alone: Understanding Mental Illness

Rejoining
The Common Reader

Essays, 1962–1990

Clara Claiborne Park

Northwestern University Press
Evanston, Illinois

Northwestern University Press
Evanston, Illinois 60201-2807

Copyright ©1991 by Northwestern University Press
All rights reserved. Published 1991
Printed in the United States of America

ISBN: cloth 0-8101-0977-8
        paper 0-8101-0991-3

Library of Congress Cataloging-in-Publication Data

Park, Clara Claiborne.
    Rejoining the common reader : essays, 1962–1990 / Clara Claiborne
Park.
        p. cm.
    ISBN 0-8101-0977-8. — ISBN 0-8101-0991-3 (pbk.)
    I. Title.
AC8.P28   1991
081–dc20   91-17272
                                                            CIP

The paper used in this publication meets the minimum requirements of American
National Standard for Information Sciences—Permanence of Paper for Printed
Library Materials, ANSI Z39.48-1984.

To David, Katharine, Rachel, Paul, and Jessica Park, from whom, severally and together, I have learned so much

Not only must art and life answer to each other, they must also accept blame for each other. The poet must remember that his poetry is guilty before the vulgar prose of life, and the human being should know that his undemandingness and the frivolity of his everyday questions are to blame for the barrenness of art. Personality must become responsible through and through. . . .

—Mikhail Bakhtin

Contents

Foreword

1

The author and I have been friends for half a century (which sounds more impressive than just "fifty years" would do), and at that distance it ought to be permissible to praise without the stigma of blurbing or burbling; for had we not respected and cared for each other's work, friendship alone could not have answered. So I am able to say straight out that hers is a beautiful and necessary book, and, having said, try to say why I think so.

For despite the pretentions of the mandates of Committees on Tenure and Promotion, despite the prose of Committees on The Curriculum and The Canon, it is remarkable that we know so little of how our colleagues teach. Not what they teach, for the college catalog will tell us that with about the ninety percent accuracy achieved each week by *TV Guide;* but how they teach; as Coleridge tells us, the ideas we think of are of altogether less import than the ideas we think with. And this book, its title acknowledging the good sense and humor of Samuel Johnson though with fewer of his magisterial certainties, gives us most valuable news of that.

Clara Claiborne Park (Clara to me) took to teaching only after raising the children (and there was a book about that, too), first at a community college and then at a more exalted institution; her observations of both, and of the likenesses and differences between them, are useful to have.

As to the likenesses first. Teaching undergraduates has ever been a kind of catch-as-catch-can business; readiness and range are more in demand than scholarly professionalism, theory, and the latest (soon to become the late) word. The pupils who arrive at the college without ever having heard of "symbolism" remain innocent for only a fortnight, after which they become so enthralled by (and expert at) "symbolism" that the idea of the literal ("he means exactly what he says") eludes them till near the end of the semester; Christ-symbolism being in the interval an especially marketable commodity.

The teacher of undergraduates will have to deal with whatever an inchoate and random-seeming authority sets down for him to teach in a given semester: Homer, Dante, Shakespeare, of course; Dostoevsky, Browning, Tolstoy and *The Lord of the Rings,* maybe; Ronald Firbank never. All the beginning teacher can be sure of is that what he knows professionally from his work on the dissertation will not be required of him ("He is our Aphra Behn man?").

As to the differences. In both the community college and the Ivy League there will be young persons of a certain cultivation, who have heard of J. Alfred Prufrock, and there will be young persons who haven't. In the community college, however, there is more likely to be a pupil who, as in Clara's favorite story, is able to wonder out loud about what is and isn't true. Clara's response, while no more satisfactory than any that might be made, dear reader, by thee and me, touches shrewdly on the life of our design: "I teach for that student, for inside every smart student there is, fortunately, a dumb one waiting to be liberated." The liberation, however, will be more difficult, and more necessary, in the Ivy League, where Derrida, Barthes, *e tutti quanti* offer possibilities of hermeneutic complication that make the seductions of Christ-symbolism look pale. Teachers, now as always, have their work cut out for them.

• 2

But if we have little impression of a direct sort about how our fellow teachers go about doing their work, we yet can identify the extremes, thus bracketing the target:

1. The "old way," as characterized by John Crowe Ransom: "'Open your books to page 50,' the professor would say. The professor . . . would read through the poem, gaze out the window for a silent moment, then say, 'Isn't that beautiful? Now turn to page 52.'" (Walter Sullivan, *Allen Tate: A Recollection*)

2. On the opening of Ezra Pound's *Cantos:* "And then went down to the ship, / Set keel to breakers, forth on the godly sea, and"—the commenter tells us that "An *and* repeating the Canto's initial *And* assures us of narrative energies still unexpended":—an

assurance doubly reassuring to the lay reader on line two of a volume occupying several hundred pages. Nor is that all: "Though the second half of the line moves more smoothly than the first—mimesis of the forward surge after launching—the line's movement does not run the words together because their junctured consonants serve to separate them. *Godly* does not sound godly, but sounds different from—clear and distinct from—*forth* and *sea*." (Hugh Kenner, *The Pound Era*)

Makes you want to divide authors into two camps and burn the camps.

I asked one of my best-ever graduate students what if anything my second instance might mean, and was answered gently but as from a great height: "It does mean something, Howard, but it would take a long time to explain to you."

All very well, but I see I have left Theory out of the account, so here is an instance of that, Umberto Eco in translation, explaining the difference between *langue* and *parole:*

3. "There is a signification system (and therefore a code) when there is the socially conventionalized possibility of generating sign functions. . . . There is on the contrary a communication process when the possibilities provided by a signification system are exploited in order to physically produce expression for many practical purposes." (quoted in William Ray, *Literary Meaning: From Phenomenology to Deconstruction*)

My definition of Deconstruction—pulling the rug out from under the figure in the carpet—might be supported by many examples, but after prolonged consideration I consider that the above may mean: 1. We have language, and—"on the contrary"? 2. We may use it.

3

The goddess Fashion is no doubt necessary, as her mother Fortuna was necessary, for things must either be made new or be made to appear so, a dispensation of Fate to keep the intelligent young fascinated enough to continue their studies even if the desirable result include such words as synchrony and diachrony (which Joyce named, in imitation of Hegel, the *Nacheinander* and the *Nebeneinander*), anciently known as Space and Time.

But against the background of new-fashioned vocabulary doing oldfangled ideas, even against the occasional new-seeming idea, Clara's essays look ever so good. You'll be aware that the following reasons are being given by an oldfangled teacher of undergraduates who teaches his graduate students exactly the same without their ever appearing to notice that they are with it while he isn't—well, here follow the following reasons.

She writes English, not English Department, and not the vast lexicon discharged through the great gut of Paris and the small gut of New Haven.

She remembers and acknowledges her own teachers; in the chapter on Werner Jaeger, John Arthos of Michigan and J. H. Finley of Harvard are also remembered.

She is memorably aphoristic: herewith a few instances.

"If you take it seriously, the absurdity of all human effort is a profoundly disturbing idea."

"We should prepare ourselves for the power that literature may have among students whom familiarity has not rendered immune to ideas found in books."

"How would we teach literature if we were in fact convinced that what we were doing could make a person different?" (Clara, I should be very frightened.)

(If the samples are all taken from chapter one, it's not that I didn't do my homework, but rather that I've been reading and re-reading from a loose-leaf typescript whose pages tend to be scattered, if not through the universe, at least around the table and sometimes the floor; and I look forward to seeing them bound in one book.)

Her range is very great, and consistently convincing from Dante and Shakespeare up through Jane Austen and Trollope and on to Richard Wilbur and James Merrill (whose difficult *Divine Comedies* I'll try again on her say-so though on my own I found them merely puzzling).

Her humor, like her learning, is quiet, but always there.

She is forgiving, both to Roland Barthes and to her freshmen, but free of the illusion that the forgiven will behave better therefor.

Her book has often reminded me of her namesake Clarissa, who begins Canto V of the *Rape of The Lock,* my own model for teaching, with excellent advice concerning good humor and good sense:

> What then remains but well our power to use,
> And keep good humour still whate'er we lose?

though ever reminded of the following line: "So spoke the Dame, but no applause ensued."

Reminds me too of Henry Adams's conclusion abut his teaching experience: "A teacher is expected to teach truth, and may perhaps flatter himself that he does so, if he stops with the alphabet or the multiplication table, as a mother teaches truth by making her child eat with a spoon; but morals are quite another truth, and philosophy is more complex still."

O yes, and I remember now that Alexander Pope modeled Clarissa's speech about beauty and merit on his own translation of Sarpedon's speech about courage and death in *Iliad* 12. Mortal stakes, as Clara says in her afterword: mortal stakes. And one more aphorism of hers to conclude the matter.

"The involuntary functioning of the English teacher as a mental health paraprofessional is only the extreme consequence of accepting the proposition that literature leads to life."

Salutations to a salutary and charming book reminding us that, whatever the fashion, what a long-dead schoolmate of ours called "the yes-they-are eternal verities" are with us still.

Howard Nemerov, November 1990

Preface

In 1925 Virginia Woolf collected her essays and reviews under the title *The Common Reader,* opening with a sentence from Johnson's life of Thomas Gray. After some rather dismissive criticism of Gray's other poems, the Doctor had been ready to praise. Of the *Elegy Written in a Country Churchyard* he wrote, "I rejoice to concur with the common reader; for by the common sense of readers, uncorrupted with literary prejudices, after all the refinements of subtilty and the dogmatism of learning, must be finally decided all claim to poetical honors."

Between ourselves and Woolf's evocation of past common sense stretch sixty-five years of literary scrutiny, years scarcely lacking in the refinements of subtilty and the dogmatism of learning. Perhaps we are ripe for a reappropriation of Johnson's magisterial judgment. So I borrow Woolf's opening, since I cannot better it.

Yet it was not from Virginia Woolf or Dr. Johnson that I learned to honor the common reader but from my students at Berkshire Community College. The title essay of this book belongs to them. Though I now teach in a different kind of college, it is less different than it seems, and I try not to forget what they taught me.

The earliest of these essays was written in the mid-1950s. I have not, however, placed it first. As I reread them, the essays seemed to talk among themselves in ways I had not anticipated, and a chronological order made less sense than one in which themes could develop, modulate, and—as themes do—repeat. I was tempted to get in on the dialogue with updates and asides, since the times change and we change with them, but I resisted as much as possible. Past and present also talk with, argue with, and sometimes correct each other. Except for a few excisions and minor changes in wording, the essays appear substantially as published. If I tell the same anecdote in three places, it is not by inadvertence. We all have our touchstones.

Every teacher owes more to others than she or he can possibly acknowledge. It is a pleasure to make even an incomplete listing of those who have contributed to my understanding, my knowledge, or the confidence without which these would have been of little use. Out of years of conversation and friendship, Monroe Engel suggested the essay that gives this book its theme, and made me believe I could write it. John Reichert, Lawrence and Suzanne Graver, Robert Bell, and the late Charles Samuels, my colleagues at Williams, gave me the academic opportunity and the encouragement without which much of the rest might have remained unwritten. As literary editor of *The Nation,* Elizabeth Pochoda played her part; so did Joseph Epstein at *The American Scholar,* and Paula Deitz and Frederick Morgan at *The Hudson Review.* Freeman Dyson and Gary Saul Morson have given me generous intellectual companionship, personal and epistolary, as have David Kramer and Eric Henry, once my students, now fellow laborers in our common vineyard. The essay on Roland Barthes profited from talks with Arthur Goldhammer and Jay Cantor, though neither need answer for any part of it.

My investigation of Shakespeare's treatment of mental illness benefits from the comprehensive scholarship of my daughter Katharine Park. She and her father, David Park, are the sources of most of what I seem to know about science, past and present. My son, Paul Park, who as a novelist has his own relation to the common reader, not only typed the manuscript but offered suggestions which, if I had been young enough to respond to them fully, would have made this a broader and more generous book.

And to Howard Nemerov, oldest of friends, who started me thinking about literature before I knew there was anything to do with it but read it, I owe a special kind of thanks. I'm grateful to all of these, and to others unnamed but unforgotten.

Yet one word more. Space, not inclination, dictated the omission of essays on Gwendolyn Brooks, Maxine Hong Kingston, Grace Paley, Salman Rushdie, and Richard Wilbur, requiring me to compress my appreciation into a single sentence. It's not enough.

C.C.P.

Williams College, September 1990

Acknowledgments

For permission to include essays originally published by them, some in slightly different form, grateful acknowledgment is made to the following.

"Rejoicing to Concur with the Common Reader," in *Harvard English Studies,* vol. 4, *Uses of Literature,* edited by Monroe Engel, Harvard University Press. Copyright © 1973 by the President and Fellows of Harvard College.

"The Mother of the Muses: In Praise of Memory," *The American Scholar* 50, no. 1 (Winter 1980–81): 55–71.

"At Home in History: Werner Jaeger's Padeia," *The American Scholar* 52, no. 3 (Summer 1983): 378–85.

"As We Like It: How a Girl Can Be Smart and Still Popular," *The American Scholar* 42, no. 2 (Spring 1973): 262–78.

"'Canst Thou Not Minister to a Mind Diseas'd?'" *The American Scholar* 56, no. 2 (Spring 1987): 219–34.

"No Time for Comedy," *The Hudson Review* 32, no. 2 (Summer 1979): 191–200.

"Trollope for Grown-ups," originally published as "Trollope and the Modern Reader," *The Massachusetts Review* 3, no. 3 (Spring 1962): 577–591.

"Henry Wilcox, Babbitt, and the State of Britain," *The Berkshire Review* 4, no. 1 (Spring 1968): 4–14.

"Recuperating Jane," originally published as "Recuperating Austen," *The Hudson Review* 42, no. 4 (Winter 1990): 643–50.

"Crippled Laughter: Toward Understanding Flannery O'Connor," *The American Scholar* 51, no. 2 (Spring 1982): 249–57.

"Merrill's Divine Comedies," originally published as "Dante on Water Street," *The Nation* 224, no. 6 (Feb. 12, 1977): 181–83, and "Where the Waste Land Ends," *The Nation* 230, no. 17 (May 3, 1980): 532–36. Copyright © 1977, 1980 by *The Nation* magazine/The Nation Company, Inc.

"Talking Back to the Speaker," *The Hudson Review* 42, no. 1 (Spring 1989): 21–44.

"Author! Author! Reconstructing Roland Barthes," *The Hudson Review* 43, no. 3 (Autumn 1990).

"Mortal Stakes," *Voice Literary Supplement* 68 (October 1988): 6.

For permission to use extended quotations from copyrighted works, grateful acknowledgment is made to the following publishers.

A Lover's Discourse by Roland Barthes, translated by Richard Howard. Translation copyright © 1978 by Hill & Wang, a division of Farrar, Straus & Giroux, Inc. Reprinted with the permission of the publisher.

The Pleasure of the Text by Roland Barthes, translated by Richard Miller. Translation copyright © 1975 by Hill & Wang, a division of Farrar, Straus & Giroux, Inc. Reprinted with the permission of the publisher.

Writing Degree Zero by Roland Barthes, translated by Annette Lavers and Colin Smith. Translation copyright © 1967 by Jonathan Cape Ltd. Reprinted with the permission of Hill & Wang, a division of Farrar, Straus & Giroux, Inc.

The Divine Comedy by Dante Alighieri, translated by John Ciardi. Copyright © 1954, 1957, 1959, 1960, 1961, 1965, 1967, 1970 by John Ciardi. Reprinted with the permission of W. W. Norton & Company, Inc.

The Iliad by Homer, translated by Richmond Lattimore. Copyright © 1951 by The University of Chicago. Reprinted with the permission of The University of Chicago.

The Changing Light at Sandover by James Merrill. Copyright © 1978 by James Merrill. Reprinted with the permission of James Merrill and Atheneum Publishers, an imprint of Macmillan Publishing Company.

Rejoicing to Concur with the Common Reader

As a general rule, people, even the wicked, are much more naive and simplehearted than we suppose. And we ourselves are too.
—Fyodor Dostoevsky, *The Brothers Karamazov*

Until I came to college there wasn't a lamp in the house you could read by.
—Community College sophomore

I first taught literature in a community college, in an old-fashioned great books course. Its reading list was frankly copied from that of a course at that time required of all sophomores at the University of Massachusetts. Our own college was only in its second year of operation, and it was both easy and helpful to suit our curriculum to the institution many of our students hoped to transfer to. Accordingly, I began with Homer, the Oedipus plays, the dialogues in which Plato tells of Socrates' trial and death. It was after this Greek exposure, while we were reading the *Inferno*, that an incident occurred which has come to embody for me the special quality of teaching literature in a community college.

The student was not one who talked readily in class, although he was not especially diffident. He was a well-set-up young man from a farm family who liked to hunt and who did his school work the best he could, which was not well. He expressed himself in short, simple units of meaning—some of them were sentences and some were not—and he could spell most of the words he knew. When he was assigned something to read, he slowly read it. One day he said something about it: "Mrs. Park. We've read what Homer says

1

about the afterlife, and what Plato says, and now we're reading what Dante says and they're all different. Mrs. Park. *Which of them is true?*"

I smile of course. I suppress, just in time, the condescending laugh, the easy play to the class's few sophisticates, who are already laughing surreptitiously. They are good students; they ask a lot of questions; I depend on them and they know it. They have reliable academic instincts, which are at the moment informing them that this is not one of the questions one asks. But the open seriousness on the boy's face encourages reflection. Who, in this class, is reading as Plato and Dante would have expected to be read? Who is asking the right questions, I and my sophisticates, or this D-level student whom I have just time to realize I shall put down at my peril? Did I really mean my students to assent to the proposition that nothing need be true where everything is interesting?

This experience could not have taken place in the college where I was an undergraduate. Such naïveté as surfaces in that kind of college is generally false. The real kind subsists, of course. But elite students hide it even from each other; they almost never expose it to their teachers. What I learned from teaching in a community college is this: that real naïveté is precious, and that it sets up changing expectations and changing opportunities for the teaching of literature.

Echoing in this incident are most of the things that make teaching in a community college different from teaching at Harvard. It is obvious that class background matters here, and that in most ways it is going to translate itself into what we advantaged ones call "cultural disadvantage." (Roughly two-thirds of our freshmen, categorized according to the usual sociological criteria, were working-class and lower-class; most of the rest were lower-middle-class.) It is obvious that the culturally disadvantaged will be culturally naive. It is obvious that the nonhomogeneity of the class, the presence of the few sophisticates, presents a complex situation, and perhaps it is obvious that it is a promising one. It is less obvious—until one has repeatedly experienced it, when it comes to seem self-evident—that the culturally naive have an intense interest in eschatology, in what Ivan Karamazov called "the eternal questions." It is less obvious that they—not all of them, but a surprising number—see their teacher as a wise person who can help them understand important things. It is perhaps least obvious that they should expect that literature can bring them important things, that what they read can matter in the way that other elements in their surroundings matter: that it can offer them something they can use. A simple assumption, simply made: that literature has uses, like other things in life. It is a loaded simplicity. One can almost imagine it turning cultural disadvantage to cultural advantage.

In graduate school I had a young professor—now a respected old one—who argued passionately against censorship. He did not argue that it was wrong (no doubt he took that for granted) but that it was unnecessary. Why should society censor literature, since literature did not influence action? Which of you, he asked his students, would actually go out and do something because of something you read? I remember feeling doubtful, but I do not recall that any of us objected.

It is probably clear that this discussion took place many years ago. The New Criticism was then in fact new, the work of art self-contained and sovereign, the artist's life and his intentions irrelevant, and the intentions and lives of us readers as well. The idea that literature affected action was represented by the crudities of the Soviet police and the remembered Nazis, and the unsophisticated directness of the Renaissance critics whom, as a matter of fact, we were then studying. They lived a long time ago, before the "rise of the historical attitude" and of that other convenient distancing mechanism, the minute concern with language. Ideas persist, however. Ellen Cantarow, in "The Radicalization of a Teacher of Literature," attributes a similar complex of attitudes to her professors:

> At Wellesley what I read moved me deeply; in so many words I was told that my feelings didn't matter, that it was "form" that did. What I read often moved me to reflect on my own experience; I was told essentially that literature was timeless, above the petty details of any one person's daily living. I loved literature; when I reached graduate school I was given to understand that loving literature had nothing to do with literary professionalism. I dimly felt that literature must give life

exaltation, specific moral sense; I was told that Western civilization dictated the values of pure form, of "universality."

Was it really that bad? Hard to believe; she can't have been taught
exclusively by mandarins. Nevertheless, a 1971 Harvard Ph.D. experienced seven years of some of the finest English teaching in the
country and came out feeling like that. Is it possible that she would
have been better off had she started out in a community college?
There the simplicity of our students, combined with our own survival instincts, must contradict each of these assumptions. Years
before we began hearing from blacks and movement theorists, our
students had instructed us: literature has uses, uses that are at the
heart of its interest and excitement.

   They did not teach us that it has revolutionary uses. That will
not surprise anyone who has had experience of students from the
lower- and lower-middle class. Revolutionary ideas are abstractions,
and the attitude that has brought most of these students to sit in our
classrooms is not abstract; it is, rather, "What's in this for me?"
Literature, for them, will offer understanding of personal processes
and events before it offers involvement in society or rebellion against
it. Teaching in a community college can be peculiarly discouraging
to the radical teacher who, if he is sensitive, becomes aware that he is
listening to his own voice rather than his students' and pulling them
in a direction they do not wish to go. The uses of literature are for
them, as they were for Cantarow before she was radicalized, primarily personal.

   The directness of its personal application can be disconcerting
as well as instructive. After the publication of *The Sorrows of Young
Werther* there was a wave of suicides; that is one of the curiosities of
literary history that one knows without believing it. We do not take
these deaths into any real account when we hear about them in our
course, "The Romantic Movement": they are felt as somewhat
ridiculous, if they are felt at all—as unconvincing as the suicides in
Zuleika Dobson. What shouldn't have occurred can't have. Contemporary distancing mechanisms work better than that; contemporary
readers know the difference between life and literature.

   Yet in my community college, within a fortnight of finishing

The Myth of Sisyphus, the finale to a rather dryly taught introductory philosophy course, one very capable student passed in a blank final, two dropped out of school, and one attempted suicide, accounting for 25 percent of the total class enrollment. If you take it seriously, the absurdity of all human effort is a profoundly disturbing idea. The moral of this is not, I suppose, that we should drop Camus from the reading list and substitute Bill Haywood's autobiography, which though more optimistic seems to have bored Ms. Cantarow's students, but that we should prepare ourselves for the power that literature may have among students whom familiarity has not rendered immune to ideas found in books.

How would we teach literature if we were in fact convinced not only that for one reason or another it matters in our own lives, the lives of a highly educated elite, but that it can matter in the lives of students? Most of the changing functions of literature in mass education follow from this question. If new claims are made on literature in a community college, they are new only in the sense that they are made by, or on behalf of, a population who before this made few claims on literature at all. In fact, these claims are very old, so old that perhaps it is time to recognize that disuse has made them new again. What the culturally disadvantaged expect of literature, when they expect anything at all, is very like what the culturally advantaged used to expect in the days of Sidney and Johnson and Arnold, and learned to stop expecting only in the very recent past. Unself-conscious and old-fashioned readers, they expect "just representations of general nature" that will help them understand their own lives and the world more truly.

It is easy to romanticize the community college student. I can already feel my tone turning Wordsworthian, with a corresponding loss in credibility. A class at a community college does not, of course, consist entirely or even preponderantly of students to whom literature matters. Many have never thought about literature at all, have read only what they were forced to in high school, hear rock music but don't listen to the words. Most of them have come to college expecting that what goes on there will help them to get a better job than they would otherwise. They are for the most part willing to believe that the English requirement will contribute to this end.

Reading and writing may be unpracticed activities, but they are what you do in school, and for the first time these students are in school because they've chosen to come. If they don't like it they'll drop out; they haven't come to rebel, or question fundamentally the value of education, which, like literature, is an abstraction of a kind they don't think about. But they will impose their assumptions, which in their simplicity have a certain self-fulfilling quality: since these students are here because they think something's in it for them, literature rises—or sinks—to the occasion.

It is hardly necessary to state that the community college is not an English teacher's paradise and would not be even if pay scales, course loads, student-teacher ratios, and fringe benefits were comparable to those at good four-year colleges. The opportunities afforded by working with students new to literature are balanced by frustrations. Simplicity is, if not always, often the more attractive face of what it is hard not to call stupidity, although we who are involved in mass education commonly find gentler words. There are plenty of times when our students' limitations make us feel we have spent the day being nibbled to death by ducks. In brief, we teach literature to students whose CEEB verbals range from 300 all the way up, but which cluster between 400 and 500. Any one of us is capable of writing an essay on the deceptiveness of board scores, embellished with an impressive group of sketches from life. Nevertheless, college board verbals reliably predict a number of discouraging facts: that a large, though variable, number of our students will read slowly and inaccurately; that their writing will be labored, crude, and incorrect; and that without our help, and probably even with it, they will neither make nor understand the distinctions and freighted allusions which are the life of language. They are aware of few of the public events of the present or the past. Their interests are narrow, although if it is opportunity and not choice which has narrowed them, they may broaden with a rapidity that astonishes the teacher and may terrify the student, who feels himself changing into someone he can hardly recognize.

For community college students have a final handicap, which both measures their receptivity and checks it: for them education is a perilous undertaking. It will not, as it does for second-generation college students, confirm them in the assured performance of roles they know and understand. It will act to change them and thus to separate them from the life in which they have been at home.

It is exactly those to whom the new experiences mean most who are most vulnerable to what is happening to them and most aware of what they have to lose. Marjorie Fallows, while teaching sociology at my college, collected a number of statements of such students, "threatened," in her words, "by the loss of the familiar without having acquired the confidence that they can adapt to the unfamiliar." "I didn't have any idea college was going to be like this. I thought you just went to college and stayed the same, except for having a diploma, but it wrenches you away from a lot of familiar things and people." Or, "I wish I could talk with my parents about what I'm doing in college. Perhaps they're not interested, but it's more like they're afraid of what I'm learning. They have a pretty rigid view of the world, and they aren't articulate. So we don't talk, because it would end up in a fight or in somebody's being hurt. Some of the kids have had to break completely with their parents but I'm trying not to do that. I still love them, even though I don't want to be like them." Or, "My back is to the wall and I'm scared because I'm out of my depth, and not just academically. This is a whole new world for me. I don't talk the same language, even. I was top in my class in vocational high school, and I think I'm bright enough to have done college work, but something's getting in the way. I don't belong. If I'm not in class some day, you'll know I couldn't take it any longer."

These people know something is happening to them. They are changing so fast it hurts, like the growth that Günter Grass's Tin Drummer experienced as his midget's body wrenched its way into maturity. Some of them flee the experience and drop back into the familiar—the attrition rate at community colleges is very large. But many will see it through and allow themselves to become different people.

How would we teach literature if we were in fact convinced that what we were doing could make a person different? Most of us do believe, I think, that education changes people, although we believe it with that kind of sickly hesitance we accord to ideas we want so much to be true that we feel we must consider them false. Such compulsive cynicism is shaken again and again in a community college. By the time a dozen human lives have taken right-angle turns before your eyes, you begin to believe your job is worth doing. Where you are, hope has been institutionalized. Being at this college can make all the difference to this student. Not that we don't think, say, Harvard makes a difference. But behind this conviction is the consciousness that if it hadn't been Harvard it would have been Amherst, and if it hadn't been Amherst it would have been Williams or Reed or Carleton or a state university, and that though each of these would have moved us differently, we would have gone on to a life in which approximately the same set of possibilities lay open. The community college alters possibilities—not only the objective options before a student, but his whole sense of what is possible for him. His life will be spent differently because he happened to come to college.

"Happened" is the word; adventitiousness is the point. For this population, coming to college is not inevitable, it is a function of cheapness, nearness, convenience, unimpressiveness—qualities that add up to physical, economic, but above all emotional availability. A student comes in from a thin Irish welfare childhood, from vocational school and the service; he hopes to rise to be a salesman. Silent and invisible in the back rows of his classes, he begins to metamorphose. For months, only the librarian notices him, sitting in the library reading *Masterplots*. Too diffident to consult his teachers on how to nurture his new excitement, he seeks out his own ways of catching up, surfacing a year later transformed from a marginal to an exceptional student—of, of all things, literature. But changed possibilities need not be measured by higher degrees and intellectual values. (This man took an M.A. at the University of Illinois and became an editor.) Another student comes in expecting to follow an admired father into the roofing business. What he learns wrenches daily his acceptance of Archie Bunker's values. He goes exploring at the University of Massachusetts, passes beyond irritation and contempt to understand his father more fully, graduates, to return home to the roofing business, but with three cartons of books and a mind enlarged and excited so that he can follow it as a respected occupation, not resent it as a prison.

Such capsule histories, though accurate, betray the rich particularity of these students' lives, and thus their quality of miracle. In the community college we assist continually at such miracles (whether we assist in the French or the English sense one never knows). I could fill this essay with such accounts, most of them less credible than these two, which were chosen particularly because neither of these students seemed in any way distinguished when we first encountered him.*

The needs of people like this affect how we use literature, when we find out how deeply they are going to use it. "I must have read that poem fifty times," the first student told me. "I *am* J. Alfred Prufrock." And Eliot's image of inadequacy and isolation stayed with him, to help him confront and surmount his own. The second student *was* Achilles—or whatever splendid image of self-destructive pride we happened to be studying. Achilles was right to stand up for his honor and his prize, for what he'd earned and had coming to him. Archie Bunker knows that. But he was wrong, too, and he found that out by suffering. It's a complex world we have to live in.

What are teachers to do with this realization, at first resisted as arrogant and rejected as incredible, that they participate in a process that changes lives? How come to terms with this new role: that of persons of influence, whose students will take seriously not only what we have told them to read but what we say about it, and about them? "Nobody expected me to go to college, and I didn't expect to go. Then the community college opened up and about five of us began tossing around the idea of whether to go or not. We finally flipped a coin. It was college or the service. College won out, but we expected to flunk out pretty quick. All my friends did flunk out. I'm

---

*It is less misleading than it appears to talk of students who go on to four-year institutions after the community college's two years. Of those who finish the two-year course at our college, about two-thirds transfer, some to elite colleges they would not otherwise have reached. The ranking graduate of Amherst's class of 1972 had transferred from Berkshire Community College; he is now a professor of Chinese at a well-known university.

the only one left. But something happened to me here. One of my teachers wrote on a paper, 'You have a good clear mind—use it!' It made me sit back and think."

Given such students, then, what and how do we teach? But things are more complicated than that. We are not simply given such students. We are given many such. Yet a community college is not more homogeneous than the Ivy League but less so. Students at my community college are mostly white, mostly young, mostly conservative though mostly Democratic, mostly Irish, Italian, Polish, or French Canadian, if they come from the city, mostly Wasp if they come from the hills about, in which case they aren't very Waspish.* Most share the values that are commonly traduced by the term "Middle American." Yet the class profile is characterized by the obtrusiveness of its variations from this norm, in age, in intelligence, in social and cultural background. Many of our most rewarding students are people who have returned in middle life to enjoy the education that has suddenly become available within commuting distance. Most of these, though not all, are women; they include ex-salesgirls, ex-secretaries, and executives' wives who married young. Among the working-class students, most commonly the ex-servicemen, are autodidacts whose commitment to high culture is more intense than their teachers' and who press us for classical languages and Pound. There are failed preppies and dropouts from prestige colleges. There are even ordinary, capable high school graduates. Such students contribute a rich variety of assumptions and experience; what do they need from us, and what can they use from literature? They would seem to have little in common; but there is one characteristic they share: a near-crippling sense of inadequacy. We have few confident students. That the "below average" will come in with a sense of failure is obvious (the Illinois M.A. was one of these). But even the "average" have no high opinion of themselves.

---

*Leonard Kriegel's "When Blue-Collar Students Go to College" (*Saturday Review, July 22, 1972*) gives an excellent picture of our students. His experience is based on Brooklyn, while mine is of a small-city college drawing from a large rural area. It doesn't seem to matter.

Progressive admissions deans may remind us that the 500 college board score is set to predict the capacity to do college work, but these students have had to do not with progressive admissions deans (who in any case would overlook their undistinguished scores only for unusual reasons), but with a high school milieu in which kids with 600s can complain that they are not good enough for a good college. Few of these average students have been treated in school as if they were either interesting or important. The older students fear they have lost whatever academic ability they had and can never compete with "all these bright young minds," while the autodidacts and the conspicuously talented are, paradoxically, the most uncertain of all.

Of course, we can only grope to meet these needs. From some, one accepts the imprecise answer, encourages the vague adumbration. For others, the relaxation of standards confirms their own self-doubt, and what they most need is that insistence on excellence which testifies to intellectual respect. What all need is continuing support for that sense of possibility which their life histories have not nourished.

It is all very personal—their relationship to us, ours to them, both of ours to literature. I can write case histories because I know what happens to my students after they leave, and I know because they come back, or write, and tell me. I learn about them through how they respond to what they read, and how they respond teaches me new things about literature. An intelligent and perceptive student of mine titled her paper on the *Odyssey* "Telemachus and My Boy Friend." The teacher who finds this intrinsically ludicrous will be out of place in a community college. He may comfort himself with irony and steady his nerves with putdowns, but to no avail. None of us can beat it; most of us join it. When we do, we find our understanding enriched, as we learn from our students to read Homer as the Greeks did, as a paradigm of human experience. "Soldiers shall never spend their idle hours more profitably than with his studious and industrious perusal. . . . Counsellors have never better oracles than his lines: fathers have no morals so profitable for their children as his counsels . . . husbands, wives, lovers, friends, and allies having in him mirrors for all their duties." The Greeks and the Elizabethans, who were not stupider than ourselves: so Chapman, in his preface to Homer.

We in the community college have little choice but to emulate that antique simplicity. We hold on to subtlety, or try to, to precision, to elegance, to linguistic astonishment. We can never predict which students may unexpectedly be ready to respond to language and to form. These, too, are necessary to survival, for our own sakes and because the autodidacts and prestige dropouts, out to prove themselves superior to their surroundings, will not be easy on a teacher they feel is talking down to them or who has the misfortune to be slower than they. But not all literary virtues need be displayed with equal prominence. Our students can use synthesis better than analysis—or rather, all close reading must be clearly in the service of synthesis. (Ponder this comment: "I really enjoyed listening to you tear those poems to pieces." That was an analysis that succeeded.)

The praise of simplicity may even expand to include the praise of superficiality; it is Goethe who reminds us that art deals with life's surfaces. A simple insistence on the importance of what happens, of event and character, is not only reassuring to weak students, but one of the most valuable things we can give our intellectual elite, who tend to try to prove their status by interpretive ingenuity. Consider Eric Bentley's warning: "In principle the drama presents human relationships—the things men do to each other—and nothing else. Other things are not presented on stage, but if 'there' at all, are merely implied. In *King Lear,* much is *implied* about Nature and the gods, but *presented* on stage are a king and his subjects, a father and his children. Dramatic criticism emphasizes the implications at its peril. Had those been the writer's chief interest, he would not have chosen the dramatic form." Accepting this, we will have more patience with students who have difficulty dealing with abstractions. Reading for the human event will get us further than reading for Significance or Symbol, in the community college, and perhaps elsewhere. The realm of Minute Particulars, where our students are at home, is the realm of the imagination.

Saul Bellow suggests that "deep reading . . . has become dangerous to literature. . . . Things are not what they seem. . . . Coal holes represent the Underworld. Soda Crackers are the Host. . . . The busy mind can hardly miss at this game, and every player is a winner. Does Bloom dust Stephen's clothes, and brush off the wood shavings? They are no ordinary shavings, but the shavings from Stephen's cross. . . . Is modern literature Scripture? Is criticism Talmud, theology? . . . Let the soda crackers be soda crackers and the wood shavings, wood shavings. They are mysterious enough as it is." Bellow complains that "It's hard in our time to be as innocent as one would like." Teaching in a community college helps a great deal.

Simplicity need not mean narrowness. The work of art leads out from its personal meanings, from "Telemachus and My Boy Friend" to the great theme of growth and initiation. Abstractions are neither inaccessible nor uninteresting when they inhere in the human event.* Through Hamlet and Edmund students can *feel* that new philosophy calls all in doubt, even if they don't *know* it. I was teaching *Dr. Faustus* the day the astronauts first went up. We had just read, "But his dominion that exceeds in this / Stretches as far as does the mind of man." That class was not mired in the particular; we felt the winds of the Renaissance blowing. What had changed since Dante, so that the devil and not God now offered knowledge? Why was he now an interesting and sympathetic companion, when Dante had found him less worth talking to than the most ordinary Florentine in Hell? Is knowledge good in itself? Why might it be forbidden? Have we a right or a duty to follow it wherever it leads? "A sound magician is a mighty god"; how do men play god? Marlowe damns Faustus; should he? Should space be explored, life created in the laboratory?

Our students have not gone stale on the eternal questions. They will wrangle for hours over the tension between God's fore-knowledge and man's free will, as *Paradise Lost* takes on an immediacy I never suspected when I was studying for my comprehensives. Teaching them, we practice perforce what George Steiner calls "the old criticism," as we try to convey the warmth of ideas, the

---

*The uses of literature in the community college are not confined, of course, to English courses. Fiction is prominent on sociology and psychology reading lists.

ways in which they inform personality and are formed by it. "Engendered in admiration," concerned with moral purpose, "above all philosophical in range and temper," the job of the old criticism is (here Steiner quotes R. P. Blackmur) "putting the audience into a responsive relationship with the work of art . . . the job of the intermediary." And Steiner's summation is a guideline for teaching in a community college: "Not to judge or to anatomize, but to mediate." What works in a community college—and the word *work* should make us think of yeast as well as of successful operation—is what Alfred Harbage sees in Shakespeare crossing every frontier: "The pervasive tone of human solicitude."

Harbage was discussing the attraction of Shakespeare for non-English-speaking readers; Steiner was beginning a book on two authors he could read only in translation, conscious that the play of their language was closed to him and yet that they still filled him with things he needed to say. A teacher new to us and fresh from a good Ph.D. program remarked that he'd never before seen teachers enthusiastic about a humanities course; didn't we feel that the fact of translation hampered our resources? These reflections lead to a principle which most of us will accept only with pain: to the degree that the meaning of a work inheres so tightly in the language that it would not survive translation, that text will not work in the usual community college class. That is what those low board scores *mean*. Many of our students cannot read a complex text with comprehension unless they look up more words than most of us have to when we read French—only they think they know their own language and are not at home with dictionaries. They are not sure enough of denotation, let alone connotation, to pick up verbal irony. They have trouble pronouncing long words or finding their way through complicated sentences, though they will respond to eloquence if well mediated—that is, read well aloud. Their weaknesses, and strengths, call for some redefinition of what is difficult reading. Jane Austen and Henry James are harder than Milton or Goethe.

Language and class combine to make this true. I taught *Emma* that first year, blindly following the university's reading list for Masterpieces of Western Lit. For the first time, protests surfaced:

why are we reading *this?* They had just finished *Faust* without complaining. But *Faust,* and *Lear,* and *Paradise Lost* had not excluded them as *Emma* did, where every character in whose life they were expected to interest themselves was a person for whom they could guess that they and theirs would not have existed even as fully as one of Shakespeare's clowns.

In order to teach Jane Austen or Henry James successfully, one would have to mediate a whole class system. Asked to name his "least favorite successful writer," Anthony Burgess named E. M. Forster. "People like Virginia Woolf and E. M. Forster belong to a kind of society which I can't understand, I can't possibly touch, and fundamentally loathe. I find it makes my flesh creep to even consider touching any member of that class. It's as physical as that. I can't help it, can't justify it, but there it is; it's just another world." Our students, less self-confident and in a society less savagely class-ridden, are more tolerant. They just "can't relate." Of course they can't. Would we give *Howards End* to Leonard Bast?

Yet—taking plenty of time—I have taught *A Passage to India* with success. And this tells us something not entirely obvious about the uses of literature in the community college: the faraway, like the long ago, may be easier, not harder, to relate to. Where differences in manners are extreme they can be confronted and recognized, leaving the attention free for deeper similarities. Remoteness in space and time need not confer emotional distance. Where all seems strange, accidents of manner subside into place. Our students may dismiss *Emma* as a snob and miss the touching vulnerability of Salinger's Esmé, but no one dismisses Antigone, though she is a king's daughter. They will identify with King Oedipus and Prince Hamlet. If they are not hurried or badgered with information on epic conventions, they will recognize in Hector not the aristocratic warrior of a legend they didn't know existed, but a steadfast exponent of middle-American values such as the literature of their own time refuses to accord them, a responsible citizen who loves his wife and baby and who fights when his country asks him to, even when he knows it's wrong. Which is to suggest that truisms about beginning with the students' own experience can be easily misapplied. Most of the books we call "great"—in a phrase more dated even than "the New Criticism"—are less bewildering to the average community college student than *Naked Lunch* or *Armies of the Night*.

This is, perhaps, no more than to say that old-fashioned readers respond to old-fashioned books. And immersion in the old-fashioned encourages old-fashioned pronouncements; as one of my students once told me, we read the classics for their universality and because they have stood the test of time. In the community college they are one solution (only one) to the problems posed by class variety. Great books, as I found out one by one, teaching that first, arbitrary list, are gut books, perennial archetypes of human effort and desire, survivors that have offered something for everybody. One student tells another, "You wouldn't *believe* what happens to that guy Oedipus." Another takes his *Odyssey* home, and his father, just retired off the assembly line, finds it the best story he's ever read. The *Iliad*, that morally and emotionally most complex of works, has a special intelligibility for athletes and Vietnam veterans. Dante holds the class elite; they respond to the ordered beauty of his passionate vision, they are interested in Medieval and Renaissance attitudes, they are satisfied to be reading a classic. They may also learn something from the simple souls who can entertain the possibility that what he says is true.

There will be no Brechtian distancing in the classroom; students transparently identify with what they read. When they can recognize themselves in a character, class and language hinder no longer. Esmé and Emma may be dismissed, but identification with Prufrock can be so strong among lower-class students as to cause a problem in interpretation: they may argue, on the strength of the one-night cheap hotels, that Prufrock's elegant attire is all a charade and that he is a social as well as an emotional outsider. Identification can make Joyce and Milton accessible. I took over *Portrait of the Artist* for that first reading list before I had reread it, and when I did I was appalled at what I had done. How could I expect insecure students, many of them of marginal competence, to sympathize with this arrogant young intellectual, hermetically sealed inside his egotism, his mind full of words they wouldn't recognize and allusions they would never trace? But they did: they were Catholic (or had been), ethnic, young, self-centered—if not all of them all of these, still enough. They understood the book much better than I had at their age. They helped me read it better, too; their sympathy taught me a little mercy.

Other surprises cause us to reevaluate our ideas of literary relevance. Oedipus's is an archetypal predicament (though our students perceive Sophocles' archetype, not Freud's). Bartleby, like Prufrock, hits home. But who could have predicted the pull of Milton's Satan? Yet when one of my apparently most impervious students came in at last to talk, it was because after days of Satan in his pride, we had come to the place in Book 4 where the sight of Adam and Eve "imparadis'd in one another's arms" strips him emotionally naked, to see "undelighted all delight." "I feel like that," said this student. "It's like I was sitting on the top floor of a house" (students often translate a poet's image into their own; I feel less confident than I used to about stopping them) "and I'm looking out and there's this bunch of children playing, and I can't feel anything at all."

This student was brilliant and deeply disturbed; two years later he was diagnosed as schizophrenic. But the next year the same passage brought in a student neither brilliant nor crazy, just conscious of a split between home and the future, who found that Milton's ambivalence toward an angel's rebellion expressed his own awareness of what it cost to challenge values that were still part of him. Our students know better than those more privileged that life pulls in contradictory ways. Though the poverty of their linguistic means makes verbal irony inaccessible to most of them, they can respond perceptively and intensely to ambiguities of content.

From such relevatory encounters we learn new powers of the works we teach. We may shy away from this particular use of literature, as a diagnostic indicator of psychic turbulence. But it is thrust upon us. We can hardly be unaware that literature can bring the hidden to light; gut books expose the guts. When this happens students look for somebody to talk to. If their approach to literature is personal, and ours has reflected it, they are likely to end up talking to us. They have a lot to talk about. The strains of social mobility are an evident source of distress, but there are many others. The conspicuously talented show the most signs of psychic tension. For the

truly gifted, the community college has functioned as a kind of
sieve, selecting those and only those who are in some sort of need.
Our society is open enough, as most European societies are not, so
that a brilliant person who has handled his life sensibly rarely ends
up in a third-rate educational institution. Accordingly, when a fine
mind turns up in one of our classes it is usually after a series of
emotional shipwrecks and disastrous choices that have left him as
much in need of support as the most marginal academic loser.

The involuntary functioning of the English teacher as a mental
health paraprofessional is only the extreme consequence of accepting the proposition that literature leads to life. Taking literature
personally means teaching personally, and if you do that, the problem—quite insoluble—becomes simply where to stop. Community
college students need their teachers even more than students do
elsewhere. A commuting college cuts out the usual opportunities
for bull sessions, particularly since most community college students
have jobs. A two-year college with a large enrollment is hard to make
friends in. It is harder still for the gifted, who are thinly spread;
unless the teacher becomes a kind of matchmaker, they may never
find each other. So the English teacher, who has been encouraging
genuineness of response since the first papers in freshman composition, reaps the predictable harvest. When the student needs a friend,
a mentor, a guru, an example of a newly conceivable life-style, the
English teacher is on hand. He's in a false position, granted; he
never prepared for this in graduate school. He can decline the
honor. But if he accepts it—well, we are back where we started, in
arrogance and terror, accepting the responsibility of making a difference to somebody's life. Such experiences make a difference to
one's own.

That sentence sounds like the end. Yet I am driven to say more
about the exceptions, who need mediation less and friendship
more. One of them reads Wittgenstein and introduces me to San-
tayana. One memorizes all thirty-two Beethoven sonatas. One
brushes up his Latin by reading Gauss. I want to tell their preposterous, unimaginable stories. That I should need so much to
bring them in shows I have not told the whole truth. I have made
our work sound too satisfying and ourselves too satisfied, and I have

not shown how often we fail. We react with irritation to our students and ourselves, with frustration at being able to teach only a little of what we know, with rage at the ignorance that meets us daily, the stubbornness, the laziness, the times when the response is beside the point or there is no response at all. So, isolated, we return to the exceptions in their isolation, with whom we have a symbiotic relationship of desperate mutual need. With them, the uses of literature are no different from what they are in any other college. Only, of course, they are, for in another college we could do without each other. For them, on stolen and uncompensated time, with corresponding intensity, we teach according to their needs and ours. Spenserian allegory, Victorian poetry, *Ulysses,* Greek—the list is as unpredictable as they are. Intellectual history is important to them; so are words. With them we can study "that absolute correspondence of the term to its import" which Pater says is the condition of all good art, and feel that we are really teaching literature. But if we push through to the end of the "Essay on Style," that most elegant articulation of the claims of form, we may be startled to find that there, of all places, the claims of substance are reestablished: "Given the conditions I have tried to explain as constituting good art;—then, if it be devoted further to the increase of men's happiness, to the redemption of the oppressed, or the enlargement of our sympathies with each other, or to such presentment of new or old truth about ourselves and our relation to the world as may ennoble and fortify us in our sojourn here, or immediately, as with Dante, to the glory of God, it will also be great art." Great art or not, that's the kind of thing we can use in the community college. At which point the claims of the exceptional and of the merely human come back together and we are back in the classroom, making the best of things, trying to use literature simply but not stupidly, rejoicing to concur with the common reader.

From *Harvard English Studies 4: Uses of Literature,* ed. Monroe Engel (Cambridge, Mass.: Harvard University Press, 1973).

The Mother of the Muses:
In Praise of Memory

Sing, goddess, the anger of Peleus' son Achilles . . .

Tell me, Muse, of the man of many turnings . . .

Yours am I, holy Muses, Calliope, rise . . .

Of man's first disobedience, and the fruit
Of that forbidden tree, whose mortal taste
Brought death into the world, and all our woe.
With loss of Eden, till one greater man
Restore us, and regain the blissful seat.
Sing, Heav'nly Muse . . .

                            & THERE ARE GOLDEN
CONTAINERS LABELED CLIO ERATO CALLIOPE
& OF THESE 9 WE KNOW ONLY THE RUSHING OF THEIR WINGS . . .

T he Muses, these goddesses who span so many centuries, whose presence, real or allegorical, has carried meaning for so many poets, who survive in our own mouths whenever we say "music"—who are they? Hesiod begins his account of the genesis of the gods by showing the Muses dancing with soft feet by a spring of violet water, then rising in mist to walk in the night, singing. They are indeed a seductively lovely assembly, if we ignore the forbidding classical polysyllables and listen to their names with a Greek ear. Calliope of the beautiful voice, Euterpe in whom we well delight, Erato the desirable, Melpomene who sings and dances, Thalia the blooming, Terpsichore who delights in the dance, Polyhymnia of the many songs, Clio the glory giver, Urania the heavenly. Who are these lovely ladies, or—since we no longer so easily personify the forces that are important to us—what are they? What are Homer and Hesiod talking about, and Dante and Milton, and James Merrill in a poem no older than yesterday? For whatever we may think about Homer and Hesiod, we know quite well that Dante and Milton and Merrill do not believe in the literal reality of the heavenly Nine. And yet if we are sensitive to when a poet's words grow warm with meaning, we know just as well that they do not invoke the Muses for mere decoration. The important place given these invocations confirms the message of the words and rhythms. To call on the Muses is a way of talking about what are, if not actual presences, still realities which poets take utterly seriously—as must many of us who have found words taking shape in our heads, and wondered where on earth (on earth?) they were coming from.

What do the Muses do? Milton continues:

> . . . Sing, Heav'nly Muse, that on the secret top
> Of Oreb, or of Sinai, didst *inspire*
> That shepherd who first taught the chosen seed . . .

They sing and they *inspire*. And most of us would agree that if they mean anything at all, the Muses are a way of talking about what we call Inspiration. For want of a better word. And when we are impelled into reaching for abstractions "for want of a better word" so we can name forces we don't understand, we would do well to wonder if what the Greeks would have called a god is hovering in the offing, and if we can explain what we are talking about any better than they did.

Or perhaps there is a better word—we could use the twentieth-century name for Inspiration: Creativity. We are just as interested in Creativity as Homer and Dante and Milton were in the Muses. "Inspiration" sounds old-fashioned, but psychological studies are made, tests are devised, books are written on Creativity. Advertising agencies have Creative Directors. Invisible as she is, Creativity must be real.

So let's strip off their gauzy robes down to the bare abstraction and say that the Muses represent Inspiration or Creativity. And then let's robe them again and recall that Hesiod gave them a parentage, as was his habit when seeking to explain his world. They are the daughters of almighty Zeus, father of gods and men, and—who? What goddess is powerful enough, full enough, fecund enough to give birth to the Muses—to music and dance and poetry and drama, to history and astronomy, even to the eloquence that a ruler needs so sorely in order to govern and that our own rulers so sorely lack? The

Muses, for Hesiod, inspire all those arts of communication that inform, delight, civilize, and link us with the past and with our fellows. *And the Muses are the daughters of Mnemosyne, Memory.* It is my antique conviction that the Greeks knew what they were talking about, that to make the Muses the daughters of Memory is to express a fundamental perception of the way in which Creativity operates.

Yet it doesn't suit us at all. Heirs of the Romantics whether we know it or not, we are more likely to think of Memory and Inspiration as enemies than as mother and daughter. Blake, for instance— in the same long poem in which he called for his bow of burning gold to build Jerusalem in England—proclaimed a new age in which "the daughters of Memory" (and of course he knew quite well they were the Muses) "shall become the daughters of Inspiration." For Blake, out of Memory could come only a cold and abstract art: "Mathematic," not "Living Form." And hordes of us agree. We ask ourselves, and our children, to remember nothing these days: not the multiplication table, for we have calculators; not the presidents or the periodic table or the great dates of history; not 1066, not 1453, not 1517, not 1789, not even, perhaps, 1914 and 1917 and 1939. We may make an exception for things we really care about— baseball statistics, for instance. The educated man, however, need not burden his memory. He has learned how to look things up. And if we do not expect to remember facts, which after all, we respect, we certainly do not expect to remember those rhythmic evocations of meaning that we call poetry.

In fact, over the years I have noticed a curious transmogrification in the spelling of the word *memory.* It now begins with an R, and it is pronounced "rotememory"—one word. Students say it that way, but not students only. One college president, talking to a *Times* reporter, called rotelearning, memorization, "the lowest form of human intellectual activity." All of us resist the work of memory, which holds so large a place in the educational practice of so many cultures and until only yesterday held so large a place in our own. We have come a long way from Hesiod's Muses; from Saint Thomas Aquinas and Albertus Magnus, for whom the cultivation of Memory was part of Prudence, one of the four cardinal virtues; from the elaborate Renaissance methods of memory training; even from the illiterate Vermont countryman of a hundred years ago who took the orders of isolated farm wives on back country roads and brought back from town unerringly the three spools of thread, the packet of embroidery needles, the pound of tea. Memory now is the marker of outmoded and sterile education. What is important, after all? Not, surely, meaningless cultural facts, still less the great stories of the past or the great weighted sentences and phrases. What is important is to *learn to think*. As for carrying around something in your head to think *about,* to think *with,* a range of language to think and speak *in*—well, what we learn today will be obsolete tomorrow; nobody can hope to keep up with the present explosion of knowledge; the task of education is not to teach us to hold on to the old stuff but to adapt to the new. And the prophecy fulfills itself as our educational practice changes to reflect our convictions. Papers substitute for examinations; exam questions are given out in advance; exams are written at home; teachers discover that they can grade their students just as readily if they give no exams at all. We license ourselves to forget. Who needs memory? Those who live by the word—politicians, commentators, TV ministers, professors—speak from prompt boards or read their texts.

But the Muses are the daughters of Memory. Hear Homer, as he prepares to sing that curious catalogue of ships in the second book of the *Iliad*—261 long lines crammed with 509 discrete facts which in a nonliterate culture he had no way of looking up:

> Tell me now, you Muses who have your homes on Olympos,
> for you, who are goddesses, are there and you know all
>   things,
> and we have heard only the rumour of it and know nothing.
> Who then of those were the chief men and lords of the
>   Danaans?
> I could not tell over the multitude of them nor name them,
> not if I had ten tongues and ten mouths, not if I had
> a voice never to be broken and a heart of bronze within me,
> not unless the Muses of Olympia, daughters
> of Zeus of the aegis, remembered all those who came
>   beneath Ilion.
>
> *(Richmond Lattimore's translation)*

Not alone, not unassisted could such a catalogue be composed and transmitted, or the almost sixteen thousand lines of the *Iliad*—not without the help of the Muses, the daughters of Memory, who know all things. And what could they do for Homer? What is he talking about?

Well, what can they do for us, on the rare occasions when we ask their assistance? How do we remember the number of days in the months? "Thirty days hath September, / April, June, and November," the rhymes and strong fourfold beat combining to give us instant recall of needed facts we might otherwise have to figure out on our knuckles? How did my mother remember the kings of England, so surely that she still knew them at eighty?

> First William the Norman, then William his son,
> Henry, Stephen, and Henry, then Richard and John.
> Next Henry Third, Edwards One, Two, and Three;
> Again, after Richard, three Henrys we see.
> Two Edwards, third Richard, if rightly I guess,
> Two Henrys, Sixth Edward, Queen Mary, Queen Bess,
> Next Jamie the Scot; then Charles, whom they slew,
> Then Oliver Cromwell, another Charles too;
> Then James, called the Second, ascended the throne;
> Then William and Mary, and William alone;
> Then Anne, Georges four, Fourth William, all passed—
> God sent then Victoria—may she long be the last!

Homer remembers in the same way. It's much more elaborate, of course. The Homeric poems are freely composed out of thousands of rhythmic verbal formulas; to quote Denys Page, "about nine tenths of the Iliad's language was supplied by memory in ready-made verses or parts of verses."

> Leitos and Peneleos were leaders of the Boiotians,
> with Arkesilaos and Prothoenor and Klonios;
> they who lived in Hyria and in rocky Aulis,
> in the hill-bends of Eteonos, and Schoinos, and Skolos, . . .
> they who held Koroneia, and the meadows of Haliartos, . . .
> they who held Arne of the great vineyards, and Mideia,
> with Nisa the sacrosanct, and uttermost Anthedon.

Not if he had ten tongues and ten mouths would Homer be able to tell his story without the Muses to remember for him all those who came beneath Ilion and what they did there. If he is to keep all that information in mind, and transmit it to others, it must be by *mousike*, music, by the beating, measured, repetitive sound patterns that preserve. "Not marble, nor the gilded monuments / Of princes shall outlive this powerful rhyme."

The Muses remember for Homer all that he knows. The bard's essential skill is to have mastered those traditional verse formulas and the information they contain so well that he can create within and around and with them as spontaneously as if the Muses were singing in his ear. The Muses are *how* he remembers. And *what* they remember is all that it is his business to know in order to be that indispensable member of his society, a poet—bard, historian, keeper of the past, who knows who his people are and where they have been, what they have done and suffered, what significances that action and suffering can bear. The Muses remember through the music that bears their name. They *sing*—that is, they put sounds and sounding meanings into an order that can please the ear, light the imagination, and accommodate the memory, so that they can reach the mind and heart and lodge there.

It is through the Daughters of Memory that Homer remembers how to make a sacrifice, how to launch a ship—those word patterns that repeat over and over again through the *Iliad* and the *Odyssey*. Thousands of bits of information are kept accessible through the Muses' rhythmic eloquence. Whatever society has a need for, the Muses are the means of remembering. Through the Muses the bard transmits the genealogies of gods and men, and the myths and legends that embody the existential and moral understanding of the culture. Through the Muses he transmits the proverbial wisdom. And the Muses are preservers of real historical knowledge too, for those who know how to listen: Clio, too, is a Muse. In Homer's own time the Mycenaean greatness he sang was long past. He himself was probably an Ionian Greek from the islands, who had never seen Greece. But Homer's Muses know the names of Bronze Age towns all over the Greek mainland, complete with details of their topography and agriculture. *The meadows of Haliartos. Arne of the vineyards.* I could not tell over the arguments about the historicity of the Homeric poems, not if I had ten tongues and ten mouths and a heart of brass within me. Not everyone agrees with Denys Page, who argues that the Muses' formulas preserve the names, even the characteristics, of a real Agamemnon and a real Achilles who led a real expedition and destroyed a real city. Not everyone trusts Clio; the Muses themselves told Hesiod that they knew how to sing false things as well as true. Schliemann dug for Troy and found walls under the hill of Hissarlik, but scoffers can point out that the gold beads he dug up were not King Priam's treasure, as he thought they were; that the Troy he found was a mere five acres in extent; and that the gold mask of Mycenae could never have been Agamemnon's. Nevertheless, Schliemann went where he went and dug where he dug because the Muses told him to, and but for their testimony the gold of Mycenae, and the shaft graves, and the burned city of Troy VII, would still be underground.

When Homer talks of the Muses, he has nothing to say about Inspiration. Certainly he knows about it. What poet does not? Hesiod, who if later than Homer was not very much later, describing that visit of the Muses which made him a poet, says that they "breathed into" him—literally *inspired* him with—the power of song, mysterious and divine, so that he might sing of things past and to come. The Muses are goddesses, and their dealings with men are inexplicable and silent; they are daughters of Zeus, and what else can that mean? That understood, there is nothing more to be said about Inspiration. It happens—who knows how? But in order for it to happen—that's where the Muses need their mother. Hesiod says just the one word about Inspiration; Homer not that. But he tells a terrible story of a bard who boasted that he could compete with the Muses in a singing contest and win. Myth after myth tells what happens to humans who make *that* kind of boast. It happened this time too. But the Muses didn't kill him, though the gods often did that to mortals who overstepped. Instead, they "in their anger struck him maimed, and the voice of wonder / they took away, and made him a singer *without memory.*" A stroke, we'd call it. They didn't dry up the springs of Inspiration; they didn't afflict him with singer's block. All they had to do was to take away that which made him a poet, his memory. He couldn't sing any more after that; he had neither the means nor the materials. With nothing in his head, what good could Inspiration do him?

But this is just an old tale, out of the long ago. It is different for us, of course. Because we can write. The Homeric bard couldn't, or didn't, so of course he needed his memory. But we can, and what a difference that makes!

What a difference indeed. Let's skip some four hundred and fifty years and listen in on one of those intellectual conversations that the Athenians delighted in, that Plato spent his life recreating, and that we call dialogues. Plato could write, of course, and did; and in his time the transition from a culture of singers, speakers, and listeners to a culture of readers and writers had begun, although it was not so far advanced that the word for uneducated had become *a-gram-matikos*—illiterate—but was still *a-mousikos*—unmusical, deaf to the Muses. In the *Phaedrus,* Plato makes the definitive statement about writing's effect on memory. Socrates is telling his young friend Phaedrus a story:

> At Naukratis in Egypt, there was one of the old gods there named Theuth. . . . He was the inventor of number and cal-culation and geometry and astronomy, and checkers and dice, but especially letters. The god Thamuz was then the king of all Egypt, ruling from that great city of Upper Egypt which the Hellenes call Egyptian Thebes. . . . Theuth came to him and showed him his inventions, and said that they should be given to the other Egyptians. Thamuz asked about the use of each of them, approving of some and disapproving others. It would take a long time to go through what Thamuz said to Theuth about each of the various inventions, but when they came to letters, "This," said Theuth, "will make the Egyptians wiser and give them better memories, for it is a specific both for memory and intelligence." Thamuz replied, "Most ingenious Theuth, he who gives birth to an invention is not the one to judge of the harm or benefit it can bring to the user. For you, the father of letters, out of paternal affection are claiming for them just the opposite of what they will do. This discovery will create forgetfulness in the learners' souls, because they will not use their memories, they will trust to the external written char-

acters, and not remember of themselves. You have found a specific not for memory but for reminding. You give your disciples not truth, but the *appearance* of wisdom; they will be hearers of many things without in fact learning them; will appear to be omniscient and will generally know nothing: they will be hard to be with, seeming to be wise when they are not."

We all recognize the phenomenon. And rereading this passage in the last of the many educational institutions through which I have passed, learning and teaching, reading and forgetting, how well I know the feeling. Hearers of many things—the easy appearance of omniscience—students and teachers, here we stand together. Someone has defined man as the only animal that buys more books than he can read.

So Socrates asks: "Isn't there another kind of word . . . far better and more powerful than this one? . . . one which is written . . . in the soul of the learner, able to defend itself and knowing whom to speak to and when to be silent?" and Phaedrus answers: "You mean the living word of knowledge which has a soul, and of which the written word is properly only an image."

It is in this context that we must understand what we have all heard: that Socrates wrote nothing, that all his extraordinary influence came through the living, spoken word. When Plato came to set down his version of the words that had meant so much to him—in writing, of course, an irony of which he was not unaware—he used all the art he possessed to communicate not mere abstract arguments but the sense of conversation, of the living human word, rooted in history and personality, contingent, supple, even contradictory. He was able to do it—to save the past alive—because, fortunately for us, and despite his opinion of poetry, he was dear to the Muses.

"The living word of knowledge which has a soul." Socrates' young friend Phaedrus understands very well what Socrates means. The story of Theuth's invention comes at the end of their conversation, but Phaedrus will not have forgotten how that conversation began. Phaedrus has come for a walk expressly to tell Socrates about a fine speech he's heard someone give about love. He doesn't want to forget it; he's been rehearsing it, and is almost ready to go through it when Socrates comes along. Socrates expects him to repeat it by heart—doubtless that is what *he* could have done at Phaedrus's age—unless, he says, it is "unusually long." But Phaedrus begs off: how can his unpracticed memory do justice to such a fine work? He offers to give, not the actual words, but a point-by-point summary by headings. But Socrates catches sight of something hidden under his cloak. Young Phaedrus has been working not from memory but from the written copy; he's brought the scroll along with him. Socrates makes him read it, since he's got it, and Phaedrus doesn't have to use his memory at all. At the end of the *Phaedrus,* in his myth of Theuth's great invention, Plato comments on the transition from an oral to a written culture; he has already dramatized it at the beginning.

Of course we shouldn't be too hard on Phaedrus. Today we should be well satisfied if a student could rehearse a speech point by point. And the speech was in prose, which is much harder to memorize than poetry. Like the *bourgeois gentilhomme,* people have always spoken prose—but only the use of writing made it possible to preserve it, and took away from the rhythms of poetry their practical necessity. The process of converting the Muses from powerful and essential goddesses into pretty ladies had already begun.

Yet Phaedrus certainly knew plenty of poetry by heart. A hundred years before him there had been no significant literature in prose. Agricultural know-how, scientific observations, philosophical speculations, all were preserved in verse. How else could they be remembered? Even in Plato's time, memory was still at the center of education. The living word written in the soul of the learner was still the primary method—poetry above all, which was why Plato was so fussy about what poetry he allowed into his Republic. But as poetry gave way to prose, means were found to memorize that too. Young Phaedrus, after all, has only had the speech a couple of hours; he hasn't had time to get it word-perfect. But with his summary by headings he's well on the way. There are plenty to encourage him; the Sophists who teach young men to compose speeches also have been developing an art of memory to help them deliver them, for who would be persuaded by a mere reading? Nor do many people have the money to acquire individual handmade copies, or imported papyrus to make notes on, while anything you jot down on a wax tablet is temporary.

It is the spoken word that lodges in the memory. Few people even today are so naturally oriented to written symbols that they can readily commit to memory a text seen merely as a text. Eidetic memory, the ability to recall a page of writing exactly as seen, is extremely rare. It is true that classical memory techniques worked by visual images: if you had a complex sequence of ideas to remember, you converted each of them into a vivid visual image and disposed them, in imagination, at specific locations in the room of a building you knew so well that you could instantly call it to mind. But the classical texts differentiate memory for subject matter from memory for words. Visual methods will keep your arguments straight, but to learn the exact words, says Quintilian, you should say them, "that the memory may derive assistance from the double effort of speaking and listening."

We do not realize how long it took—not just hundreds of years, more like a thousand—for the word even to begin its separation from its sound in the ear and its feel in the mouth. Eric Havelock describes how slowly "the new habits of literacy" penetrated a wholly oral culture; Plato's relation to writing, Havelock says, was more like Homer's than like ours. There was no speed-reading of manuscripts in which there were no capital and lowercase letters, no separations between words, no marks of punctuation—all introduced in postclassical times. Only the living voice could translate the marks on stone or wax or papyrus back into the words they signified and bridge the abyss between marks and meaning. We take for granted that writing implies not a speaker but a reader. But it was not always so.

"Among the Greeks," writes Moses Hadas, literature was "something to be listened to in public rather than scanned silently in private." Even after books and private reading became more common, "the regular method of publication was by public recitation." Not only Plato's dialogues, then, or the exchanges of Greek drama, but "all classic literature . . . is conceived of as a conversation with, or an address to, an audience." Herodotus recited his history—at the Olympic Games, no less—for more publicity. Horace tells us that he "recites to no one except friends, and then under constraint; not just anywhere or in the presence of just anyone"; on the other hand, Ovid complains that in his Black Sea exile he can't find the kind of audience that would appreciate him. Roman prose writers recited too. The Emperor Claudius "gave constant recitals through a professional reader." Philosophers complained of audiences who shouted and swayed, "impassioned by the charm . . . and rhythm of the words," but paid no attention to the philosophy.

But we are, after all, familiar enough with lectures and poetry readings. We know that in the Hellenistic and Roman worlds book-sellers grew common. We know of libraries, including the great library at Alexandria, and we think we know how the private individual reads for his own purposes. Silently, how else? Only clods move their lips. But listen to Saint Augustine describe an extraordinary sight—his master, Saint Ambrose, reading. It is A.D. 384. Augustine is thirty years old, a well-known teacher of rhetoric, versed in all the literature of his day. He has studied and taught for years in the great intellectual centers of Carthage and of Rome. *And he has never before seen a man read silently.* When Saint Ambrose read, "his eyes glided over the pages, and his heart searched out their meaning, but his voice and tongue were at rest." It's hard to explain such a phenomenon. "We thought perhaps he was afraid if the author he was reading had expressed things obscurely that it would be necessary to explain it for some perplexed but eager listener, and if his time were used up in such tasks, he would be able to read fewer books than he wished to. However, the need to save his voice, which easily grew hoarse, was perhaps the truer reason for his reading to himself. But with whatever intention he did it," says Augustine, still a bit suspicious, "in such a man it was good."

From Homer to Plato, by our impressionistic dating, is some four hundred and fifty years; from Plato to Augustine, some seven hundred and fifty more. More than a millennium of writing, and the word was still living in the mouth. It is in the sixteen hundred years *since* Augustine that the real change has taken place. It took a long time, but Theuth's invention, writing, has fundamentally changed the conception of literature, starting with the word itself, in which the word for "letters," *litterae,* is so embedded that we do not question its presence. Enamored of the text, we are scarcely able to imagine what Augustine's anecdote makes plain: that all classical literature, Thucydides and Cicero and Caesar as well as Sophocles and Sappho and Catullus, though it was transmitted in writing, existed in the sound of the human voice. That means Euclid too, and Aristotle, uneuphonious as we may think them. Why not? Augustine had seen people reading philosophy and mathematics too.

I don't know when silent reading became common. It's clear from his description that Augustine himself didn't imitate Saint Ambrose, even after he had observed him. But I suppose that if Saint Ambrose could do it, Saint Thomas did, nine hundred years later; and when I imagine Dante poring over his manuscript of Virgil, in the classical Latin that at first he found so hard to understand, I should imagine him studying in silence. But once he got the hang of it, I'm not going to imagine him *reading* it in silence. Being a poet, he didn't read it any faster than he could say it. I imagine that he said it *as* he read it, as we still exhort the freshmen to do, knowing full well that they aren't going to do any such thing. For Dante says he knows the whole of the *Aeneid, tutta quanta,* which must certainly mean "by heart." It is not such a feat if you love the words and value their meaning; I myself knew a blind man who knew by heart the whole *Divine Comedy.* But it can't be done through disembodied congress between page and mind. To get a passage by heart, of poetry or prose either, requires the aid of tongue, mouth, and ear, a full synesthetic response to meaning and sound and feel and rhythm, the gifts of the Muses.

I'm only guessing, of course. I don't know how Dante read, or Chaucer, or how much of what they knew they knew by heart. Nor do I know what people did with Shakespeare's "sugared sonnets" as they passed them about in manuscript or read them in the first printed copies—whether they read them aloud and how rapidly, whether they moved their lips. But we do know how much of the Elizabethan lyric poetry that we read in our anthologies, silently and too fast, was truly, literally *lyric*—written to be sung.

> Come unto these yellow sands,
> And then take hands.
> Curtsied when you have, and kissed
> (The wild waves whist),

> Foot it featly here and there,
> And sweet sprites, the burden bear.

How can we *read* these lines, least of all silently? And the songs are the least of it. Throughout Shakespeare's life his plays existed primarily in the mouths and memories of actors. And we remember Prince Hamlet himself, who told the players that he had heard that speech about Hecuba only once. He would like to hear it again; he asks the player, "If it live in your memory, begin at this line." But in fact it's Hamlet himself who begins, groping at first, then coming out with a line: "The rugged Pyrrhus, like th' Hyrcanian beast—." But that's not right. "'Tis not so, it begins with Pyrrhus"—then he gets it: "The rugged Pyrrhus, he whose sable arms, / Black as his purpose, did the night resemble. . . ."

Hamlet carries it on for thirteen lines; he stops only when Polonius interrupts him, to praise, not his memory, but his delivery. If it seemed plausible to an Elizabethan audience that Hamlet could speak off an indefinite number of lines he'd heard only once, years before, how much poetry—speeches, fragments of speeches, floating lines—did the Elizabethan playgoer himself carry around with him, preserved by that powerful gift of the sixteenth-century British Muse, blank verse?

But we know that actors memorize their lines even if we don't; we expect drama to be spoken. But epic? *Arma virumque cano:* "Arms and the man I sing." Virgil, and Dante after him, talked about how they sang; but they wrote their epics. They composed for the speaking voice, but they did not compose orally. When Milton invoked his Heav'nly Muse, not quite sixty years after *Hamlet,* the old bards we began with, who carried the whole culture of a people in their heads, were long gone. Homer, the first great European oral poet, was also nearly the last—and Homer was more than two thousand years in the past in 1658. Yet Milton, too, was an oral poet. It seems obvious enough, yet it is exactly the obvious that is most likely to escape us: like Homer, who also, tradition has it, was blind, Milton *wrote* not one of the 10,564 lines of *Paradise Lost*. All were first communicated to the ear, dictated to him, as he says, by the Heav'nly Muse, his Christian Urania, she who inspired Moses

and whose "Voice divine" will lead Milton above Olympus, above
the achievements of Homer and Virgil into the Heav'n of Heav'ns.

> Descend from Heav'n Urania, by that name
> If rightly thou art call'd, whose Voice divine
> Following, above th' Olympian Hill I soare,
> Above the flight of Pegasean wing.
> The meaning, not the Name I call; for thou
> Nor of the Muses nine, nor on the top
> Of old Olympus dwell'st, but Heav'nly born,
> Before the Hills appeared, or Fountain flow'd,
> Thou with Eternal Wisdom didst converse,
> Wisdom thy Sister, and with her didst play
> In presence of th' Almighty Father, pleas'd
> With thy Celestial Song. . . .

Blind though he is, and "fall'n on evil days, / In darkness and with
dangers compass'd round," Milton is a poet still; his Heav'nly Muse
visits him unimplored; she dictates to him nightly and inspires Easy
his unpremeditated verse. In the morning he himself dictates it to
the waiting amanuensis, who copies it down, preserving his pauses
and special pronunciations in the punctuation and spelling of the
printed edition, which of course Milton never saw. So we can hear
Milton's own voice and know that those who still say "heighth" for
"height" speak with Milton's seventeenth-century authority.

Certainly, if we call "the meaning not the name," the Muse is
Milton's Inspiration. She is his poetic skill too—and, like her classical avatars, she too is Memory's daughter. Can we imagine how
stocked Milton's mind was, had to be, with what he needed to make
his poem—stocked with the Bible, whose words are everywhere
recognizable in *Paradise Lost;* stocked with names, ideas, facts, images, references; with all the materials of his astonishing erudi-
tion—in order for his song to well up, easy and unpremeditated, by
night? Lucky for him that the cultivation of memory was still, in the
Renaissance, an essential part of education—as it has been in every
time and place until the advent of today's sophisticated eye-and-
print culture. Those old enough to remember know how things
have changed. My mother read to her sisters while they sewed; they
didn't mind setting in the sleeves and she did. Even I had a college
friend whose father still read the family a chapter of Dickens every

night as they sat around the dinner table. For all the Gutenberg revolution and the spread of literacy, it's within our lifetimes that Socrates' prediction has been fully justified, and that poetry has moved out of its ancient and accustomed locus—ears, mouth, and gut—and into the place where D. H. Lawrence thought sex ought not to be—the head.

I suspect I'm not the only person over fifty-five who can sing along with these lines:

> Then up spake brave Horatius,
>   The keeper of the gate;
> "To every man upon the earth
>   Death cometh soon or late.
> And how can man die better
>   Than facing fearful odds
> For the ashes of his fathers
>   And the altars of his gods?"

And certainly this:

> Breathes there a man with soul so dead,
> Who never to himself hath said,
>   This is my own, my native land!
> Whose heart hath ne'er within him burned
> As home his footsteps he hath turned
>   From wand'ring on a foreign strand?
> If such there be, go, mark him well;
> For him no minstrel raptures swell.
> High though his power, mighty his fame,
> Boundless his wealth as wish could claim,
> For all his pride of power and pelf,
> The wretch, concentred all in self,
> Living, shall forfeit fair renown,
> And, doubly dying, shall go down
> To the vile dust from whence he sprung,
> Unwept, unhonored, and unsung.

I may not have those lines quite right; I've never seen them in print. For years I didn't know who wrote them. I heard them before I was old enough to read poems in books, and when I faltered, trying to recall them, an older colleague was able to supply the lines—from memory. They reached me entirely through oral tradition, as poetry still could in that age of innocence—not as literary *Ding an sich*, still less as a "text," but as what all poetry was once: sound artfully patterned, a familiar, nourishing rumble.

Full many a flower is born to blush unseen. Man is born to sorrow as the sparks fly upward. The Assyrian came down like a wolf on the fold. Say not the struggle naught availeth. This above all, to thine own self be true. I am the master of my fate, I am the captain of my soul. The moving finger writes, and having writ. . . . My grandmother, from whom I first heard most of these lines, never went to college. She was no better educated than the average gentlewoman born in 1856. But lines like these were part of her common speech; they lay in her consciousness, a rich, undiscriminating cultural humus, the verbal deposits of a lifetime. Those to whom literature was really important could do much better; they carried whole anthologies in their heads, as we are told that Borges did—blind, like Milton and Homer. The central place still held by the spoken word ensured that most people who had been to school, and many who had only been to church, possessed a stock of words, figures, phrases, sentences, that deviated satisfyingly from everyday speech but with which they felt at home—portable, personal, usable belongings.

"Every student in the class was required . . . to memorize and recite long poems and chapters from the Bible." James Earl Carter is describing the educational methods current in his boyhood in Plains, Georgia, and paying tribute to Miss Julia Coleman, a "superlative teacher," he calls her, who "heavily influenced" his life. I will not, I suppose, make many converts by calling on Jimmy Carter's Muses. We have left that kind of education behind, and we have made real gains in doing so. It did not require understanding; it did not invite questioning; it did not insist on a discriminating response—though we are wrong if we think that it precluded these good things. But it did make elevated language a familiar possession. In December 1979 Jimmy Carter had a grave matter to talk about on television: an embassy attacked, citizens held hostage. So he dredged up two lines of poetry from the long ago, and spoke them with unusual feeling:

> God is not dead, nor does He sleep;
> The right is strong, and shall prevail. . . .

Not the first lines of Longfellow's poem, not particularly famous, and so not likely to be the contribution of a speech writer—Miss Julia's legacy, rather, waiting in the memory bank.

Certainly it's not our kind of poem; it's a shade inspirational for our tastes. Miss Julia's poems, like my grandmother's, tended to be like that. It's poetry, though—and I would argue that there is a sounder, more genuine relationship to poetry attending the natural use of these two lines than in all the elaborate and self-conscious presidential noticing of poets that began with John Kennedy. We need the words, we reach for them, they are there, we use them. Should poetry be useful? Why not? "Art for art's sake" was born yesterday. The classical dictum was that poetry should profit and delight—both together. Homer was so useful that Greek education was based on his poems for hundreds of years. Milton considered *Paradise Lost* to be of the greatest utility; he wrote it to justify the ways of God to men. Dante told his patron explicitly that he wrote his *Comedy* for a practical purpose: to lead souls from darkness into light. These are grand uses. My grandmother had small ones, though perhaps the human need for capsule inspiration or comfort is not entirely insignificant. It takes all kinds. And it's true that those who use poetry naturally will naturally misuse it—get it wrong, misunderstand it, or misapply it—as Socrates "misused" Homer when he quoted, three days before his death, Achilles' words, "On the third day you shall reach fertile Phthia," though Achilles clearly wasn't thinking of death at all. But Socrates was, and at the time it was *his* poem.

Our own relationship to poetry is much more respectful. More anxious, too; we have been made aware that poetry has many pit-falls, that we can get things wrong, and that most of us will. One of the more interesting dates of literary history must surely be the date when someone was first graded on his reading of a poem. It certainly wasn't in my grandmother's time. For me it wasn't until graduate school in the late 1940s, though I. A. Richards must have been putting his students through it years before that. The method works, and works well; it made two generations of students—and teachers—better readers. Grading concentrates the mind wonderfully, as Dr. Johnson said of hanging. We learned, in those years, to respect the poem, to read it for itself, in itself, to value it for itself, and not for what we wanted it to do for us. This was an immense gain. But it was a loss too. In truly secure relationships, respect and easy intimacy are compatible, between person and person and between person and poem, too. But that kind of security is hard-earned; few of our students attain it. In most relationships, respect entails a certain distance. We may respect poetry too much, treat it too carefully. If we do, it is no longer fully our own.

I do not suggest that today's readers do not value poetry. Today the Muses frequent colleges, indeed are seldom found outside them. And our colleges have done their work well. There are as many people as ever, perhaps more than ever, for whom poetry exists, and exists with a freighted seriousness my grandmother and Miss Julia never imagined. But even for these it exists only partially. We teach from the printed text, inculcating attentiveness and accuracy, analyzing structures, exploring metaphors, searching out hidden linkages, conscientiously attending to tone. Tone? That's a word I didn't hear even in graduate school; now it's such a necessary concept that we teach it to freshmen. "Descriptions of tone," we tell them (I quote from the *Norton Introduction to Literature*), "try to characterize the way the words of the poem are (or should be) spoken when one sensitively reads the poem aloud."

Aloud—the sound of the human voice is unexpectedly recalled. But now the important thing is not to speak the poem ourselves or listen to it, but to learn to characterize in writing how it should be spoken. It's not easy, for the freshmen or for us. The limits of the English adverb are quickly reached. "Playfully"? "Seriously"? "Sarcastically"? (The freshmen love that word, though they don't know what it means.) "Ironically," most treacherous of all? It's surprising how well we manage, when you consider the difficulty of the task and how little time is left to spend actually saying the poems. So gifted senior English majors, who read with a depth and intelligence that was never asked of me in an undergraduate English course, can still stun me by asking what I mean when I say a line doesn't scan. There are brilliant graduates of fine doctoral programs in English, lovers of poetry, who know less poetry by heart than Jimmy Carter, and who possess, therefore, texts, or intellectual-emotional reconstructions, or paraphrases, but no poems. A paraphrase is not a poem; English teachers work very hard to teach exactly that. But without memory we grope for "That time of year thou mayst in me behold" or J. Alfred Prufrock's mermaids—but they slip away, and all we are left holding are our ungainly paraphrases. Which is why some of us are now surprising our students by asking them to memorize poetry.

There is a memory for fact, of course, and memory for language. Homer's Muses did not distinguish them, and I have mixed them up cavalierly here and left no space to sort them out. But they do connect, in our time as well as Homer's. Creative thinking of any kind requires more than just knowing where to look things up; you have to know they're there before you know you need them. The mind is the greatest of computers, and it works its marvels best when well stored—with facts: names, dates, places, events, sequences—and also with language: words, phrases, sentences, the tongues of men and of angels. Perhaps language is the most important of all. We all notice the contraction in the range of reference of the young. But facts can be looked up, that's true, and if we get a grant, our servants can do that for us. What's harder to acquire—in adulthood hard indeed—is that intimacy with language, that sense for different ways of using it, which grows naturally when we carry Shakespeare and the Bible, Jefferson and Lincoln, Eliot and Yeats, Edward Lear and P. G. Wodehouse in our heads. In our heads or, better, in another part of the body, where we "learn by heart"—in the unconscious, where the Muses sing to us darkling, and all the richness of what we know and value can come together in unexpected, unheard-of combinations. Memory is not the enemy of Inspiration, or of thought either. Today, as always, it is the essential prerequisite of both.

From *The American Scholar*, Winter 1980–81.

At Home in History:
Werner Jaeger's Paideia

. . . m'insegnavate come l'uom s'etterna. . . .

H ow man makes himself eternal. It is what Brunetto Latini
taught Dante, learning he found so important that he remembered his gratitude even in Hell, even returned from Paradise. I
first heard the words not in a course in Dante but in the mild
Rhineland accent of Werner Jaeger of the Harvard classics department, in a course on Aristotle's *Nichomachean Ethics*. I was a refugee
from the philosophy department, majoring in an eleventh-hour
mocked-up combination of Greek and English, in deference to the
fact that I knew too little Latin to major in classics and that it was
possible to read quite a lot of English at the last minute. I had no
desire whatever to learn more about Aristotle. I knew enough, however, to know that I ought to take a course with Werner Jaeger—it
didn't matter what.

It didn't. I would have liked it to be a course on Homer, of
course, or Sophocles, or Aeschylus, whom Jaeger always wanted to
write a book about but never did; I liked poetry. Having already
learned from John Finley to see history as tragedy (it was 1943), I
would have liked it to be a course on Thucydides. I liked history
too; I couldn't but know that my own ideas and those of all my

friends took their origin and half their meaning from the web of personal and political and social events around us as we emerged from the Depression and moved into the war. But in the Harvard philosophy department it did not seem to be so. If Spinoza erected his lonely thought into a great cathedral where a philosopher could be at home, no one encouraged us to think that this had anything to do with the perceptions and needs of a Jew in Amsterdam in the mid-seventeenth century, grinding lenses for a living, cut off both from his own people and from the culture around him. Certainly Aristotle came after Plato; how else could he have criticized the Theory of Ideas? We learned all that and wrote it down. But that he lived and worked in an Athens where the values of the Greek polis had already collapsed, that he was Plato's student until he was almost forty, that he wrote a poem as an altar offering in Plato's memory, that we actually possess it, that it concerns not Ideas but "Holy Friendship" for "the man whom it is not lawful for bad men even to praise"—no one had told us these things as we studied the four kinds of causes and the idea of the mean and learned how different Aristotle was from Plato.

From Jaeger we learned that the work of Aristotle and Plato was anything but pure thought. It was not only that their thought had developed in time, both personal and public—any member of the philosophy department would have conceded that—but that we could not understand that thought without imagining ourselves into the personal and historical, into what it must have been to be Aristotle or Plato. For a Greek, he wrote later, "theory and life must always go together." Theory issued from life, and returned to renew it. The philosophy of Aristotle, as of Plato, was a practical, public activity, the activity of a whole human being, alive in society. It was that central synthesis of act and thought and value, of history and poetry and philosophy that he called, as the Greeks did, "paideia." It means something between "education" and "civilization," and its aim for Plato and Aristotle was, he told us, no less than *soteria,* their culture's safety and salvation.

Meaning inheres in history; Plato, recreating in the loving circumstantiality of his dialogues the society of his youth, "confesses it in every line." Socrates, he wrote in his monumental *Paideia,* "breathes the air of history and is lit up by its rays." And Plato's whole work, he told us, was an attempt to explain a world in which Socrates *had* to die: "Around that fact he builds up the broadening circles of his philosophy." "It is impossible to separate his life from his work." Suddenly the chill marble took on the tint of living flesh.

Recent and remote, the presences of the past were all around us as he talked. Aristotle continued a tradition; he was not like Nietzsche, who "broke the tablets." (Jaeger had occupied Nietzsche's chair at Basel, but of course we did not know that.) And out of the past, the thought of Aristotle stretched forward into a future he could not know. But his future was our past, shaping us whether we knew it or not. The very first day Mr. Jaeger told us, who had thought we were among Greeks, that the fundamental difference between Catholicism and Protestantism is expressible in their opposite attitudes to Aristotle. Luther thought Aristotle had made Aquinas pagan, but as soon as Lutherans had to build up a church and a dogma they found they needed him again. History's tablets are not so easily broken.

Professor Jaeger did not simplify the past, nor did he sentimentalize it. He insisted, as only a true historian can, that we see it in its own terms and not ours, and cautioned against the easy game of drawing contemporary parallels. Yet he always gave us the sense that we lived surrounded by the greatness of a past compounded of achievement and tragic failure and renewal in history. Living in time, we lived also *sub specie aeternitatis*. I heard those words first from him; he did not tell us they were Spinoza's. He may have thought we knew; he was always generous. But he was also realistic; he knew he couldn't tell us everything.

Sub specie aeternitatis. Come l'uom s'etterna. Curiously, I do not find the words in my notes, though I was the kind of student who wrote everything down. I had not yet, apparently, unlearned what is so well inculcated in college—that the definition of *irrelevant* is "not likely to be on the exam." But even though Dante was irrelevant, I remember how Mr. Jaeger, teacher as well as scholar, imagined our presuppositions and spoke to them: that knowing Dante was a Christian poet we would assume that "eternal" must carry its customary Christian meaning. But here it doesn't: that way of making ourselves immortal has nothing to do with life after the death of the body. It describes the life of philosophic *theoria*, which Dante and his teacher got from the tenth book of the *Ethics*, from the tradition of Greek *paideia* as it still lived in thirteenth-century Florence.

At that time Jaeger had not yet written the little book *Early Christianity and Greek Paideia* that he called a "down-payment" on the work he doubted he would live to complete, the "comprehensive book on the historical continuity and transformation of the tradition of Greek paideia into the Christian centuries." Not until forty years later (fifty years after it was first published), preparing for this writing, did I read the astonishing essay on Tyrtaeus, in which that warlike poet's simple idea of a citizen's *arete*, his soldierly virtue, is traced through its ethical transformation in Xenophanes and Plato, to emerge transfigured in the rhythms of 1 Corinthians 13. But in his class we began to experience some inkling, according to our readiness, of what it might be to feel all time eternally present.

Exam time came. Two very young women bending over blue books, slowly puzzling out our translations, we looked up startled as the door opened. The exam was not half over; we had still an hour and a half to go. Nothing in our years of Harvard education, not even four months of Professor Jaeger's courtly friendliness, had prepared us for what we saw: his pale, luminous presence advancing upon us in soft benignity, bearing a tin of wafers. They were delicate, long, thin cylinders with chocolate inside; I cannot imagine how he had acquired such quintessentially European confections in wartime America. Hardly believing in the reality of this incursion, we partook and returned to our blue books.

Our astonishment at so simple an act needs some explanation in an era when small classes are demanded as if by right, and intimacy and first names have become cheapened by familiarity. As a Radcliffe student, my classes had generally been small, for Harvard and Radcliffe remained segregated by gender until the last year of the war, and students then as now did not crowd into upper-level courses in philosophy and Greek. Small or large, however, the lecture reigned supreme at Harvard; what in most small colleges would be considered teaching was left to graduate students with other things on their minds. I was accustomed not to being taught but to being lectured at, from notes yet unpublished or yellowed with age, brilliantly or dully, but always from a distance, whether I sat in a group of two hundred or (as in Ralph Barton Perry's course in ethics) at a table within three feet of the professor. It may not have been always so at Harvard; I had a friend who said he played tennis with a professor. But at Radcliffe the distance between student and teacher was unbridgeable. If there were office hours, I did not know them; Radcliffe undergraduates did not even know the names of most of the buildings in which their professors might have been found. The Widener Library was not open to us in those days, though a little reading room was provided for seniors working on theses. It would not have occurred to me to seek out a professor, nor do I remember ever asking a question in class.

Teachers could suffer from this institutional perversity as well as students; I recall with shame John Wild, then in what must have been his early years of teaching, trying—not to start a discussion, there would have been no chance of that—but to elicit from his class on the *Gorgias* the obvious parallel between rhetoric, as Plato excoriated it, and modern advertising. He had breached Harvard etiquette; he must have studied elsewhere. We sat silent, sourly complacent at withholding the answer we knew he wanted, and after a sickening interval he had to supply it himself. But most professors seemed well content. So we were totally unprepared for a teacher who seemed to think it natural to offer us refreshments, to ask his classes—even the larger ones—to tea at his home, the only home of a Harvard professor I ever entered.

It was the more astonishing because of the aura of eminence with which Jaeger had come to Harvard. If Harvard's finest were out of reach, what could we expect from a Herr Professor in the full tradition of European formality, an international luminary who had been lured, we had heard (incorrectly) from Chicago to be a University Professor, free to teach anything he wished, with the unheard-of stipend of twenty-five thousand dollars a year? We had heard other things too. "Man must eat fables," wrote Edward Dahlberg, "or starve his soul to death," and students feed on heroic fables. Our story was that Mr. Jaeger had been Rector of the University of

Berlin before he came to America, that he had refused to dismiss a Jewish professor, and that a Nazi gauleiter had slapped him in the face. This cannot have been so; biographical entries make no reference to a tenure as Rector, and though I cannot imagine Professor Jaeger failing to defend a colleague, the rest of the story remains equally without confirmation. Certainly, even if true, he would not have told it. The closest he ever came to commenting to us on the tragedy of twentieth-century history was in the dark May of 1944 (he had, I learn, become an American citizen the year before), when he mused, in some fifth-century connection I have forgotten, "And those who want to find their paradise on earth will find hell sometimes." Nor did he, who could imagine himself into the personal life of Plato and Aristotle, ever speak of his own. The autobiographical sketches he wrote late in life contain only a few muted sentences through which one can glimpse the reality of a political choice that meant loss and exile.

Even as a child, history was his starting point, a history, as he made clear, far too rich for nationalism. He was born into a Lutheran family in a corner of the Catholic Rhineland that had once been part of the Spanish empire: "The nearby borders of Holland and Belgium were a constant reminder of 'Europe'; so too was the palpable proximity of the Low German, Dutch, Flemish and French languages." At eight he began Latin, then five years later Greek, at a Catholic school named for Thomas à Kempis, "author of the *Imitatio Christi,* the best known and most translated of books." (That it is now no longer the Thomaeum but the Werner Jaeger Progymnasium would, I think, have elicited his most complex smile.) "All around me," he wrote, "stood the old walls and castles and thousand-year-old churches of the Middle Ages, the excavated fortresses and military highways of the Romans, the builders of the Rhenish cities. . . . From the beginning, the Roman empire in its final Christian and universal form was presented to us as a simple fact." The lower Rhineland still flew the red and white flag of the Church; only "a few newcomers . . . raised the black[,] white and red flag" of the German Empire. The roads over which he wandered as a boy "had not yet been usurped by the youth movement of a later day." That was as close as he came to mentioning Hitler.

Still, when that later day came, as a scholar of antiquity he might have lived quietly even in the world of National Socialism, protected by his nonpolitical eminence. He chose not to. We cannot know all the reasons, but one of them, recorded in the Harvard faculty memorial minute, suggests that there was a kernel of truth in our student legend, less flamboyant and more characteristic. Jaeger's luminous generalizations always rose out of minutely comprehended texts (often those he had himself established); in determining meaning, every phrase, to its last echo, must be weighted into its context. He was surrounded by texts when I last saw him, joyful over two manuscript pages, one in the Vatican and one in Cambridge, that he had just demonstrated belonged together—one more fragment of the eternal past salvaged for the future. So it is appropriate that the true story concerns the alteration of a text.

In 1936, Jaeger had held for fifteen years the chair of the great classical scholar Wilamowitz at Berlin. There was no more honored position in all Germany; he had reached it when he was barely thirty-three. Nineteen thirty-six was the Harvard tercentenary year, and he was delegated to represent the Prussian Academy of Sciences at the observances in Cambridge. His address was to end with a reference to the peaceful competition of America and Germany "in the service of humanity." The Ministry of Education censor required that he delete those last five words.

It was with a detachment worthy of Epictetus that he wrote, much later, the single reference, in all his published work, to what he had lost. "The writer of this paper found himself forced to give up the professorial chair of E. Curtius and Wilamowitz and, like some of the ablest young men and like my revered older colleague, Professor E. Norden, go into exile abroad." (The reference to other colleagues is characteristic; he would have been the last to claim uniqueness.) One of his first publications after he came to America was a lecture he could not have delivered in Germany, a characteristically detailed and original exploration of the earliest Greek references to Jews and Judaism. But he spoke to us no more of anti-Semitism than he did of twentieth-century politics. Only now, looking him up in the *Dictionary of American Biography*, do I find that his wife was Jewish.

It is not a dramatic story. Many things combine to force such a decision, and professors live like professors, not like heroes. But though the young love drama, I think we would have accepted the revision of our legend. Besides his classes in Greek, Professor Jaeger gave a yearly course open to the whole college; in it he explored what he told us was "the central idea of all Greek culture: the development of human *arete*." That was what his paideia—and *Paideia*—was all about: human excellence, changing yet constant, as the warlike heroism of the Homeric heroes was enriched and refined over centuries into that heroism of mind and spirit that Plato experienced in his own great teacher and memorialized for times to come. "Other nations made gods, kings, spirits; the Greeks alone made men." We had learned enough from him, even then, to understand that for him the simple words "in the service of humanity" could not be expendable.

I have gone rather long without giving those details of manner and appearance that are supposed to lend portraiture conviction. In a brief memoir written during the last year of his life, Professor Adele Fiske evokes the outer man, unchanged in the twenty years since I had known him—briefcase, beret, umbrella, rubbers (yes, I had forgotten the rubbers, the rubbers bring him back)—a likely professor, an unlikely hero. But once beyond such accoutrements, a certain indefiniteness of feature, a softness of expression—of body, even—make description difficult. It was an indoor face, very pale, in some ways tentative, lips not firmly set even when closed, expressing not determination but a kind of responsive readiness. The year he died, someone took four photographs of him, in series. It is characteristic that they show not a state but a process, the gradual realization of a smile. Certainly he was always ready to smile with us at some instance of the penetrating yet gentle humor that, while not rare, we somehow never expected from him. Gentle, modest, unassuming, mild, benign, serene—the words that present themselves are accurate and unavoidable yet radically misleading. The fault, of course, lies not in them but in us if they suggest the weak and wishy-washy. For Mr. Jaeger's serenity was a positive, an educative force—among other things, it educated the turbulent and demanding young to realize that there might be some meaning to the words we

read in the *Ethics,* that the most perfected human happiness is to be
found in the activity of contemplation, *theoria,* intensive *seeing,* and
that it is in this activity, being closest to the divine, that we can
athanatizein, achieve a life beyond mortality—as far, injects Aristotle, ever the realist, as is possible for a human being. (It was at this
point that Professor Jaeger told us about Ser Brunetto.) I might as
well, then, give over physical description. What comes to mind,
rather than any image, is a color—a steady, shining grey, so milky
and so luminous that it is hardly a color at all.

This scholar's serenity had not always been his. In the Germany
of the Weimar Republic, in those years of the twenties that he once
said future historians might see as our century's most creative period, he had been a public figure, fighting to influence German education, founding a magazine to bring classical culture to the layman,
defending what came to be called The Third Humanism against the
ever-encroaching emphasis on the practical and the contemporary. It
was hard, as Professor Finley said in his memorial address, even for
his Harvard colleagues to see the public man of Berlin in "the serene
figure . . . in the golden summer of his Cambridge years," whose
world seemed to be the manuscript-filled study at the top of Widener. Students, of course, could not see it at all. But we sensed that
there was nothing negative in his detachment. He had quoted a
pregnant sentence of one of the Seven Wise Men, like him an exile,
as so many were in the turbulent world of antiquity: *Omnia mea
mecum porto.* All that is mine I carry with me. What he carried with
him was his paideia.

Mr. Jaeger was unique among the professors I have known in
the harmony—the identity, indeed—between what he professed
and what he was. Paideia was the subject of the more than fifty years
of his scholarship, the Hellenic paideia realized first in itself, and
later as it was transformed into what he called "the paideia of
Christ." He was a teacher, and he conceived the entire cultural history of man—poetry, philosophy, natural science, the whole heritage
of written self-expression—as teaching. The English subtitle of
Paideia is *The Ideals of Greek Culture.* Faithful enough to the con-
tents of the book, it misses, as Jaeger later pointed out, the emphasis
of the German subtitle, *Die Formung des griechischen Menschen.*

What concerned him was the *forming* of a human being. In *Early Christianity and Greek Paideia* he shows how Gregory of Nyssa, "the most truly Greek of the Christian fathers," reverts constantly to the basic image of *morphosis,* formation. It implied, for Gregory and for him, "the essential identity of all educational activity and the work of the creative artist, painter, and sculptor." This was the central meaning of his scholarship and of his teaching: the making, not of gods or kings, but of fully human beings. He quotes in *Paideia* that culminating section of Plato's *Apology* which is Socrates' description of his "service to God": "For all that I do is to go round and persuade young and old among you not to give as much of your attention to your bodies and your money as to the perfection of your souls." Jaeger comments: "Socrates says that he 'philosophizes.' Obviously, he does not mean by this that he engages in abstract thought, but that he exhorts and teaches." And, for Plato, he observes, "All human effort to reach the truth is ultimately justified . . . not (as for the great natural philosophers of the era before Socrates) by the urge to solve the riddle of the world, but by the necessity of knowledge in maintaining and shaping human life." Plato's work was a public, a political, activity, he told us, as all Greek literature had been, its aim "to bring the true society into being as the proper milieu for the achievement of the highest virtue possible to man." It was "inspired by the educational spirit of Socrates, whose aim was not only to see the true nature of things, but to do good."

Socrates, Plato, Aristotle—all were teachers. So were those last voices of the Greek polis, Demosthenes and Isocrates. So was Thucydides, who wrote his terrible dissection of a society at war as a *ktēma es aiei,* a possession for always, that men might be taught and remember how like causes produce like effects. (In 1943, Professor Jaeger spoke to us of Thucydides' chapter on how the pressures of war corrupt moral standards and the meaning of words together. He advised us to learn it by heart. I wish I had.)

The Greek tragedians were teachers, too, their characters wrestling out insoluble conflicts of ideas and values before an audience of thousands of citizens. (Are Antigone and Creon both right and wrong, Professor Jaeger asked us, contradiction being, as Hegel thought, the essence of reality? Or is Antigone innocent, as Jebb claimed, and Creon a criminal, misusing a political power in itself inherently bad? "And you will go on answering this question," he told us, "as long as you live.") Poets were teachers, their singing voices essential to the understanding even of political revolution, Homer first among them and fundamental, "the educator of Hellas."

Mr. Jaeger had the quality that Aristotle noted in Homer, of seeing human beings in the integrity of their individuality, as fundamentally not mean but noble. However the preoccupations and programs and values of those contentious Greeks contrasted and conflicted, he entered into each of them with equal sympathy. "I have already been a boy and a girl, and a bush, and a bird, and a dumb fish out of the sea." Empedocles, wrote Jaeger, "speaks of all these various forms of life with the loving inflexion of one who has felt their existence from within, and to whom none of them is any more remote than he is remote from himself." Coming across these words long after I had known him, I seemed to understand for the first time that curious indefiniteness—the modesty of the chameleon-scholar, responsive, like Keats's chameleon-poet, to the manifold shapes of arete. That luminous grey was the color of Negative Capability.

Paideia was for Jaeger a human relationship. That was what the chocolate wafers affirmed. Greek paideia taught through exemplars; rereading *Paideia* for this article, I recognized what his had been. "Unless we realise to the full Socrates' concern for the individual to whom he is speaking, we cannot understand *what* he is saying. Although the philosopher may consider that relationship unessential in the abstract, academic sense, Plato shows that for Socrates it was essential." Plato's Socrates "holds friendship to be not only the chain that binds every political association, but the real form [the Platonic Form, what else?] of every productive connection between men. That is why he does not speak of his 'pupils,' as the sophists do, but of his 'friends.'" Jaeger's students wrote him letters; he always answered, in the regular and beautiful script that seemed another mark of his life's unhurried harmony. He was uniquely accessible.

The undergraduate writer of a *Crimson* Faculty Profile recorded with
Harvard-earned incredulity that "he will stop work to talk for
hours—literally hours—with any student who comes in on any
pretext whatever," and added that he always knew the names, abilities, and problems of his students, "unlike many insignificant section men." Some student essays, never picked up, are preserved
among his papers in the Harvard Archives. One, which did not
receive a high grade, is gently criticized for its loose organization, a
fault, he added, for which its originality went far to compensate.
There was no conflict between encouragement and rigor in his harmonious paideia.

During his American years, the theme of Christian paideia
moved from the periphery to the center of his scholarship. As he
worked on the great edition of Gregory of Nyssa that Wilamowitz
had suggested to him in 1909 while he was still a student, Jaeger was
deeply drawn to the Father whose word for the monk's life was
"philosophical" and for whom the Bible was "not law but education." As a master of that close reading which today's students must
learn via the techniques of the New Criticism but which is inherent
in the interpretation of classical texts, Jaeger found in Gregory's
vocabulary the manifestation of his continuing theme. "Instead of
saying 'the prophet says' or 'Christ says,' as would be most natural
for us, he writes innumerable times, 'the prophet Isaiah educates us
or the apostle educates us' (paideuei)." In Gregory's mind, "the way
in which the Spirit speaks to the human race in the Scripture is that
of the wise educator who never forgets the narrow limits of his
pupils' capacity."

Professor Jaeger knew our limits well enough; he wrote in 1960,
the year before his death, that to learn what classical scholarship was
like in a country where classical humanism did not exist, one must
come to America. Stumbling through our Greek or Latin—or
worse, studying through the veil of translation words on the un-
translatability of each one of which he could have given a full lecture—we were not like the students he had had, that he might still
have had, in Germany. Yet he never made us feel our inadequacy. If
our Greek was imperfect and slow, very well, he would have us buy
the Loeb with its double text; important as the words were, more

important was what could survive translation. If Dante, or Hegel, or
Nietzsche, or Saint Thomas were only names to us, he would give
us a phrase or a sentence or a reflection to make us vow that one day
they would be more. Like all great teachers, he met us where we
were, selecting from his vast storehouse what we were ready for,
which was, of course, a tiny proportion of what he knew, of what
was relevant, and even, surely, of what he deemed essential, recognizing that each stage of learning has its integrity. He did have some
students on the graduate level in whom he could take a scholar's
satisfaction; anyone who read the notes that are, as he always insisted, an essential part of his books—containing the arguments too
detailed for the general reader who was always in his mind—will
note the generous references to the monographs of his students. But
like the great Wilamowitz, whose name we learned to repeat with
reverence, he was content to give "lectures of general interest for a
wide audience of nonclassicists." One does not limit access to
paideia. *Paideia* itself was written for that wide audience, all quotations willingly translated out of the originals. He wrote to Professor
Fiske, after a happy week spent with her students at Manhattanville,
his credo as a teacher and, perhaps, as a Christian:

> What I can do for another human being and its growth has
> always been for me of first importance since it is my natural
> way of communicating with the world outside me and the
> strongest root of my existence. Without it the *Paideia* would
> never have been undertaken or become possible at all. Mere
> technical scholarship would not be enough to create it. And so
> everything I have written is part of my life. The religious and
> theological problem also has been there from the start, it is not
> a recent addition.

He told the girls—"the choir of muses," he wrote to one of them
afterward—

> To study Greek is to go to the very source, as Cicero tells us to
> do, *ite ad fontes;* to the ultimate source, Homer, the lyric and
> tragic poets, Plato, thus living again the development of the
> human spirit, seeing the whole breadth and depth of human
> experience taking form and shape for the first time. What does

"Literature" mean? letters? writing? No, it means the form of human life; to experience what it means to become human . . . to see like Lucretius the walls of this world recede, *moenia mundi discedunt*, the universe open up before you. It is something no one can understand who has not experienced it, it is liberation, a revelation of what it really means to be free.

It is, of course, the meaning of liberal education, the education proper to the arete of free human beings.

The word *radiance* keeps coming forward. The Harvard colleagues who spoke at his memorial service, John Finley and Krister Stendahl, both used it; writing to me at his death, another of his students spoke of "the radiance of his mind and soul." John Ciardi, translating Inferno 15, made Ser Brunetto "a radiance among men"; it was years before I came to the original and realized that the words were Ciardi's own addition. I did not grudge him them; he must have had such a teacher. Of course it is natural to think of the mind's influence in metaphors of light. I think of Finley himself—an electrical storm of ideas and passion—as immediate, as exciting, and as personally remote; of John Arthos of Michigan, layers of cloud with flashes of brightness rewarding the eager glimpser. Radiance is different—steadily, equally *there*, to be experienced by all within its range. Where else does the idea of the halo come from?

Hagiography, alas, entails a concomitant loss in credibility. Yet our teachers can give us nothing more precious than the capacity for admiration; hagiography today is a genre too much neglected. After forty years I write still as a reverential undergraduate, in no position to sketch in the warts and deficiencies that now seem requisite to carry conviction. The biographical note in the *DAB* recalls a review of *Paideia*, pointing to an elitism that a rabid nationalism could misuse; the note emphasizes, rather, his book on Aristotle, "which changed all subsequent study of the philosopher," and notes that though *Paideia* was thought in his lifetime to be his great achievement, "the volumes are rarely read by scholars today." I am not a classical scholar and I cannot say. They don't seem outdated to me. Certainly Jaeger's paideia had its limits; we live now in a wider world for which a wider past determines an even more uncertain future. I cannot think, however, that widening horizons have made obsolete the ancient definition of the cultured man with which Jaeger introduced the first volume: the philologue "is he who loves words and is serious about paideia." "Is serious"? There is no translation for *spoudazōn*, one of those wonderful Greek words in which an adjective or a noun takes on all a verb's dynamism, converting being to action, reminding us that, as Aristotle said, virtue is not a mere settled state, but an activity, an *energeia*. *Athanatizein*. To achieve immortality. *Philokalein*. To love the beautiful. *Philosophein*. To love wisdom. Werner Jaeger lived to teach us that here was once a culture, a paideia, in which these were single, necessary verbs, and that we are its heirs.

That culture seems even more expendable now than when he fought for it in Berlin, even in colleges that proclaim the liberal arts. Hardly anyone studies Greek, of course, or has any idea why one might want to do so. The Great Books courses that opened so many minds in the postwar years are now difficult to find. Unless pursued with "before 1800" requirements, students avoid courses in the past, even of their own culture; one of my students, a theater major, complained that Shakespeare has "a writing style which is practically foreign." The economy contracts and vocationalism reigns. Yet I find that students still respond when I tell them what Boris Pasternak wrote in *Doctor Zhivago:* "that man does not die in a ditch like a dog, but at home in history." Though they may not know why, they know what it is to be homeless. Pasternak, who translated Shakespeare for Mother Russia, who combined both Jewish and Christian paideia, knew in himself what I learned from Professor Jaeger. The history we cannot do without is the paideia we share, the record of the developing, resilient experience of human arete as our culture has given us to understand it. We may seek—and find—new perspectives to enrich that tradition, but we abandon it to our inexpressible loss, a loss no less devastating because so many cannot miss what they never had. Without our paideia we make ourselves what Werner Jaeger could never be, exiles of the spirit.

In the first essay in *The American Scholar*'s series on great teachers, Edmund Wilson closed his tribute to Christian Gauss with Dante's words. They are words for which our need is permanent.

Che in la mente m'è fitta, ed or m'accora,
    la cara e buona imagine paterna
    di voi, quando nel mondo ad ora ad ora

m'insegnavate come l'uom s'etterna;
    e quant'io l'abbia in grado, mentr'io vivo
    convien che nella mia lingua si scerna.

In Ciardi's English:

For that sweet image, gentle and paternal
    you were to me in the world when hour by hour
    you taught me how man makes himself eternal

lives in my mind, and now strikes to my heart;
    and while I live, the gratitude I owe it
    will speak to men out of my life and art.

From *The American Scholar,* Summer 1983.

As We Like It: How a Girl Can Be Smart and Still Popular

In the major literature there are no useful bildungsromans for girls. A boy's development into manhood through testing experience is one of the oldest themes in literature; Homer's Telemachus presents the first model of how to grow into the kind of man one's society approves and has need of. From the *Odyssey* to "The Bear," literature affords a long procession of raw youths; almost all manage to become men. Girls, however, had to wait out a twenty-five-hundred-year history before anyone made fiction of their growth. When Evelina and Emma did at length appear on the scene, a capable girl—let us imagine, for example, the young Florence Nightingale—might have been pardoned for feeling that whatever else they did, these characters scarcely enlarged her sense of possibility. The scope of their activities was even more restricted than that of the ladies who created them—who did, at least, write books. Only the dearth of images of the possibilities open to a developing girl can explain the immense influence of a novel that most males never read, Louisa May Alcott's *Little Women*.

Yet young females, like young males, create themselves according to the models their society provides for them; and, like young males, those who read look in literature for images of what they could and ought to be. Stories of female trial and initiation are by their nature difficult for male writers to provide, and we should remember that from Sappho—*floruit* 600 B.C.—to Jane Austen, there were hardly any writers who were not male. Male writers, of course, can and do provide models for females, but not very many. A cursory check of the dramatis personae of any Elizabethan play will demonstrate what is still true of modern fiction: female characters are greatly outnumbered. (A London director has estimated that there are five times as many parts for actors as for actresses.) Still, quantity is not everything. Literate girls could find without difficulty images which, although they lacked the dimension of development, still provided a warm variety of ways of being female. They could—like everybody else—read Shakespeare.

As classics go, Shakespeare isn't bad reading for a girl. The conventions of tragedy and romance offer horizons considerably wider than those available in Fanny Burney and Jane Austen; the courts of Europe and the seacoasts of Bohemia provide backgrounds in which a girl can imagine herself doing far more interesting things than she could at home. It is true that, unlike those paradoxical dramatists of male-chauvinist Athens, Shakespeare never allows a woman a play of her own. He provides neither *Antigone*s nor *Medea*s; no feminine name appears in his titles except as the second member of a male-female pair. Yet a girl can read Shakespeare without calling upon the defenses necessary for Milton or Hemingway, or Lawrence or Mailer—writers she must read callused for survival, a black in Mr. Charlie's land. Shakespeare liked women and respected them; not everybody does. We do not find him, like Milton, luxuriating in the amoebic submissiveness of an Eve in Paradise, and we can surmise that he would have found little interest in the dim Marias and complaisant Catherines whom Hemingway found nonthreatening. He is not afraid of the kind of assertiveness and insistence on her own judgment that Eve displays when she gets busy bringing death into the world and all our woe; the evidence of the plays is that he positively enjoyed it.

From Mrs. Jameson on, critics, male and female, have praised Shakespeare's women. "The dignity of Portia, the energy of Bea-

trice, the radiant high spirits of Rosalind, the sweetness of Viola"—
William Allan Neilson's encomia can stand for thousands of others.
Juliet, Cordelia, Rosalind, Beatrice, Cleopatra, Hermione, Emilia,
Paulina—Shakespeare's girls and mature women are individualized,
realized, fully enjoyed as human beings. His respect for women is
evident in all the plays, but it is in the middle comedies that the
most dazzling image recurs. It is an image significant for what it can
tell us about the extent—and the limits—of acceptable feminine
activity in the Shakespearian world, a world which in this as in
other things remains, over time and change, disconcertingly like our
own.

Limits? What limits? It would seem that no girl need feel herself
diminished when she reads *As You Like It, The Merchant of Venice*, or
Much Ado. Rather, she is given a glittering sense of possibility. Who
would not, if she could, be beautiful, energetic, active, verbally
brilliant, and still sought after by desirable men, like these Shakespearian heroines? Hebraic and Pauline tradition might subordinate
the female; secular codes might make her, like Juliet and Portia, her
father's to dispose of as he wished, to a man who, once her husband,
could exercise over her the same absolute dominion. Yet Juliet and
Portia, like Rosalind and the ladies of *Love's Labour's Lost*, clearly
think of themselves as autonomous people. Submissive mildness is
not lacking in Shakespeare: Bianca and Hero and Mariana would
content a Milton and reassure even a Mailer. But such characters are
never central to the action—logically enough, because they do not
act. Apparent exceptions are seen to prove the rule: beneath Cordelia's gentleness is a strain of iron stubbornness that Milton would
probably have welcomed much as Lear did.

Bianca and her like do not interest Shakespeare. When he does
bring this kind of woman to full individuality it is, significantly
enough, not to present her as an effective human being but to offer
her to our sympathies, as he does with Desdemona and Ophelia, as a
helpless victim. What catches his imagination in *As You Like it, The
Merchant of Venice*, and *Much Ado* is a young woman of an entirely
different kind: one who, by her energy, wit, and combativeness,
successfully demonstrates her ability to control events in the world
around her, not excluding the world of men. Perhaps we should not

be surprised that the greatest Elizabethan was attracted by the qualities of his sovereign, who told her lords that "though I be a woman, I have as good a courage answerable to my place as ever my father had. . . . I thank God I am endued with such qualities that were I turned out of the realm in my petticoat, I were able to live in any place in christendom."

But perhaps we should be surprised; there are no such women in Marlowe or Jonson or the other dramatists who could have been expected to remember the qualities of the Virgin Queen. In drama as elsewhere, men find such women hard to handle, and often hard to take. Shakespeare knew how to manage them—at least on stage. That he could create women who were spunky enough to be fun to be with, and still find ways to mediate their assertiveness so as to render them as nonthreatening as their softer sisters, is one of the secrets of his perennial appeal. His is one of the surer methods of keeping a love story from liquefying prematurely, durable enough to remain serviceable to Yale professors who write best-sellers—as we shall see.

We should note at the outset something that Shakespeare's wide-ranging geography and tapestried history can easily obscure: that whoever and wherever they are, the sphere of action he allows his women is severely limited. As Betty Bandel shows in her fascinating 1951 Columbia dissertation, "Shakespeare's Treatment of the Social Position of Women," Shakespeare never dramatizes, even peripherally, a learned woman (although women may be, even should be, "wise"). Nor, in so many plays that deal with politics, does he ever present a woman who is active in politics on her own behalf, in spite of the example of the sovereign under whom he spent his formative years. The type of "la très sage Héloïse" interests him no more than Joan of Arc does, and although his women often intervene forcefully in political matters, it is always in the interest of the male to whom they are attached, whether husband, lover or son; and usually—as with Lady Macbeth—their influence is for the worse. Professor Bandel points out that even when a tradition of independent action clearly exists, as with Cleopatra, Shakespeare does not use it; he leaves undeveloped Plutarch's suggestions of the queen's political ability and power. "The play is not the play of a

woman ruler; insofar as Cleopatra is concerned, it is the play of one
of the sisterhood 'that trade in love.'" Similarly, it would have been
easy, in *All's Well That Ends Well,* to give Helena the credit for the
skill that cures the king of France; the knowledge of herbs and
simples was an acceptable part of the feminine role. Instead, she
merely administers the medicine bequeathed her by her father the
physician.

But what Shakespeare does not do is far less immediately striking than what he does, and what he does is to glorify as never before
the image of the bright young girl. In *Much Ado,* in *As You Like It,* in
The Merchant of Venice, the image recurs, lovingly differentiated, but
the same in its essentials: a young woman who is to delight the
audience by her beauty, vigor, self-confidence, and wit.

It is Beatrice and Benedick who provide the real interest of
Much Ado. As we have seen, when Shakespeare himself couples a
masculine and feminine name, the feminine comes last; but although Juliet follows Romeo and Cleopatra, Antony, in the mouth
of both common reader and critic Beatrice precedes Benedick. From
the beginning, it is Beatrice who determines the tenor of the relationship: "I wonder that you will still be talking, Signior Benedick.
Nobody marks you." Benedick's parry is instant—"What, my dear
Lady Disdain! are you yet living?"—but it is a response to her
initiative; the lady has taken the offensive, and Beatrice will give as
good as she gets. The young woman and the young man are endowed with the same kind of wit and the same enjoyment of verbal
competitiveness. The pleasure of watching them lies in the equality
of the match.

It is significant that Shakespeare went to the trouble of inventing Beatrice and Benedick; there is no trace of them in the Renaissance originals. It is already clear in *Love's Labour's Lost* that he
enjoyed this kind of relationship, and this kind of woman. Born in a
merry hour, when a star danced, Beatrice clearly is delightful to her
creator. The older men in the play also find her attractive and charming; although her uncle warns her she will never get a husband if she
"be so shrewd of her tongue," the tone of the reproof is light and
leads merely to further cheerful repartee. Don Pedro considers her
"a pleasant-spirited lady" and actually makes her a semiserious pro-

posal, to which she replies that so grand a match would only do for Sundays. Like Benedick, she has a good time making jokes against marriage, and there is no tinge of bitterness in them. Both are good-natured beneath their repartee; they are obviously well suited, and it's no wonder their friends decide to bring them together.

Beatrice's capacities match Benedick's; so does her cheerful self-assertion. That, it would seem, is the point of what's going on; that is what Shakespeare intends his audience to enjoy. Yet if we examine more closely this apparent glorification of equality between the sexes, we shall discover that what it in fact demonstrates is exactly what its glitter obscures: that if the bright young girl is to be made acceptable—to audiences, to readers, perhaps even to her creator—ways must be found to reduce the impact of her self-confidence, to make sure that equality is kept nominal.

There is an undercurrent of uneasiness in the audience's response to Beatrice. Ellen Terry warned that Beatrice's encounters with Benedick "can easily be made to sound vulgar and malicious" and cautioned the actress taking the part to speak with "the lightest raillery with mirth in voice and a charm in manner." Don Pedro may find her charming, her uncle may value her gaiety, but young males are more vulnerable. *Much Ado* is not out to test the limits of our tolerance for feminine assertiveness. Shakespeare's bright young girls are meant to please, not to make us uncomfortable. A way must be found to mitigate this lightest of threats. We need some reassurance that Beatrice cannot hurt us, and Shakespeare will provide it.

Beatrice and Benedick are both scoffers at Cupid, and as their personalities are similar, so the stratagems that are to make them fall in love seem at first glance strictly parallel. Equally matched, male and female apparently are to be treated with strict equality. Their friends arrange for each to overhear a put-up conversation; planted in it is the information that, in spite of all appearances, each is hopelessly in love with the other. We might expect that the two conversations, parallel in their effects, would also be parallel in content, but this is by no means so. Benedick merely overhears a circumstantial account of how much Beatrice is in love with him. Beatrice, however, must hear herself accused of scornful carping which "turns . . . every man the wrong side out," of disdain, of pride, of egoism. "Her wit," says her cousin Hero,

> Values itself so highly that to her
> All matter else seems weak. She cannot love,
> Nor take no shape nor project of affection,
> She is so self-endeared.

Although she and Benedick have been presented up to this point as two of a kind, Benedick is not thus criticized. Young females are expected to temper their behavior to the vulnerability of the male, and those who fail to do so expose themselves to the censure of their peers. We remember that earlier, although Beatrice bore up well under Benedick's taunt that she got her wit from a joke book, her retort (that he was called "the Prince's jester") sent him off to complain to his friends that "she speaks poniards, and every word stabs." Merry Beatrice is no Katharine, but she is tainted with shrewishness. Although her cousin's criticism is touched with hyperbole, Beatrice is evidently meant to take it to heart. And so she does. Benedick does not hear her recantation, delivered in soliloquy, but the audience must.

> What fire is in mine ears? Can this be true?
> Stand I condemn'd for pride and scorn so much?
> Contempt, farewell! and maiden pride, adieu!
> No glory lives behind the back of such.
> And, Benedick, love on; I will requite thee,
> Taming my wild heart to thy loving hand . . .

At the end she is still joking; when Benedick tells her that he takes her for pity, she replies that she yields only to save his life. But the audience can feel quite comfortable. The slight ambiguity of her character need never be resolved. We need not decide whether or not there is a bit of the shrew in Beatrice; since we know that she will need no taming, it does not matter.

This is, of course, the ideal: the high-spirited woman who will tame herself. She offers both men and women that most precious of assurances—that they can have it both ways. To women, a girl like

Beatrice affirms their bright potentialities, but also the warm safety of a conviction that these should never be displayed in any way that could threaten men. The men in the audience—like the men in the play—can enjoy her company, free from both the threat of insubordination and the necessity of putting her in her place. Only the most flamboyant of Petruchios enjoys playing the tyrant; it is much pleasanter not to have to.

If Beatrice is delightful, Rosalind is even better. Neilson (who, as president of Smith College, occupied a privileged position for girl-watching) describes her as having "the wit of Portia and Beatrice softened by the gentleness of Viola"—exactly as we like it. In *As You Like It,* however, Shakespeare does not hesitate to tip the equal balance that affords the fun of *Much Ado* in favor of the lady; in wit and energy, Rosalind has no male rival. Insofar as any other character is able to match her repartee, it is Celia, who although she is usually remembered as the gentle foil, the "other kind" of girl, turns out to have a surprising number of the snappy lines. Orlando is merely a nice young man.

Rosalind, however, is more than witty. *As You Like It* is her play. This, of course, is unusual in Shakespeare. Heroes act, but heroines commonly do not, which is why, unlike Antigone and Lysistrata, none of them gets a Shakespearian title to herself. Neither does Rosalind—although Thomas Lodge had accorded her one—but nevertheless it is she who moves the play. She is energetic, effective, successful. She has the courage to accept exile; she decides to assume male dress, and, playing brother, she guides her friend to the Forest of Arden. The late comedies no longer present these forceful young women, and the faithful Imogen of *Cymbeline* retroactively exposes the extent of Rosalind's autonomy. It is not Imogen but her husband's servant who originates the idea of male disguise; the necessity for her journey originates not in her own position but in her relation to her husband, and as soon as she lacks a man to guide her, she gets lost. Her complaint at this point measures her distance from Rosalind: "I see a man's life is a tedious one." (Her previous remark to Cloten also bears thinking about: "You put me to forget a lady's manners / By being so verbal." Through Imogen we can appreciate the unique position of Rosalind in her play. Rosalind's

decisions control the progress of *As You Like It,* and it is through her
agency that the four couples assemble in the concluding nuptial
dance which, as in *The Boke of the Governor,* "betokeneth concord"
and embodies for the audience the harmony restored that is the
essence of Shakespearian comedy.

Yet Shakespeare arranges for her to do all this without making
the ladies censorious or the gentlemen nervous. He has various
methods of rendering her wit painless and her initiatives acceptable.
The most obvious way is to confine them to love matters, a proper
feminine sphere. Rosalind is a political exile, but she shows no
disposition to meddle in politics; it is not through her agency that
her father is restored to his rightful place. Her wit is not, like Portia's, exercised in the service of sensible men engaged in the serious
business of the world, nor are her jokes made at their expense. Her
satire is, in fact, narrowly directed at two classes of beings—sighing
lovers and women. In the course of the fun she works her way
through most of the accusations already traditional in a large anti-
feminist literature (inconstancy, contrariness, jealousy, unfaithful-
ness, and so on)* to the point where Celia tells her, "We must have
your doublet and hose pluck'd over your head, and show the world
what the bird has done to her own nest." Add that we know all
along that she herself is the butt of her own jokes, being herself both
lovesick and female, and it would be a fragile Benedick indeed who
could feel himself stabbed by her poniard.

The most useful dramatic device for mediating the initiatives of
the female, however, is the male disguise. Male garments immensely
broaden the sphere in which female energy can manifest itself.
Dressed as a man, a nubile woman can go places and do things she
couldn't do otherwise, thus moving the play out of the court and
the closet and into interesting places like forests or Welsh moun-
tains. Once Rosalind is disguised as a man, she can be as saucy and
self-assertive as she likes. (We can observe a similar change come
over sweet Viola of *Twelfth Night* as soon as she begins to play the

---

*The survey of this tradition is one of the most valuable contributions of
Professor Bandel's dissertation, which reviews the position of women in English
literature from Anglo-Saxon times to Shakespeare.

clever page.) The characters, male and female, will accept her behavior because it does not offend their sense of propriety; the audience, male and female, because they know she's playing a role. With male dress we feel secure. In its absence, feminine assertiveness is viewed with hostility, as with Kate the Shrew, or at best, as with Beatrice, as less than totally positive. Male dress transforms what otherwise could be experienced as aggression into simple high spirits.

The temporary nature of the male disguise is of course essential, since the very nature of Shakespearian comedy is to affirm that disruption is temporary, that what has turned topsy-turvy will be righted. It is evident that Rosalind has enjoyed the flexibility and freedom that come with the assumption of the masculine role, but it is also evident that she will gladly and voluntarily relinquish it. "Down on your knees," she tells the proud shepherdess who scorns her faithful swain, "And thank heaven, fasting, for a good man's love." Rosalind, clearly, is thankful for Orlando's, and although she is twice the person he is, we are willing to believe that they live happily ever after, since that's obviously what she wants.

Portia is another lady who outweighs her man. Bassanio is one of the most firmly nonmemorable of Shakespeare's characters, but Portia is nonetheless delighted with him. It is true that she has more excuse than Rosalind. Bassanio may be no more than a pleasantly affectionate incompetent in need of a rich wife to free him of his debts. But Portia is not free to choose her husband; Shakespearian fathers may dispose of their daughters as they will, and she must marry the fellow who chooses the right casket. Among suitors who include a drunken German, an Englishman who speaks no European language, and an African prince in whose negritude she finds no appeal, Bassanio looks good. She can, after all, make up what he lacks in intelligence and force. His improvidence and poor judgment have put his friend's life in jeopardy, and he lacks the wit to extricate him. It is not he who possesses the resourcefulness to pass himself off as a lawyer, or the brains to find a technicality to win on. Portia sends her newly wed husband off to Venice to bid goodbye to the friend he has ruined, since this is evidently all he is capable of. She herself posts off to assume the male attire that will make possible her triumph over Shylock.

Portia recalls Beatrice and Rosalind, but, unlike them, she is allowed to engage her intelligence with matters more serious than the pairing of lovers. The law, the quality of mercy, the survival of a man—alone of Shakespeare's heroines, Portia is allowed to confront a man over matters outside a woman's sphere, and to win. (A somewhat similar confrontation occurs in *Measure for Measure*—not mediated by male dress—but Isabella's opposition to Angelo is swiftly reduced to sexual terms, and she thereafter loses the center of the stage.) Even the male disguise will hardly be enough to render harmless such a formidable lady. We may expect that special means will be necessary to mitigate this unusually serious threat.

One way is to reduce the significance of her male adversary. Shylock is a man, but one with whom the audience was not expected readily to identify. The Elizabethan response to Shylock was far less ambiguous than our own. Shakespeare's audience unquestionably would have found it reassuring that the man Portia confronted and vanquished was not a person of her own status in society, but a misbelieving Jew.

The audience, however, needs more explicit reassurance than this. It is provided. Here, in the only play beside *As You Like It* where Shakespeare allows a woman's action to control the outcome,* Shakespeare makes sure that Portia does not have her day in court until she has explicitly affirmed her subordination to her husband-to-be. Portia's betrothal speech to Bassanio rivals in its length, its emphasis, and its poetry even the locus classicus where Shakespeare showed the proper attitude of a girl whose assertiveness was unmitigated by charm and good nature toward a husband likewise not notably endowed with either. Katharine's submission to Petruchio is famous:

> Thy husband is thy lord, thy life, thy keeper,
> Thy head, thy sovereign; one that cares for thee. . . .
> Such duty as the subject owes the prince

---

*If *Macbeth* and *Antony and Cleopatra* present themselves as exceptions, we should reflect both that the actions of Lady Macbeth and Cleopatra do not uniquely determine the outcome and that the outcome is catastrophic. As much can be said of Volumnia in *Coriolanus*.

> Even such a woman oweth to her husband;
> And when she is froward, peevish, sullen, sour,
> And not obedient to his honest will,
> What is she but a foul contending rebel
> And graceless traitor to her loving lord?
> I am asham'd that women are so simple
> To offer war when they should kneel for peace,
> Or seek for rule, supremacy, and sway,
> Where they are bound to serve, love, and obey.

And a great deal more of the same. Katharine's speech, considering what she's just been through, might be considered a bit overwrought. Portia's, however, seems to well up quite spontaneously, and it is just as strongly phrased. She wishes herself "a thousand times more fair, ten thousand times / More rich" just to be good enough for Bassanio. Yet, says this lady who is about to astonish the Venetian courts,

> . . . the full sum of me . . .
> Is an unlesson'd girl, unschool'd, unpractis'd;
> Happy in this, she is not yet so old
> But she may learn; happier than this,
> She is not bred so dull but she can learn;
> Happiest of all is that her gentle spirit
> Commits itself to yours to be directed,
> As from her lord, her governor, her king.
> Myself and what is mine to you and yours
> Is now converted. But now I was the lord
> Of this fair mansion, master of my servants,
> Queen o'er myself; and even now, but now
> This house, these servants, and this same myself
> Are yours, my lord . . .

"Thy lord, thy life, thy keeper, / Thy head, thy sovereign"—or "Her lord, her governor, her king." But this is not an admission wrung from ill-natured, headstrong Katharine, this is Portia speaking, brilliant Portia, confident Portia, who will soon be off to accomplish what no male Venetian seems able to. She speaks in this vein for twenty-four lines; Katharine's submission takes forty-four. No audience, as far as I know, has complained of the length. It is in-

teresting, then, to compare Shakespeare's treatment of one of the
rare occasions when a man submits. In such a case, our patience is
assumed to be short. In *The Merry Wives of Windsor* Master Ford
makes an apology to his wife for having incorrectly suspected her
virtue. He imprudently begins, "Pardon me, wife. Henceforth do
what thou wilt." This is too much; he scarcely gets out four more
lines before Master Page interrupts him: " 'Tis well, 'tis well; no
more. / Be not as extreme in submission as in offence." Once again
we are shown that when the sexes are reversed, parallel situations
lose their similarity.

Brilliant and fascinating women are a pleasure to watch, once
we can be sure they will accept the control even of the Bassanios and
Orlandos of the world—at least this was so in Elizabethan England.
That was, however, a long time ago. Shakespeare's feminine models
certainly can be seen as significant to the pre-twentieth-century
reader. But today's young girls have never heard of Rosalind and
Beatrice. To consider that Shakespeare's comic heroines have something to tell us about the twentieth-century feminine image would
seem to be academicism gone overboard.

And yet—have you by any chance seen *Love Story,* or read it?
Millions have, if you have not; for many, the story of the doomed
love of Jenny Cavilleri and Oliver Barrett III stands as an epitome of
what the relationship between young male and young female should
be. The popularity of Erich Segal's *Love Story* is genuine and significant; it expresses what a very large number of people believe. If we
scrutinize it we will discover something that we may find encouraging or disconcerting: Segal has demonstrated that the Shakespearian formula is still a winner.

Invent a girl of charm and intellect; allow her ego a brief pre-
marital flourishing; make clear that it is soon to subside into voluntarily assumed subordination; make sure that this is mediated by
love. Today, however, the archetypal bright young girl is to be
found, not in courts or forests, but in the Radcliffe library.

When a likely Harvard jock tries to borrow a book, Jenny, like
Beatrice, takes the offensive. "Do you have your own library?" she
asks, and the parry and thrust that follow impart a sense of dèjá vu.
It glitters with I.Q., and the heroine wins it. It is only the first of a

series; she wins them all. However tricky her Benedick's riposte, she always tops it. She's lovely when she takes off her glasses; she is brilliant, but she is nice too, sweet and warm and young, and the audience cries at the end much as it did when Juliet died some years ago in another successful love story. We who teach college students, especially female ones, had better watch out how we knock *Love Story;* those tears are wet, and as many of our students have told us, they don't care what we say, it's a beautiful story. And if we take the unaccustomed trouble to consider it from a young girl's point of view, we must concede that it is a compelling one: who wouldn't want to be beautiful, clever, and good, like Jenny?

Like Shakespeare, Segal writes for the box office, and like Shakespeare in the romantic comedies, he writes not to disturb, but to reassure. Oliver and Jenny are no more likely to disrupt the social order than are Florizel and Perdita. The Harvard they inhabit is as remote from today's vexed colleges as the Forest of Arden. *Love Story* is built to last—on the hypothesis that demonstrations and demands for relevance are temporary phenomena, but that images of youthful brilliance, generational misunderstanding, love, and early death are likely to retain their traditional interest. So, evidently, is the bright young girl. We may refuse to accept Jenny as an avatar of Rosalind and Beatrice, but we are bound to recognize her, complete with the assertiveness, the charm, and the fundamental acquiescence in traditional sex roles that allow us to have our cake and eat it.

Jenny's verbal one-upmanship must not be allowed to mislead us. Her aggressiveness is only apparent, part of the delightful game that assures us that this prize is worth having. Since Jenny wins each verbal passage, her Benedick has to discover this in bed, the minimal measure of how far the social mores have progressed since Shakespeare. The necessary reassurance comes with the required explicitness: "Our first physical encounter was the polar opposite of our first verbal one. . . . This was the real Jenny—the soft one, whose touch was so light and loving." The real Jenny is as different from the clever one as the "unlesson'd girl" is from the shyster lawyer. The clever Jenny has a scholarship to study in Paris; the real Jenny gives it up without hesitation when Oliver asks, "What about our marriage?" The clever Jenny keeps up the repartee and never loses a set, but the real Jenny has given up all for love. When Oliver is disinherited by a stern father, Jenny teaches music to support him through law school. She gives up participation in music groups. "She came home from Shady Lane exhausted, and there was dinner to cook." Woman's work is never done. Oliver, after all, is making a sacrifice too; he has had to give up football. There is no suggestion that the independent exercise of her highly trained abilities gives her the slightest satisfaction; her work is obviously temporary. When Oliver lands the lucrative job proper to an all-Ivy jock who has graduated third in his class, the only Wasp in the top ten, Jenny retires contentedly into an expensive apartment on East Sixty-third Street and assumes the activities proper to a woman whose husband is supporting her. She cooks for him (even later, when she's dying, she fends off his attempts to help because that isn't "man's work"). She goes to work on getting pregnant. And she obediently enters upon the conspicuous consumption that he sees as the blazon of his triumph.

It pleases us to see that, like Rosalind and Portia, Jenny is wiser than her man, and it's made clear that she uses her charge accounts, as she does everything else, only because he wants her to. We are allowed to understand that her own values are less crudely materialistic, but that she is too wise not to indulge her husband's fierce competitiveness in these unimportant matters. For all the verbal victories are kept carefully only verbal. The one matter of substance on which she and Oliver disagree is his implacable refusal to understand his father, and although she is shown to be absolutely right when she calls her husband a heartless bastard, she obediently abandons her attempt to soften him, and the final reconciliation between father and son is brought about only through her death. Jenny, we are given to understand on the last page, is more than a tender memory, she is an enduring influence—but an influence of the traditional womanly kind, whose strength is in its gentleness and willingness to give way.

So Jenny dies, and millions weep for her, including many who will not afterward admit it. I teach at an extremely unsophisticated college,* but unsophisticated students are not without perspicacity.

---

*The reader will note that many things have changed since 1972, when this was written, among them where I teach.

The force with which my students insist on the enduring beauty of *Love Story* is intensified by a certain irritation growing out of their suspicion that their sophisticated teachers are, as usual, trying to put something over on them. They suspect that we are quite simply lying; that either we did cry at *Love Story,* or that if we did condescend to read it, we would. I suspect they are right. Our need for images of brightness and beauty, fidelity and tenderness, is insatiable. Sophisticated modern literature refuses to give them to us, and rightly; the cleverer we are, the surer it is that we will repudiate in today's fiction the patterns that free us to weep at *Romeo and Juliet* and smile at *As You Like It.*

Yet love stories are hardy, as Segal knew when he chose his title. Stereotypes do not necessarily detract from their durability, for truth, unfortunately for us sophisticates, is an essential component of stereotypes. Women commonly do smooth their assertiveness into acceptability, and it is those who do so who are experienced as charming—by men and by women. Women frequently do exercise a softening influence on the extremes of male competition; they do, like Portia and Isabella and Jenny (and Antigone) speak out for mercy and the relaxation of the lethal rigidities of men. Literature is not unrealistic in representing this as one of the most satisfactory ways in which women interact with men; and Shakespeare may not be unrealistic, either, in bodying forth the repulsion of the race when even women abandon gentleness for ambition and aggression. "Proper deformity shows not in the fiend / So horrid as in woman." Theodore Roszak has recently called for a liberation of "the compassionate virtues"—in men as well as in women—and has warned that the world will not be better if women exercise their indubitable right to be "every bit the brutes and bastards men have been. . . . Courage, daring decisiveness, resourcefulness are good qualities, in women as much so as in men. So, too, are charity, mercy, tenderness. But ruthlessness, callousness, power, lust, domineering self-assertion . . . these are destructive, whether in man or woman."

Literature, however, which is still overwhelmingly produced by males, has not been very helpful in providing the young girl with the bildungsroman that would show her how to combine the compassionate virtues with the expansion of ego-strength that is her due as a human being. Shakespeare does better than the rest; as accurately as if he had died yesterday, he represents the limits a girl can reach and still be sure of the approval of her society. But it remains true that no major writer since those curious, woman-obsessed Athenians has made a woman's active heroism his or her central concern, and that a girl who wants, in George Eliot's words, "to make her life greatly effective" can search the literature of her own civilization and find, even in George Eliot, only treatments of how to fail in the attempt. The point of the male bildungsroman, however, is that it deals not with failure but with success. *The Mill on the Floss* and *Middlemarch* come as close to the model as the feminine situation has allowed, yet Maggie is destroyed by her surging emotions, and Dorothea Brooke is explicitly presented as a balked Saint Theresa with no convents to found. George Eliot wrote *Middlemarch* to show the forces that prevent a woman from being a hero. Unless or until these forces lose their strength, the best a girl can hope for is to be a heroine, while waiting for the new literature that will render *Love Story*—but not, we hope, Shakespeare—hopelessly out of date.

From *The American Scholar*, Spring 1973; reprinted in *The Woman's Part: Feminist Criticism of Shakespeare*, ed. Carolyn Ruth Swift Lenz, Gayle Greene, and Carol Thomas Neely (Urbana: University of Illinois Press, 1980).

"Canst Thou Not Minister
to a Mind Diseas'd?"

I n the tragedy by Euripides, Heracles comes home in triumph after the heavy labors inflicted on him by the goddess Hera. His wife has been waiting for him for a long time. They have a brief and happy reunion. Then, totally without warning, he goes mad and slaughters her and his two young sons, only to awaken to the inexplicability of what he has done. It is a not unfamiliar kind of event; however little we may know of Heracles, we watch the evening news. A psychotic episode is what we would call it today, and we would anticipate a successful insanity defense. Euripides sent Madness—Lussa—herself onstage to show the characteristic sudden onset. He made clear that Heracles himself had done nothing to bring on this pointless horror; it occurred merely because Hera hated him—for her own thoroughly personal, thoroughly contemptible reasons. So difficult is it to understand where madness comes from.

Mental illness is as endemic in literature as in life. The hero Ajax, in Sophocles' tragedy, suffers the same kind of sudden, destructive attack, after which, in shame, he commits suicide. Unlike the madness of Heracles, his is called a divine illness—a *theia nosos*.

Like Heracles', it is inflicted by a goddess—ironically, Athena, the goddess of wisdom. She had a good reason, however, unlike Hera. Sophocles was a pious man, as Euripides was not; he was not out to challenge received explanations, but to confirm them. Ajax, for all his greatness, had made a very serious error: he had boasted that his achievements were his own. All the stories show that it is a mistake to claim that your strength owes nothing to the gods. For Sophocles, madness and death are seen as punishment for such hubris.

The cases of Heracles and Ajax invite reconsideration of an idea, once radical, that has grown familiar to the point of cliché. Twenty-five years ago Thomas Szasz proclaimed that mental illness is a myth, a label our conformist society puts on a person who is different from ourselves, to devalue him, stigmatize him, cast him out, or lock him up. Michel Foucault's *Histoire de la folie,* published in America in 1965 as *Madness and Civilization,* presented a variant; invoking the trinity of Nietzsche, van Gogh, and Artaud, he saw insanity as a kind of splendid freedom. The history of psychic intervention was a history of repression by society. Two years later, R. D. Laing's *Politics of Experience* popularized these ideas for the receptive children of the sixties. Primitive societies, we were told, are wiser and kinder; there, the right hemisphere of the brain dominates; there, they recognize the value of the madman's visions; there, he is the shaman, the prophet. *The madman*—those who embraced this reinterpretation of the phenomena of psychiatry tended to revert to the word *madness,* long out of use in referring to the insane or mentally ill. Poetic, archaic, Shakespearean, the word *madness* lent to mental aberration an aura of romance. No one wishes to be thought insane, schizophrenic, psychotic. But are we not all a little mad? Medical terms exclude and frighten us, but *madness* opens to include us all.

Madness is an enduring experience, whether we call it Lussa or Mania or Paranoia as the Greeks did, or insanity or schizophrenia or psychosis. Every society recognizes it. As Fuller Torrey points out in *The Mind Game* (1972), every language has a word for "crazy." Even primitive societies have noted that animals go mad and that people do too. The same tribes that honor the shaman also have their plain lunatics. As with us, they are sometimes treated humanely, sometimes cast out and ridiculed. Everywhere, crazy people tend to outnumber prophets. Every culture must recognize the existence of a class of people who behave in unpredictable, yet reasonably characteristic ways—ways that range from the disconcerting to the terrifying. They are rarely treated just like other people, because the things they say and do seem to demand some kind of special treatment. The issue is, what kinds of special treatment have different societies thought appropriate, and why?

But do we not know the answers to that question, at least for our own tradition? *Daimonie!* say Homer's heroes to each other when one of them has made a crazy statement. God bless you! say we, when one of us sneezes, to encourage the demon's departure. *Daimon* is the intermediate kind of spirit, neither human nor fully divine; transformed as *demon,* the Greek word permeated the languages of Christian Europe. We have seen that fifth-century Greeks, contemporaries of Socrates, thought madness was inflicted by the gods. Scripture concurs: God sent an evil spirit upon Saul, and Jesus had the power to cast out devils.

> And one of the multitude . . . said, Master, I have brought unto thee my son, which hath a dumb spirit; and wheresoever he taketh him, he teareth him: and he foameth, and gnasheth with his teeth, and pineth away. . . . And [Jesus] asked his father, How long is it ago since this came unto him? And he said, of a child. And of times it hath cast him into the fire, and into the waters, to destroy him. . . . And Jesus rebuked the foul spirit . . . and the spirit cried, and rent him sore, and came out of him; and he was as one dead. . . . But Jesus took him by the hand, and lifted him up, and he arose.

Demons existed—fallen angels; demons could enter human souls and bodies; demons could cause mental and physical illness. If the mentally ill are thought to be possessed, will they not be treated accordingly? Do we not know that in the past—exactly when is uncertain, as we shall see—the mentally ill were tortured or burnt at the stake by superstitious Inquisitors, or, if they escaped that, chained and scourged and prayed at to get the demons out? As the psychiatrist Gregory Zilboorg wrote in 1935 in *The Medical Man and the Witch during the Renaissance,* still for most psychiatrists and psychologists the authoritative history of psychiatric treatment, "The differentiation [among] a mentally sick person, a witch, and a heretic became less and less definite, so that towards the middle of the thirteenth century these became synonymous in the mind of man."

Seventy years before the Salem witch trials, in the era of Galileo and Bacon, Robert Burton reported the case of a girl who "purged a live eel . . . a foot and a half long," which "afterwards vanished," as well as "great balls of hair, pieces of wood, pigeons' dung," and much else; "they could do no good on her with physic, but left her to the clergy," since "Wierus, Skenkius, Scribanius all agree" that such things "are done by the subtilty and illusions of the devil . . . to try us and our faith . . . 'tis for our offenses, and for the punishment of our sins, by God's permission they do it. . . . So did he afflict Job, Saul, the lunaticks and daemoniacal persons whom Christ cured."

The agreement among Wierus, Skenkius, and Scribanius is rivaled by the modern consensus on how mental illness was explained and treated in the olden days by our naive and superstitious forefathers. The theory of demonic possession has become a commonplace in the half-century since Zilboorg published his book, one etiology at least on which psychoanalysts, behaviorists, and neurologists agree. Thus Frederick Kiel, writing in 1975 in *The Center for Behavior Modification Newsletter,* refers casually to "the eighteenth-century view that schizophrenics were possessed by demons"; thus in 1985 Dr. Bruce Price, working on Alzheimer's disease in the neurology unit of Boston's Beth Israel Hospital, tells an interviewer for Harvard's alumni magazine that "in the 1800's any kind of mental aberration was seen as possession of some sort— demonic." One can imagine the surprise of Philippe Pinel or Benjamin Rush or Daniel Tuke, or any of the other eighteenth- and nineteenth-century physicians who concerned themselves with the treatment of the insane.

To condescend to the past is both tempting and pleasurable, and all too easy amid the frightening ahistoricity of our education. Yet we need not study the intellectual history of the past two hundred years to suspect generalizations that import medieval demonology into the minds of the medical contemporaries of Voltaire and the Encyclopedists, or indeed into the minds of the physicians who treated our own great-grandfathers. The past remains present if we look and listen, not in scholarly (or unscholarly) histories, but in texts that reach every high school. Shakespeare, says Jan Kott, is our contemporary, and what everybody knows about how madness was regarded in the days of yore is blankly inconsistent with what we know about Shakespeare and Shakespeare's people.

Insanity is endemic in literature. Two centuries and more before readers shuddered at the madwoman in the attic, they laughed at the mad knight of La Mancha. Shakespeare was also Cervantes's contemporary: the Renaissance, as Kenneth Clark and Erwin Panofsky have pointed out, shows a new and intense interest in mental aberration. In three of Shakespeare's four great tragedies, major characters are called mad or lunatic, or are seen as treading the border of madness; madness is an issue in several of the comedies as well. Mental processes and behavior are described exactly enough so that a modern psychiatrist may diagnose their symptoms with a fair degree of precision. We need only think about King Lear, and Lady Macbeth, and Ophelia, and Hamlet, about what they did and said and how other people in the plays responded to them—how, in short, they were *treated,* in both the ordinary and the medical sense of the word—to discover that our capsule history of psychiatry won't do. History is both more complicated and more interesting than that historical sediment that settles into received myths and collective fictions. The familiar texts, looked at without preconceptions, will give us, if possible, even greater respect for the wisdom, breadth, sophistication, and humanity of our forefathers, and leave us with even less respect for our own self-congratulatory oversimplifications. What we know—not as specialists or scholars, but as ordinary readers and playgoers—about Shakespeare's most famous characters is only a beachhead on the immense continent of the history of Renaissance psychology and medicine, but it is one we hold securely, and we can explore it with no more special knowledge than we already possess.

All four of Shakespeare's major tragedies present abnormal psychological states, and madness—actual mental illness—is an issue in three of them. Yet nobody, at any time, anywhere in *Macbeth*, *Hamlet*, or *King Lear*, so much as hints that any of the famous sufferers from a mind diseas'd is possessed by a demon. Such treatments as they receive are clearly medical in nature, prescribed and administered by physicians, and conceptually closely akin to treatments administered today. To confirm this, we need only reread the plays. Only in the context of psychiatric pseudohistory could anything so obvious need underlining.

Consider Lady Macbeth. We all know that it is she who will crack, but the first audiences must have been astonished. For, both before the murder and after, it is Lady Macbeth who is practical, matter-of-fact, controlled, while it is Macbeth who experiences what he is doing so deeply that he seems on the edge of breakdown. When, after he has murdered Duncan, he looks at his bloody hands and says, "This is a sorry sight," she briskly answers, "A foolish thought, to say a sorry sight." When he speaks—surely not literally—of hearing a voice cry out that he has murdered sleep, her reaction is coolly obtuse. Hearing voices? "What do you mean?" she says. "Who was it that thus cried? Why, worthy thane, / You do unbend your noble strength to think / So brainsickly of things." Brainsickly—the word itself refutes the demonists, with the vocabulary of illness—moreover, of illness with a physiological base in the brain. It is Macbeth who acknowledges "the torture of the mind" and the "terrible dreams / That shake us nightly." His wife tells him that "things without remedy should be without regard," and calmly explains his horrified reaction to the ghost of Banquo in strictly medical terms.

We should note that, although hallucinations, auditory or visual ("Is this a dagger that I see before me?"), were then as now recognized as psychiatric symptoms, seeing a ghost is not a sign of madness in the terms set by the play, any more than it is in *Hamlet*, where the ghost is visible to the soldiers and Horatio before it is to the prince. Macbeth sees Banquo's ghost; he doesn't just think he sees it. We see it too: *Enter the Ghost of Banquo and sits in Macbeth's place.* But Lady Macbeth *does not* see it, and she must explain her husband's behavior not only to the assembled thanes, but to herself.

Macbeth has just addressed what appears to all of them as empty air:

> Thou canst not say I did it. Never shake
> Thy gory locks at me.

When a tactful courtier says, "Gentlemen rise. His Highness is not well," Lady Macbeth intervenes with:

> Sit, worthy friends. My lord is often thus,
> And hath been from his youth. Pray you keep seat,
> The fit is momentary, upon a thought
> He will again be well. . . .

She presents his condition, in fact, as an epileptic fit—epilepsy being an illness well known since ancient times. Ignore it, she adds; paying attention to it will only prolong it. But since she is perfectly aware that he has *not* been subject to seizures from his youth, she needs a second explanation that she herself can find satisfactory. Again, it is a perfectly natural one: illusion caused by fear and emotional stress. The sight "might appall the Devil," says Macbeth; she answers, "Oh, proper stuff!"

> This is the very painting of your fear.
> This is the air-drawn dagger which you said
> Led you to Duncan. . . .

She tells him to be a man and pull himself together, which he does—since he is not crazy—as soon as the ghost leaves. He even has the presence of mind to pick up her cover story and reinforce it, telling the guests of his "strange infirmity, which is nothing to those that know me." At the end of the disastrous evening, as they go out together, his wife suggests to him the final medical explanation—he has not been getting enough sleep, "the season of all nature"— which, of course, with the kind of dreams he has been having, is perfectly true. Insomnia is still a commonly noted precursor of psychiatric illness.

But of course it is not Macbeth who is going to be the patient. It

is Lady Macbeth, though Macbeth seemed again and again so much
closer to breaking. We may find Shakespeare's implicit explanation
in what Malcolm says to Macduff when Macduff hears the news of
the massacre of his family and covers his face without speaking:

> What, man! Ne'er pull your hat upon your brows.
> Give sorrow words. The grief that does not speak
> Whispers the o'erfraught heart and bids it break.

It is one more manifestation of Shakespeare's human and psychological insight that, unlike her sensitive husband, Lady Macbeth
gives words neither to sorrow nor to guilt until—well, she does not
go mad, although it is easy to assume she does. She would indeed
be mad if she said while awake such things as she says while walking
in her sleep. But the responses of her gentlewoman and her doctor
make clear that, although she needs "light continually by her" even
by day, she lets slip no such revelations in her waking state. Only in
sleep does this cool and unimaginative woman lose control of the
thoughts she has so effectively suppressed.

Well before we see her, we see the doctor who has been called to
attend to her. He is a true professional; he wishes to establish the
actual symptoms. "Besides her walking and other actual perfor-
mances, what, at any time, have you heard her say?" Her gentlewoman will not repeat it, since, of course, it is highly incriminat-
ing. The doctor reminds her of medical confidentiality, established
since fifth-century Greece in the Hippocratic oath: "You may to me,
and 'tis most meet you should." But in a moment he hears for
himself, and like a careful shrink immediately begins to take notes,
"to satisfy my remembrance more strongly."

Later Macbeth asks him how his patient is doing, using just that
word—*patient*. His agonized question prefigures our modern hopes
that psychiatry can work miracles:

> Canst thou not minister to a mind diseas'd,
> Pluck from the memory a rooted sorrow,
> Raze out the written troubles of the brain,
> And with some sweet oblivious antidote
> Cleanse the stuff'd bosom of that perilous stuff
> Which weighs upon the heart?

Macbeth is appealing for the application of the medical model to a mind diseas'd. He wants the doctor to accord his wife the "sick role," which confers diminished responsibility and which can only be bestowed by a physician. Moreover, sickness may be cured; that is the doctor's job. "Cure her of that," he demands. "Disease," "cure"—this is the vocabulary of medicine.

The doctor, however, demurs. Although he has earlier told the gentlewoman that "this disease is beyond my practice," by this time he is less sure of the word; she is "not so sick, my lord, / As she is troubled with thick-coming fancies / That keep her from her rest." The physician is reluctant to trespass on the border regions of human responsibility. He has heard Lady Macbeth "speak what she should not," though he can scarcely say so to Macbeth. It is not the physician's function to erase the troubles written in the brain by murder. Nor are guilt-caused nightmares and somnambulism madness; the doctor is a courageous man, and with the authority of his profession, he tells Macbeth, "Therein the patient / Must minister to himself." *Patient* is Macbeth's own word, the one he wants to hear, the one the very presence of the doctor establishes. The doctor will use it, but this sickness is spiritual, and he knows that for matters of conscience his skills are irrelevant. He has already told the gentlewoman, "More needs she the divine than the physician"— not, as we might hastily assume, for exorcism, though religious rituals existed (and exist) for the casting out of spirits, but for confession and repentance. The drugs that will help King Lear are useless here; no sweet oblivious antidote can cleanse this bosom. Macbeth has failed of what he wanted: "Throw physic to the dogs, I'll none of it."

The prominence given to naturalistic explanation (which, of course, includes the workings of guilt) is particularly striking in this play. Lear may be more sinned against than sinning, but no one will say that of Lady Macbeth. If there was ever a case where it would have been appropriate to attribute emotional disturbance to demonic possession, it is here, where the whole action has been precipitated by the powers of darkness. *But Shakespeare does not do it.* It was left to a dramatist of our own tormented era, so much less sure of its own rationality, to do what Shakespeare chose not to do, and assimilate Lady Macbeth to the witches. Charles Marowitz, in his modernized version *A Macbeth,* makes a striking effect and a striking point by giving Lady Macbeth Hecate's lines to speak, thus making her the Queen of Hell as well as of Scotland. But his point is not Shakespeare's. The pathology that Shakespeare created for Lady Macbeth is psychologically wholly probable. Everything she says, though it exhibits the fragmentation and irrationality of sleep, refers clearly to what she has literally experienced, and if she says, "Hell is murky," she has good reason. Shakespeare can horrify us with the horrors of our own nature. But while he may allude to the bizarre and the grotesque, and use it to catch his audience's interest, he never luxuriates in it himself. Like Homer and Tolstoy, we can count on him, when faced with horror, to see it, and ask us to see it, in the light that is most reasonable, most decent, most humane.

Hamlet and Ophelia are conceived equally naturalistically; it goes without saying that they are not possessed. It is unnecessary to add to the thousands of pages already extant on the subject of his problematic and her indubitable madness, especially since neither becomes a patient. Though Macbeth summons a doctor to his castle, Shakespeare has dramatic, and Claudius human reasons for not introducing one into Elsinore. Note, however, that Claudius's prescription for Hamlet, a trip to England, though its purpose is hardly hygienic, would seem a natural treatment to everyone at court, since travel, especially sea voyages, had been a recognized therapy for madness since the Greek physician Soranus prescribed them in the second century B.C. The Renaissance doctor would find Hamlet's character type equally familiar. The melancholy man, wrote Timothy Bright in *A Treatise of Melancholy,* is "witty," "excels others," has "dreadful dreams." Above all, though such men think of death "as a terrible thing . . . , notwithstanding, they often desire it . . . eagerly," to the point where it is hard to prevent them from destroying themselves. Bright's description preceded Shakespeare's by fifteen years; otherwise, we might take it for a thumbnail sketch of the brilliant prince who, except for his dreams, could think himself king of infinite space and who longed for his flesh to melt away.

Cordelia gives the unforgettable picture of King Lear:

> . . . mad as the vex'd sea, singing aloud,
> Crowned with rank fumiter and furrow-weeds,
> With hardocks, hemlock, nettles, cuckoo-flowers,
> Darnel, and all the idle weeds that grow
> In our sustaining corn.

In its central paradox it is an emblem of madness, beautiful, yet deviant—the wild garland, various and lovely, yet recognized nevertheless as idle weeds among the necessary, cultivated uniformity of the sustaining corn. Here, as so often, Shakespeare gives everything its due value and proportion. We are about to meet Lear, raving mad; to live through—burn through, said Keats—the great scene with Gloucester, in which the king rises to a level of insight into "how the world goes" that he never reached in eighty years of sanity.

> Plate sin with gold,
> And the strong lance of justice hurtless breaks;
> Arm it in rags, a pigmy's straw does pierce it.

"Reason in madness," as Edgar says, weeping. Edgar weeps, as Cordelia does—for Shakespeare never tips over into the merciless romanticism purveyed by R. D. Laing, who tells a public all too vulnerable to romanticism that "schizophrenia is a reasonable response to an unreasonable world," and that, in a mad world, the schizophrenic alone is sane. It is true that once wrenched out of his normal world Lear sees with new eyes and speaks truths he never knew. Yet however lovely the cuckoo flowers, however searing the mad king's vision, we must at last rely on the sustaining corn that gives us our daily bread. So Cordelia asks what everyone who loves a real mentally ill person (and not a romantic abstraction) must ask, and she asks a doctor:

> What can man's wisdom
> In the restoring his bereaved sense?
> He that helps him take all my outward worth.

The doctor answers reassuringly, prescribing drugs and rest, what most psychiatrists today would prescribe for an acute schizophrenic reaction in a previously well-functioning individual—exactly that class of patients, as Shakespeare's doctor knows, for which the prognosis is most favorable. "There is means," he tells her, "many simples operative" to provoke repose, "our foster-nurse of nature." Cordelia answers:

> All blest secrets,
> All you unpublish'd virtues of the earth,
> Spring with my tears! be aidant and remediate
> In this good man's distress.

And the simples do remediate, along with music, which from the time of Hippocrates—and Saul—had been prescribed to temper "the untun'd and jarring senses" into harmony again. "Louder the music there!" calls the doctor, and Lear wakes, himself again, though it takes him a little time to know it. There is, of course, no suggestion that his illness has been caused by any supernatural agent, by anything but overwhelming emotional and physical stress—the tempest in his mind and the tempest on the heath. Certainly there is no suggestion that his recovery is not to be welcomed, that the awakening of the insane is, as Michel Foucault sees it in *Madness and Civilization,* an "authoritarian intervention" into the madman's "dark freedom."

Throughout, Shakespeare takes a medical model for granted. Lear's poignant outcry, "Keep me in temper, I would not be mad!" directly reflects the contemporary etiology of mental pathology. Though Lear is an irascible man, that "temper" is not anger but its opposite, the tempering, the equable mixing, the Galenic *krasis* of the body's elements that maintains the balance of the temperate soul, its *equanimity.* The benign and competent doctor, when he is ready to wake the old king, "doubt[s] not of his *temperance.*"

But what about Tom-o-Bedlam? "The foul fiend follows me," he says, poor Tom, "whom the foul fiend hath led through fire and through flame, through ford and whirlpool. . . . Peace, thou fiend! . . . The Prince of Darkness is a gentleman." And later, "Five

fiends have been in poor Tom at once: of lust, as Obidicut; Hobbidi-
dence, prince of dumbness; Mahu, of stealing; Modo, of murder;
Flibbertigibbet, of mopping and mowing." At length the fiend is
actually described. The crazed beggar has led the duke of
Gloucester, as he thinks, to the cliffs of Dover; Gloucester, blind and
suicidal, is led to believe he has cast himself over and—mirac-
ulously—has escaped unharmed. He is asked then:

> Upon the crown o' the cliff what thing was that
> Which parted from you?

Gloucester, for all the talk of fiends, answers reasonably and with
sympathy: "A poor, unfortunate beggar." His interlocutor, whom he
does not yet know, creates for his father's blind sockets the complete
picture of a devil, eyes like full moons, a thousand noses, "horns
welk'd and waved like the enridged sea." Gloucester replies,

> That thing you speak of,
> I took it for a man. Often 'twould say
> "The fiend, the fiend"—he led me to that place.

We could not have a better example of a madman, demon and all,
every possible received idea included.

Of course. Because this Tom-o-Bedlam, as we know, though
easily forget, is not a madman at all. He is Gloucester's son Edgar in
disguise. Edgar has put together every cliché of madness to make his
persona convincing to his father, who has already been shown to be
an unusually credulous and suggestible old man, finding portents in
eclipses and ready in a moment to believe his loyal son is out to kill
him. Edgar does convince his father. But he should not convince us
that he is anything more than the idea of a madman, expressly
concocted to appeal to the naivest superstitions of Gloucester—and
the audience in the pit.

Shakespeare was fully conversant with the idea of possession
(he worked up the names of Edgar's foul fiends from a recently
published book). He was equally aware of treatments of mental
illness far less benign than those prescribed by Lear's physician,

treatments in which "they must" (as Rosalind says jokingly in *As You Like It,* and as is actually done in *The Comedy of Errors* and *Twelfth Night*) "be bound and laid in some dark room." But such etiology and such treatment Shakespeare situates firmly in a context of superstition and bad faith. When, in *The Comedy of Errors,* "Doctor" Pinch (no physician, but a schoolmaster) charges Satan to come forth from Antipholus of Ephesus and commands the darkness treatment, the audience, who knows Antipholus is sane, is called upon to agree that Pinch is a "doting wizard." (The Abbess will later explain the supposed madness sensibly and naturalistically.) When Sir Toby and the Clown, in *Twelfth Night,* shut up Malvolio in the dark house and try to make him believe that he is vexed with a "hyperbolic fiend," even a groundling cannot take seriously their appeals to popular superstition. The interview between Malvolio and Feste, falsely masquerading as a priestly exorcist, represents, as the nineteenth-century psychiatrist J. C. Bucknill remarked in *The Mad Folk of Shakespeare* (1867), "a caricature of the idea that madness is occasioned by demonic possession."

Clearly, that idea was common enough; so far the pseudohistorians are right. James I, at whose command *Macbeth* may well have been produced, would not have been in the least surprised to see Lady Macbeth's symptoms attributed to a devil. He might even have taken it as an authorial compliment, since he himself had written a *Daemonology* and called for greater public vigilance against witchcraft. The Bible itself left no room for doubt. In the story of the Gadarene swine (Mark 5:1–20), the unclean spirit tells Jesus, "My name is Legion; for we are many." In Shakespeare's time, the Prince of Darkness was no gentleman, no urbane Mephisto for an eighteenth-century skeptic. Still less was he a metaphor. His power was deadly serious reality—deadly in the old sense of bringing death. For many people it still is. An evil spirit was cast out in my town, while I was writing this, not a mile from my desk—and like King Saul's, it did not stay cast out.

When salvation and damnation are ultimate realities and devils are known to be legion, they must be taken seriously. Those who tortured old women to confess witchcraft and then burned them did not act out of simple cruelty. Confession and punishment in the here and now might save a soul in the hereafter. No believing Christian, Catholic or Protestant, could deny the power of Satan and his hosts. It is no wonder that Sir Thomas Browne, in his tolerant and charitable account of "a doctor's religion," wrote in 1635: "I have ever believed and do now know, that there are Witches; they that doubt of these [note that people did doubt, in the age of Bacon and Galileo] do not only deny *them*, but Spirits; and are obliquely and upon consequence a sort not of Infidels, but Atheists." In Christian Europe there was ample reason, even without cases like that reported by Burton, to agree with Doctors Wierus, Skenkius, and Scribanius that mental (and physical) illness could be caused by demonic possession.

Why, then, was Shakespeare able to perceive madness so astutely? Was it that he was particularly large-minded—as of course he was? That he was ahead of his time? That, it seems, he was not. What was it, then, that tempered the religiously sanctioned, indeed scripturally mandated, belief in demonic possession, so that for the sensible, reasonable mind it was not the primary, evident explanation for mental illness but the explanation turned to last, to explain the inexplicable after everything else had been ruled out? As Burton wrote: "They could do no good on her with physic, but left her to the Clergy."

Let us hope that Beth Israel's neurologist was misquoted, that he never told *Harvard*'s reporter that "the first scientific inkling that there might be any relationship between [mental] aberrations and brain disorder was Alzheimer's [1906] report." For two hundred and fifty years before Shakespeare doctors had been anatomizing the brains of humans. (The great Greek physician Galen, in the second century A.D., had only dissected animals.) Even before the Renaissance brought the rediscovered Greek medical texts to the West, the philosophers and physicians of the Middle Ages had had Aristotle to set beside the Scriptures. Living in the heyday of Hippocratic medicine, Aristotle took a disease model of mental illness for granted, as in the *Nichomachean Ethics* (1149:7), when he speaks of "those who lose their reason from some disease, as epileptics (*epileptikas*) or the insane (*manias nosematodeis*)." That way of thinking was never lost. In Shakespeare's time there was Galen (whose heavy volume is visible onstage in Marlowe's *Dr. Faustus*), as well as recent medical texts. Doctors opened the brain, examined its fluids, mapped its ventricles, and discussed which part of the brain governed which faculty of the mind. These medical texts regularly contained sections on diseases of the head (*de morbis capitis*)—that is, mental illnesses. These were regularly attributed to disorders of brain function and to faulty body metabolism—imbalances among the elements of the body (hot, cold, moist, and dry) and the four humors (blood, black bile, yellow bile, and phlegm). It is, of course, from the Greek for black bile—*melaina cholē*—that the word *melancholy* comes. Hamlet, along with Dürer's Melancholia, is its definitive Renaissance image.

Renaissance medical texts are heavy and long and in Latin, mostly untranslated. They are hard to find and no more fun to read than medical textbooks today. *The Anatomy of Melancholy* is much more entertaining, a pop psychology book that went through six editions in sixteen years, each with enthralling new material. Also full of excitement is the *Malleus Maleficarum,* or "Hammer of Witches," by which two superstitious Dominican monks mobilized the sixteenth century against witches. It is not surprising that a psychoanalyst who decided to brush up his Latin and look into the history of mental illness could not get his mind off demons, witches, and the Inquisition.

But even Burton, who was a minister, not a doctor, and who repeated some of the most lurid tales of demonic possession, devoted four times as much space to the natural causes of mental illness as he did to the supernatural. In discussing the causes of melancholy—which term, as used in the Renaissance, has a much broader meaning than simple *depression,* taking in most of what we call mental illness—Burton leads his list of causes with God, as is appropriate for a divine. Then comes "A Digression of the Nature of Spirits, bad Angels or Devils, and how they cause Melancholy." Next comes "Of Witches and Magicians," and how they cause it. Nevertheless, "how far the power of spirits and devils doth extend," remarks Burton, "and *whether they can cause this or any other disease*" (emphasis added), "is a serious question, and worthy to be considered."

Even in this section, Burton pays his tribute to rational medicine: he agrees that the devils must work *through* the humors—that is, by physiological means. It is a mechanism of which Hamlet, with his university training, is fully aware as he reflects that the ghost "may be the devil," who abuses him to damn him, not directly, but "out of my weakness and my melancholy, / As he is very potent with such spirits." He uses the word *spirit* here not as a synonym for *ghost*, but in the sense universal in sixteenth-century medicine, of vapors, rarefied yet material, that course through the body and link it with the soul. So Donne in "The Ecstasie" explains:

> . . . our blood labours to beget
> Spirits, as like souls as it can,
> Because such fingers need, to knit
> That subtle knot which makes us man.

Once Burton has delivered himself of our story of the vanishing tapeworm, he gets down to the natural causes of melancholy: the stars; old age; parents, by which he means, not what modern psychiatrists do, but "hereditary disease" and the transmission of the emotional *temperament* from parent to child. Melancholy can be caused by bad diet; constipation; bad air; idleness; passions and perturbations of the mind; envy, malice, hatred; emulation or desire for revenge (Hamlet!); anger; discontents, cares, miseries; love of gaming and immoderate pleasures; self-love, pride, overmuch joy, and the like; and (a very important cause) too much study. Accidental— we would say environmental—causes included bad nurses (via the milk); bad upbringing in the home and school (a relatively minor cause); terrors and affrights; scoffs, calumnies, bitter jests; and a few sociological causes, including poverty, a popular cause today.

Yet Burton was far more open to the idea of supernatural causes than the average Renaissance physician. In 1593, the Jesuit Delrio felt called upon to counter the effect of a book written by Dr. Johann Weyer (the same Weirus cited by Burton). "Weirus hereticus" had found the *Malleus Maleficarum* "full of silly and often godless absurdities"; he had denied that "the childish old hags whom one calls witches . . . can cause any harm to men or animals"; he had said they needed no punishment, since "their illness itself is a sufficient pain." "If doctors were to express their opinions," complained Delrio, "no one would be burned."

Yet to oppose enlightened physicians to a simpleminded and superstitious clergy would be to substitute one oversimplification for another. The sixteenth-century preoccupation with demonic possession and the persecution of witches was, in fact, a kind of aberration for the Church, as shown by its very late appearance. Christian doctrine from its beginnings had richly woven together Greek rationalism and Christian grace, the two strands of the Western heritage. Faith and natural reason were seen as complementary, not conflicting. *Sic enim fides praesupponit cognitionem naturalem:* "Faith," says Aquinas, "presupposes natural reason." It was as a Christian that Dr. Weyer criticized *The Hammer of Witches*. It is true that his book was put on the Index of Prohibited Books. But it was also republished within a year with a congratulatory letter from a Benedictine abbot. There was ample Christian precedent for using your mind, and only the credulous and superstitious confused faith with credulity and superstition.

What, then, was the source of this tradition of natural causes and humane treatment? The received wisdom does know that. Long ago, before Christianity ushered in the Dark Ages, there was Hippocrates, the father of medicine, and he knew what he was about. We need only fill in: the influence of Hippocratic medicine never died out, but was passed on by Galen and Arab physicians, available through Aristotle even to the Middle Ages: rediscovered and extended in the Renaissance, it continued to provide a model for how to think about the mysterious and frightening phenomena of mental illness.

Of course it was only a model. Mental illnesses are still mysterious, and there is, if anything, less agreement within the psychiatric profession about etiologies than there was four hundred years ago. The legacy of Greek medicine, as of Greek natural philosophy, was not the explanations themselves—the four humors have gone to join the demons. It was the idea, the *model* of what a medical explanation should be, and the confidence that one existed and could be found, and when found would determine treatment.

So what did the boy that Jesus cured suffer from? Luke and Mark are a far cry from the Hippocratic writings, but even so the symptoms are clear enough for diagnosis: a condition existing from childhood; sudden, intermittent seizures; foaming at the mouth and gnashing of teeth. It is epilepsy, "the falling sickness"—the oldest of psychiatric diagnoses.

And in fifth-century Greece, too, there were people to ascribe this disorder to supernatural causes, to call it "the sacred disease" to point to the jealousy or anger of the gods—although the Greeks were mercifully free from the idea of a devil who took possession of human beings for evil. A Greek physician, perhaps Hippocrates himself, addresses such folk. He wrote toward the end of the fifth century, very close to the time when Sophocles and Euripides were writing their tragedies of heaven-sent madness. Euripides, of course, did not really think madness was heaven-sent. He could only be revolted by the idea of divinities who sent such afflictions; he makes that bitterly clear. We can be sure he was aware of the Hippocratic writings; as Werner Jaeger has shown (in volume 3 of his monumental *Paideia*), medicine, its theory and practice, was one of the strongest intellectual influences in the Athens of Euripides and Socrates. We can see why, reading these words in which a doctor two and a half millennia ago spoke for his profession:

> The disease called sacred . . . appears to me no more divine or sacred than other diseases, but it has a natural cause from which it originates like other diseases. Men regard its nature and causes as divine from ignorance and wonder, because it is not at all like other diseases. And this notion of its divinity is kept up by their inability to comprehend it. . . . Those who first referred this malady to the gods appear to me to have been just such persons as the conjurors, purificators, mountebanks, and charlatans now are. . . . Such persons . . . using the divinity as a pretext and screen of their own inability to afford any assistance, have given out that the disease is sacred. . . . Men ought to know that from nothing else but the brain come joys, delights, laughter and sports, and sorrows, griefs, despondency, and lamentations. And by this . . . we acquire wisdom and knowledge, and see and hear, and know what are foul and what are fair . . . and by the same organ we become mad

and delirious, and fears and terrors assail us, some by night, and some by day, and dreams and untimely wanderings, and cares that are not suitable, and ignorance of present circumstances, desuetude, and unskillfulness. All these things we endure from the brain. . . . So that there is no necessity for making a distinction and holding this disease to be more divine than the others, but all are divine, and all are human.

It is no great leap to the Renaissance doctor Paracelsus: "The insane and the sick man are our brothers, let us give them treatment to cure them, for nobody knows whom among our friends or relatives this misfortune may strike."

From *The American Scholar,* Spring 1987.

No Time for Comedy

A long time ago, back at the beginning of literature, Achilles got angry. Out of that came destruction, for enemy and friend. Odysseus, on the other hand, kept his cool; he got to eat his cake and have it too. The *Iliad* and the *Odyssey* are the fundamental narratives of Western consciousness, even for those who have not read them: two masks, two modes, two stances; minor chord and major; two primary ways of meeting experience. The *Iliad* sets the type of tragedy, as Aristotle tells us, where greatness shines amid violence, error, defeat, and mortality. The *Odyssey* celebrates survival among the world's dangers and surprises, and then homecoming, and order restored. It is the very archetype of a prosperous outcome, of Comedy.

Comedy? Laughs are not the point. It is that primary sense of comedy that Dante explained to his patron:

> It differs, then, from tragedy in its content, in that tragedy begins admirably and tranquilly, whereas its end or exit is foul and terrible . . . whereas comedy introduces some harsh complication, but brings its matter to a prosperous end. . . . And hence it is evident that the title of the present work is "the Comedy."

Evident from the Inferno's first lines, in which Dante tells us what he means to do: to give account of the *good* he found in that dark and harsh and savage wood where he had lost the straight way.

Tragedy and Comedy: the masks are two. *Iliad* and *Odyssey* go together, and not only as they trip off the tongue. One requires the other. A reading of Homer that stops with the lament for Hector must be in every sense partial. As surely as we experience the *Iliad* in the knowledge that Achilles will die and Troy will fall, we must experience it in the awareness that there is another kind of story to be told, that Odysseus will survive the war and the journey and make it home.

Tragedy and Comedy: though the words are paired, their order is not reversible. We do not speak of Comedy and Tragedy, *Odyssey* and *Iliad*. "To make a sombre action end happily is easy enough," writes Northrop Frye; "to reverse the procedure almost impossible." The direction of this statement runs directly counter to what our gloomy age expects. Yet it tests true. We can imagine *Iliad* and *Odyssey* in only one sequence. To turn back from the long voyage home to the fall of the city, from Odysseus in Penelope's arms to Hector dead and Achilles' death to come, would be to turn experience upside down. It is not merely chronology that forbids it, or arguments from archaeology or technique, but the requirements of the imagination itself, as it balances What Is and What Should Be to make the kind of sense we call art—sense which is enough more than the first to take on shape, and enough less than the second to be felt as real. Historically indeed, but above all emotionally, the *Odyssey* comes last.

Last—as Sophocles at ninety, his proud city collapsing around him, in defeat returned to the bitter legend and brought old Oedipus to the healing grove of Colonus, insisting that though suffering is disproportionate, it is not meaningless but mysteriously confers blessing; last, as Matisse with crippled fingers cut singing color into immense shapes of praise. Not everyone survives, of course. But those who do have a bequest to make. Shakespeare's sequence makes the same statement; what comes last is not the sovereign "Nothing" of *King Lear,* but the benign vision of *The Winter's Tale* and *The Tempest*.

Perdita, Miranda; Nausicaa, Telemachus—in comedy the young
grow up, the lost are found, the separate joined, as the rhythms of
renewal are recognized, and luck, and wonder.

> How many goodly creatures are there here!
> How beauteous mankind is! O brave new world
> That has such people in it!

The comic spirit knows well enough that the goodly creatures Miranda sees are only ourselves, the clowns and criminals and honest
men that Prospero has assembled for what Eric Henry, speaking of
the characteristic comic ending, calls "that burst of good will in
which, at the close, the aberrant society is forgiven and invited to
rejoin the mainstream." "Tis new to thee," says Prospero to his
only daughter, whom he has just betrothed to his enemy's son.
Prospero's revels are near ended, and he knows that. Yet here on
stage stand Miranda and Ferdinand, undertaking once more to live
happily ever after—the young, our own, that simple investment in
the future we're all capable of, our built-in second chance. For them
the tragic past is only a story the grownups remember. Untenden-
tiously, insouciantly, they will go about their business, the business
of comedy, making new beginnings of our bad endings, showing us
that they were not endings at all, that there are no endings. Even
Odysseus has one more journey to make. But though there are no
endings, we are not trapped in stasis either, since boy gets girl, the
prince and the princess marry and renew the world. Whatever com-
peting structures of enmity and loss we have taught ourselves to call
deep, this is one we cannot do without. What Prospero wished for
he has accomplished. Ferdinand and Miranda will make their fathers' errors good. Odysseus will come home and when he does,
Telemachus will fight at his side and succeed him, making his father
glad. The story of Oedipus is not the only story we know. Our
*Odyssey*s and *Tempest*s stand, permanent challenges to Ivan Karamazov's terrible question, "Who doesn't desire his father's
death?", reminding us to read it, not as the late-revealed archetype
of all human development, but as Dostoevsky took the trouble to
write it, the cry of a mind diseased.

What is at issue today is whether we have grown too conscious and too clever for comedy's burst of good will. In every age but this the creators of our great fictions have regularly accorded us happy endings to stand beside those others that evoke our terror and pity. Happy endings still exist, of course. But they have lost their ancient legitimacy. Diminished into trash and Tolkien (not, of course, at all the same thing), they awaken in the intelligentsia an automatic distrust. Though we'll greet any cheap irony with adolescent acceptance, for a contemporary work to end happily seems in itself enough to make us refuse it full intellectual respectability. At least let it be ambiguous—as some critics convert even the ultimate "Yes" of Joyce's great modern Odyssey into fashionable dubiety. Art accommodates itself to our educated expectations; for all the romantic cult of the outsider, writers are as anxious to be thought respectable as readers, nearly as anxious as critics. And so for the first time since the beginning of our literature there is no major artistic mode to affirm the experience of comedy: healing, restoration, winning through.

In the wilderness, a few voices are newly audible. John Fowles makes his Daniel Martin reflect "how all through his writing life, he had avoided the happy ending, as if it were somehow in bad taste. . . . It had become offensive, in an intellectually privileged caste, to suggest publicly that anything might turn out well." Is the writer's creative freedom, he asks, "compatible with such deference to a received idea of the age that only a tragic, absurdist, black-comic view . . . of human destiny could be counted as truly representative and 'serious'"? In *Daniel Martin* the hero is denied disaster, or even the copout of the "open ending," in a refreshing authorial decision that there is no sufficient reason why intelligent and privileged people, even those who have not "fulfilled their promise," even those whose somber fate is to have become highly paid screenwriters, need permeate our fictions with narcissistic bellyaching. Saul Bellow attacks the same orthodoxies in his Nobel Prize address (the general neglect of which eloquently illustrates its thesis):

> Essay after essay, book after book . . . maintain . . . the usual
> thing about mass society, dehumanization, and the rest. How

weary we are of them. How poorly they represent us. The pictures they offer no more resemble us than we resemble the reconstructed reptiles and other monsters in a museum of paleontology. We are much more limber, versatile, better articulated; there is much more to us; we all feel it.

Our claims to *angst* override realism, common sense; they override our own experience.

Consider the ending of Joseph Heller's *Something Happened*. The unpleasant, trapped, pathetic musings of its unpleasant, trapped, pathetic narrator cannily suppress until the last few pages what is offered as the climactic fact: what's happened is that this suburban father has somehow managed to kill the little boy who is the one creature he loves in the world. Our interest in whether it was a true accident or consciously or unconsciously willed shrivels before the event's blank incredibility, even in its own fictional circumstances. The ending is absurd indeed, but in no cosmic sense; it is merely implausible. We have come full circle. In a hundred years, the unhappy ending has become as gratuitous as the conventional happy conclusion the nineteenth century novelists came to find so confining.

"Fairy-tale endings" we have come to call them—the phrase itself is a repudiation. In *The Uses of Enchantment* Bruno Bettelheim made another old man's bequest; he tried to give us back fairy tales. He dressed his insights in the oedipal garments of twentieth-century respectability, but they shine brighter naked. "The fairy tale leaves no doubt in the child's mind that the pain must be endured and the risky chances taken"; it can do this because "despite all anxieties, there is no question about the happy ending." "The message that fairy tales get across to the child in manifold form [is] that struggle . . . is an intrinsic part of human experience—but that if one does not shy away, but steadfastly meets unexpected and often unjust hardships, one masters all the obstacles and at the end emerges victorious." Yet children are not the only ones among us who have deep uses for archetypes of success. Bettelheim quotes Schiller: "Deeper meaning resides in the fairy tales told to me in my childhood than in the truth that is taught by life"; he reminds us that "only if a fairy tale met the conscious and unconscious requirements of many people was it repeatedly retold." It was not children who invented these stories. The message of fairy tale is the message of the *Odyssey*—the indispensable message of comedy.

Yet even Schiller's tribute reinforces the conventional opposition between the meanings of fairy tales and "the truth that is taught by life." To speak of a fairy-tale ending is another way of saying "untrue," an assertion that the story ends, not according to our experience but our wishes. Dying gods may rise again and winter give place to spring—a secular society knows, if only from anthropology, that people might think that. But even those who recognize the ancient emotional uses of such mythic happy endings will concede, all too readily, that the mythic is also mythical in the common sense: false. The most they dare claim is that the truth of comedy is somehow deeper than the real world's. The hard-nosed simply reiterate "untrue."

Yet mythic need not mean mythical. Stories can be archetypal, and still show us how people and events can interrelate for good in a world we recognize, how character attracts luck and makes the prosperous outcome not only wished-for but likely. It is important to distinguish a kind of happy ending different from those of fairy tale or myth, where miraculous escapes and supernatural assistants invite the hard-nosed to dismiss them (or ghetto them into innocent, old-fashioned art forms like the Tolkein romances). From Homer on, there have always been fiction makers who have interested themselves in what may be called *earned* happy endings. Putting their resources of language and invention to dramatizing the qualities of personality that conduce to happy outcomes, they have been fascinated by the human capacity for adaptation, moderation, for perseverance without obsessiveness, by the quality that bends but does not break.

Comedy can contain pain. The name "Odysseus" comes from the same "pain" root which gives us "anodyne," and every Greek knew that to be Odysseus meant to have more than one man's share of trouble. In the *Odyssey*, we are made to wait through five books to meet the hero; when we do, he is sitting on the shore, his eyes "never dry, weeping for a way home," weary of adventures and

Calypso. Almost all those familiar adventures—Cyclops, Sirens, Circe, Hades, and the rest—took place in the first eighteen months of his ten-year voyage. They are crammed into a small fraction of the *Odyssey*'s twenty-four books: more than half the action takes place in Ithaca. The *Odyssey* is a poem of wandering, but primarily of homecoming, its prosperous outcome seconded by luck but earned by intelligence. It is mythic and realistic at once. It offers all the accoutrements of fairy tale—giants and witches, magic beasts and herbs, supernatural helpers. Yet it displays in its array of survivor characters—not Odysseus only but wise Penelope and prudent Telemachus, sleek old Nestor, Menelaus and the lady Helen—the personal resilience that is a necessary aspect of the power to endure.

That resilience may include a certain deviousness; more kindly we might call it tact. We need continually to be reminded that too strong an integrity, however it may command admiration, can work devastation, like Cordelia's and Lear's. Odysseus himself, joined later by the versatile slave of New Comedy (resurrected in *A Funny Thing Happened on the Way to the Forum*), shows the alternative type. Like the slave, Odysseus in the Cyclops's cave is not in a position to fail grandly. The tragic poets were fascinated by the Antigones and Creons, who will die—or kill—rather than disguise what they are or compromise what they are sure they know. The comic vision contemplates and celebrates the reverse. These are the characters who have all the luck, who are happy-accident-prone. Comedy shows us how they make their luck. If Shakespeare, in his late comedies, affirms the mythic vision of restoration, his earlier comedies, as Hugh Richmond has shown, interest themselves in the flexibility, adaptability, the willingness to climb down from preestablished positions that is necessary to earn happy endings. It is the quality that Richard Wilbur has noted in Molière's comedies, of those who respond to life and do not coerce it.

These are the happy endings in which we can believe. We think of Trollope, who applied himself seriously and successfully to the task of investigating what behavior in human beings tended to bring about the kind of endings his public demanded and he himself would wish for his characters. His modest gifts did not include mythmaking. But he accepted, as Dickens never did, the responsibility for imagining the prerequisites for happy endings which should be organic and not imposed.

It is a grand claim we make when we reject happy endings: that we are very special, that whatever songs previous ages could sing, in our terrible century all success is shallow or illusory, all prosperity a fairy tale; that the only responses to our world which can command adult assent are compulsive ironies and cries of pain; that the world which seems to lie before us like a world of dreams, so various, so beautiful, so new, hath, in short, really neither joy nor love nor light, nor certitude, nor peace, nor help for pain, and we are here as on a darkling plain waiting for Godot. But what is true enough when recognized as half the story rings counterfeit when it aggrandizes the whole. Since misery loves company, it will find it. But second-hand misery is as inauthentic as second-hand cheerfulness, and far less attractive. It used to be possible to laugh at melancholy Jacques.

In the world of unparalleled safety and comfort which most contemporary readers and writers inhabit, it takes real chutzpah to deny that there can be true tales of victory, unscrambling, fortunate coming together, that literature can weightily concern itself with imagining a world in which luck is frequently on our side and with dramatizing the social wisdom that knows how prosperous outcomes are commonly brought about. Was Homer's vision—Chaucer's—Shakespeare's—Molière's—so much less searching than our own? There is an ugly arrogance in the insistence that our age, alone among all, is too terrible for comedy. In the city of York, in the years when Shakespeare was writing, only 10 percent of the population lived to the age of forty. Aristocrats indeed did better; they had nearly an even chance. We cannot imagine what the words "the shadow of death" meant to our forefathers. The Thirty Years' War left two of every three in Germany dead. Chaucer's pilgrims rode to Canterbury through a countryside which a generation before had been devastated by the Black Death. In 1348 Oxford lost two-thirds of her academic population. It was not out of his prosperity that Dante wrote of the good he found. Any realistic consideration of the life of the past, both in its day-to-day precariousness and its vulnerability to repeated holocaust, will show up our claims to unique misery as uniquely self-centered.

"It is incorrect," wrote Auden, "to say . . . that all men have a right to the pursuit of happiness. . . . Happiness is not a right; it is a duty. To the degree that we are unhappy we are in sin (and vice versa)." The idea is old enough to be ready for rediscovery. In Kierkegaard's formulation, Despair is Sin, related like all other sins to Pride, first of the deadly company. Happiness is our business. Hope is not the lucky gift of circumstance or even disposition, but a virtue like faith and love, to be practiced whether or not we find it easy, or even natural, because it is necessary to our survival as human beings.

Christian thinkers, of course, go further. Survival suggests safety, and the other way to say that is salvation. "My duty to God," continues Auden, "is to be happy." It is what Dostoevsky's Father Zosima says to silly Mme. Holakhov, when on the day before his death she tells him how well and happy he's looking. He understands his illness, and does not deceive himself or her. "But if I seem happy to you, you could never say anything that would please me more. For men were made for happiness and anyone who is completely happy has a right to say to himself, 'I am doing God's will on earth.' All the righteous, all the saints, all the holy martyrs were happy."

Poignant enough, since Dostoevsky himself so evidently was not. But to cite the Christian version of the comic imperative is unnecessarily to limit the application of what Homer knew as well as Chaucer and Dante and Shakespeare. Plato and Aristotle knew it too: Aristotle saw happiness as virtue's serene by-product, and Father Zosima's cheerfulness before death pays its debt to the Socrates of the *Phaedo*. The art that affirms survival reaches through rite to reality; that babies are born, that pain passes, that spring comes again, is as sure as that the sun will rise tomorrow. It is, says Frye, speaking of Shakespearean comedy, an archetypal function of literature to visualize "the world of desire, not as an escape from 'reality,' but as the genuine form of the world that human life tries to imitate."

Nor need one be religious to speak up for happy endings. Georg Lukács, that gallant and sensitive Marxist, demonstrates how our time's great secular locus of faith imposes the same demands. For Marxism, like Christianity and Judaism, establishes for history a direction that gives life meaning beyond mere process. Speaking of the fruitfulness of "justified historical optimism," Lukács carefully distinguishes it from that "schematic optimism" which gives rise to unearned happy endings. He writes impatiently of the gift for misery of the modern existential hero, "basically solitary . . . , constitutionally unable to establish relationships with things or persons outside himself," trapped in a world in which it is considered "impossible to determine theoretically the origin and goal of human existence." In *The Meaning of Contemporary Realism*, Lukács, discussing the literature of *angst*, refuses to accept it as a justified response to a decadent and oppressive capitalism. Rather, it is "a rejection of reality," "an escape into nothingness." He castigates the glorification of the pathological which is now everywhere around us, as "distortion becomes the normal condition of human existence . . . the formative principle of art and literature." He sees in Kafka and Beckett, for all their marvelous inventiveness, an apotheosis of impotence and paralysis, which makes "the denial of history, of development, the mark of true insight into the nature of reality." And when "the static nature of reality and the senselessness of its surface phenomena" are accepted as "absolute truths requiring no proof," "*angst* becomes supreme."

For the artist, whether bourgeois or socialist, has an obligation to the whole truth. "The question," for Lukács, "is not: is *x* present in reality? But rather: does *x* represent the whole of reality?"

> What counts is the personal decision . . . : acceptance or rejection of *angst*. Ought *angst* to be taken as an absolute or ought it to be overcome? Should it be considered one reaction among others, or should it become the determinant of the *condition humaine*? These are not primarily, of course, literary questions—they relate to a man's behavior and experience of life. The crucial question is whether a man escapes from the life of his time into a realm of abstraction—it is there that *angst* is engendered in human consciousness—or confronts modern life determined to fight its evils and support what is good in it.

Bellow is more Platonic, but he comes out in the same place:

> The value of literature lies in these "true impressions." A novel
> moves back and forth between the world of objects, of actions,
> of appearances, and that other world from which these "true
> impressions" come and which moves us to believe that the
> good we hang on to so tenaciously—in the face of evil, so
> obstinately—is no illusion.

Tragedy and Comedy: the masks are two. *Iliad* and *Odyssey*
require each other—or rather, it is we who require them both. It is
imperative to hail winners as well as heroic losers; to refuse credence
or admiration to those who manage to get what they want and want
what they get announces a perverse and envious romanticism. It is
that sulky refusal of good that Dante knew, according it no grand
extremes of fire or ice but the unlovely muck of Styx. "Tristi fum-
mo"—"Sullen were we in the sweet air the sun made glad, bearing
within us a sluggish smoke."

Since there are no endings, tragedy can be no more *final* than
comedy. In every fiction, the pause we call an ending has been
imposed by a mind, and reflects a choice. Our solemn rejection of
happy endings would be lethal, personally and socially, if it were not
by nature partial and temporary. Yet it may most sanely, perhaps, be
seen as comic, comic in the familiar sense—ludicrous. We may recall
the cry of the Frenchman at the beach resort in that story gram-
marians used to tell to illustrate the difference between "shall" and
"will," in the days when people still cared about such things: "I will
be drowned, and nobody shall save me!"

From *The Hudson Review,* Summer 1979; reprinted in *Comedy: Meaning
and Form,* 2nd edition, ed. Robert W. Corrigan (New York: Harper &
Row, 1981).

Trollope for Grown-ups

One wants some sort of excuse for reading Trollope—a long convalescence, or an ocean trip. Without it, it is hard not to suspect the motive for immersing oneself in this reassuring ambience of decency, money, and ease. The Trollope revival is partly simple envy of our opposite numbers a hundred years ago; we readers are, in general, the privileged, with money in the bank and correct grammar, and Trollope's vanished amenities once seemed to be our heritage. Trollope made ordinary upper-class life interesting. Time has made it into Arcadia.

It is hard to take Arcadia seriously. The voice of F. R. Leavis is the voice of conscience: "If the criterion is the achievement of work addressed to the adult mind, and capable of engaging its full critical attention . . ."—intimidated, we hasten to agree that life is not long enough for Trollope. Trollope addressed himself not to the adult mind but the buying public. He did not expect to engage their full critical attention. He obliged them with easy sentence structure and happy endings. We can only be suspicious. We have no business with happy endings. Compulsive disaster is our stock-in-trade—in personal relationships, in politics, and in fiction. We are used to it and we respect it. Trollope had a low opinion of disaster, and his novels are full of expedients for avoiding it. Consequently, a taste for Trollope, though easy to acquire, is hard to justify.

Ideas did not interest him. His novels about clergymen neither discuss nor dramatize religion; his novels about politicians contain hardly one recognizable political issue. Hundreds of characters talk through book after book with an effect of the greatest cultivation, but they do not talk about history or sin or the nature of man. And what does Trollope offer instead? Even an addict hesitates to admit it—he offers love matches.

There are dozens of them. Love matches between ladies and gentlemen with widely differing amounts of money and slightly differing levels of birth—brought almost uniformly, over weakening opposition, to a happy conclusion. Mary Thorne and Frank Gresham, Lucy Robarts and Lord Lufton, Grace Crawley and Major Grantly, Lady Mary and Frank Tregear, Lord Silverbridge and Isabel Boncassen—the same thing over and over. And worse, the same style, which at first seems leisurely and soothing, but which sooner or later will suddenly infuriate with its trivial irony, its shameless padding, its total lack of intellectual seriousness.

Trollope repeats—situations, explanation, phrasing. He irritates us with clichés, jocose biblical language, comic names. Again and again by some trick of style he confounds his defenders by undercutting the value or significance of what he is saying. Yet no novelist is more habit-forming. For the fortunate lovers are part of a complete and compelling world. Once entered, it claims us like our own family, who may not be very intellectual either.

> Have you ever read the novels of Anthony Trollope? They precisely suit my taste—solid and substantial . . . just as real as if some giant had hewn a great lump out of the earth and put it under a glass case, with all its inhabitants going about their business, and not suspecting they were made a show of.

Hawthorne recognized Trollope's achievement, and Trollope can use praise from a novelist whose somber preoccupations pass muster with "the adult mind." But Trollope did not merely quarry his own experience, and although he is in general the despair of those concerned with the technique of the novel, there is a technical reason for the engrossing reality of his work.

Trollope added the dimension of time to the "three-dimensional" character. Before our eyes his young people grow tame and settled, his strong old men release their hold on life and die. We lose sight of our esteemed acquaintance, Plantagenet Palliser, for a few years, but when we next meet him, in another novel, he is not the same; and though his life is only intermittently the subject of the books, he bears its weight upon him as if he continued it without his author's assistance. Like Tolstoy, Trollope presents what it is to mature, not as a result of a single experience or complex of experiences that can provide a neatly delineated plot, but as a natural result of imagined life. Uncharacteristically, Trollope was aware that he had made an innovation. In his *Autobiography* he calls it "the state of progressive change"; but as he undervalued himself, others undervalued him, and a real extension of the possibilities of the novel went unnoticed.*

Yet this kind of success is not enough for the voice of conscience. Leavis is devastating on what he calls "the talk about 'creating characters' and 'creating worlds' and the appreciation of Trollope and Mrs. Gaskell and Thackeray," but a pundit is at liberty to find this less impressive than a working novelist like Hawthorne. It is true that there is a whole class of addicts who would like nothing so much as to walk into the Barsetshire Arcadia and never come out. They have produced a curious body of subcritical literature that deals with Trollope's world as if it were in fact real, gloating over the well-loved scenes and speculating on things the master didn't get around to describing. For a time they had their own novelist, Angela Thirkell, and even their own magazine.

But Trollope's reputation would have got along better without the Trollopians. He has suffered more than he has gained from this kind of praise, since he gets no other. Yet there remains a nagging feeling that not everything has been said—that behind the want of ideas there is an idea, beneath the avowed lack of message some insistent message, so obvious to the writer, by his age so safely

---

*Tolstoy noticed, Gary Saul Morson tells me. He even suggests that the English novel Anna Karenina is reading, "the ethos of which does not appeal to her," can be identified as *Can You Forgive Her?* and that Karenin is modeled on Plantagenet Palliser.

assumed, that it is only in our altered world that we can perceive it.
Trollope is offering us something which can "engage our full critical
attention."

It is this that explains why even the happy marriages still interest. In them the unconscious, omnipresent message is most obvious. For marriages are made on earth, and Trollope knows all the
adjustments and sacrifices that make possible the loving couples at
the end of Volume Three. Trollope, almost alone, tells us what we
need to hear: be reasonable, be moderate, in action, in desire, in
expectation, and you will be fairly happy. In this bloody and immoderate age, Trollope is the laureate of compromise. Underlying every
conflict, every tension that is to provide the framework of a story, is
the assumption, all the more solid for being unconscious, that a
successful adjustment is possible.

Typical of the novels in which love conquers all is *Dr. Thorne*.
Here the loving couple, which forms the subplot of so many of the
novels, is central to the story, and here the differences in class and
money which provide their problems are as intense as Trollope ever
allows them to be. And since the effect of the main plot is reinforced
by two subplots that also involve significant class differences, with
any writer but Trollope one might assume a conscious intention of
writing a novel about the class structure. For that is certainly the
subject of *Dr. Thorne*.

The class of gentlemen and gentlewomen in Victorian England
admitted of infinite gradations. On these Trollope plays his variations. Compromises are necessary if a lord's mother is to accept his
marriage with her parish clergyman's sister, if a duke is to allow his
son to marry an American whose grandfather was a laborer, a Lady
Amelia to marry the family attorney. (One of the useful facts we
learn from Trollope, later to be brought up-to-date by C. P. Snow, is
that between an attorney and a barrister there is a social chasm.) But
Mary Thorne's position is harder to deal with. She is engaged to the
squire's son, Frank Gresham, soon to be "the first commoner of
Barsetshire" by right of lineage and tradition. Yet she is not merely
illegitimate, but connected through her mother with the two great
threats to the stability of Trollope's agricultural paradise, the labor-
ing classes, and the new capitalists of Manchester. She has two
uncles: Dr. Thorne, poor but proud of his Saxon blood, and Roger

Scatcherd, the common laborer whose sister the doctor's brother seduced. The laborer killed the seducer, served his time, became a contractor, a millionaire, a baronet, in retirement buying up the land of the improvident gentry and drinking himself to death. His wealth and his knighthood have declassed him; powerful but uncouth, he is isolated both from his former class and his new one. He is a moving figure, and though Trollope intermittently laughs at him, he is not too snobbish to treat him as one.

Here is a problem novel set out; the girl, brought up with all her uncle's family pride and kept in ignorance of her history, accepts the standards by which the squire's family find her wanting. Mary Thorne is one of those characters in Trollope who have a compulsion to question themselves and their position. His real heroes are all harassed by self-doubt; it is their peculiar virtue. And quite properly, since no situation can be adjusted if its principals are adamant in their own righteousness. The Warden feels he cannot keep his sinecure, the Prime Minister fears he is not fit to govern, the Reverend Mr. Crawley thinks he may indeed have misappropriated the cheque. Mary Thorne's attempts to think through the questions of value implied in her situation lift her above the simple ingenue she would otherwise be and make her problem not merely a romantic one but a matter of conscience. One can imagine some of the possible solutions—rebellion, suicide, emigration. But Trollope knows how to make tragedy evaporate, and with it the searching novel of class structure. Mary inherits Sir Roger's wealth, marries Frank, and the threat from Manchester is painlessly absorbed as Manchester money restores the fortunes of the squire and returns to the land.

A fairy-tale ending—the Trollopian may accept it, but the adult mind? Yet it really happened:

> After 1832 the old landowning aristocracy steadily lost power, but instead of disappearing or becoming a fossil they simply intermarried with the merchants, manufacturers, and financiers who replaced them, and soon turned them into accurate copies of themselves.

George Orwell did not believe in fairies, and this sentence of his might stand as an epigraph for all of Trollope. Couple by happy couple, he shows us how it was done.

Proletarian blood mingles with the First Commoner's. Dr. Thorne surrenders his pride of birth without even noticing its loss. Usually Trollope is only too ready to inflate the number of his pages with elucidations of what the narrative makes obvious; here he forgoes comment. Compromises are best made imperceptibly. But he underscores the whole thing in a later novel by marrying off the doctor to a patent-medicine heiress. Duty, affection, and decency are the solvents—and of course money. Trollope treats people as people, rather than as the representatives of an abstraction, whether of class, race, or principle; and his characters, insofar as they find content-ment—Trollope's very limited brand of salvation—must learn to do the same.

Henry James, in what is still after nearly a century the best essay on Trollope, spoke of "the good-natured, moderate, conciliatory view" and "the natural decorum of the English spirit." The English are by nature resistant to the lure of the abstract. They resisted even Liberté, Egalité, Fraternité. England has, nevertheless, lurched for-ward measure by measure, without benefit of ideology, carrying the impedimenta of her aristocracy and her monarchy, to achieve a gov-ernment that is a monument to compromise, to reasonableness, and to lack of dogmatic principle. Liberalism is not a creed. It is men of goodwill engaged in muddling through, an unprepossessing meth-od of shaping events that has been successful beyond expectation. Trollope is its unassuming representative. It masters him as it has no other novelist. It is manifest in all his work, this flexibility in the face of complex personal and social phenomena, this reasonableness which is the antithesis of French rationality. With individuals it is possible to come to terms, once the mind is free to deal with them instead of what they symbolize. "The personal is all that matters" is the motto of one of Trollope's more respectable heirs. It is Trollope's, too, but he would not have framed it abstractly.

Not all Trollope's couples, in his own rather contemptuous words, "have two children and live happily ever after." Class, money, and family opposition are potent forces, but the internal hazards to marriage present an even greater challenge to the philosophy of adjustment. Decency and kindness, as psychiatrists know, are not always sufficient. Trollope's remedy is more old-fashioned than theirs, and cheaper. It consists of self-discipline in conformity with a rigid code.

Trollope's couples had no choice. Real and fictional, they operated within a limitation that was absolute. Divorce was practically, if not theoretically, impossible in nineteenth-century England, and even a legal separation had to meet such stringent requirements that it was only rarely possible. A mistaken marriage, therefore, is irrevocable (which partly explains the inordinate interest taken by Trollope's audience in the problems of courtship); it stands for life as a challenge to the participants to effect a successful adjustment by means of the British virtues of common sense, decency, affection (not passionate love), and self-control. Trollope rewards those of his couples who successfully transcend their temperamental incompatibility, and punishes those who refuse to make the effort.

His model marriage is that of Plantagenet Palliser and Glencora McCluskie. Presented over thirty years, it forms the continuing interest of the Parliamentary Novels, and Trollope, in an uncharacteristic access of critical judgment, called it "the best work of my life." Palliser and his wife are fundamentally incompatible. Their instincts and actions are at war and break out in continual tension during the years of their marriage. "Planty Pall" contrasts completely with the jaunty nickname his fellow MPs give him. Oversensitive, reserved, conscientious, without humor, he is a man of principle and patriotism, a dedicated public servant whose entire interest lies in the government of his country. Anxious to do the right thing by friends, wife, and children, he is dangerously unskilled in human relationships. On the recommendation of others, he has married a spirited and passionate girl, witty, rambunctious, and indiscreet. She, too, married him because she was told to, knowing that the young man she loved was thoroughly unsuitable. Trollope here recognizes that true love does not always resolve problems. Even money and good will may fail of their healing effects; her lover, who eats paté de foie gras for breakfast, can dispose of any amount of money, and though both are passionately in love, he has not the stamina to respond to the situation with common sense or self-discipline.

Glencora gives him up, but the marriage of convenience becomes unbearable as the responsive and irrepressible girl realizes her isolation from a man whose heart, such as it is, is in the House of Commons. Feeling his silent reproach as the months pass and she fails to conceive an heir to carry on the almost royal house of Omnium (Palliser is the coming Duke), she becomes more and more unhappy, begins to oppose his kind rigidity in trivial matters, and ultimately, of course, to see her lover. She is at the point of running away with him, which would carry her irrevocably out of her own world and Trollope's into a classless and degraded limbo, but Palliser belatedly responds to the situation and sacrifices his political interest to an attempt at a closer relationship. Glencora disciplines herself to respond with affection, becomes comparatively tranquil, and pregnant. There is no pretense of ideal happiness. Sacrifices have bought this adjustment, and sacrifices that will have to be continually repeated, though no new crisis will be as acute. Nevertheless, catastrophe has been avoided, and although, as Trollope summed it up in his *Autobiography*, "the romance of her life is gone, there remains a rich reality of which she is fully able to taste the flavor." It is, after all, something to have four children and be Duchess of Omnium.

The Palliser marriage is Trollope's most careful exposition of the techniques of satisfactory living. Those who willfully neglect these techniques pay for it, and like the Pallisers, fulfill their roles as exemplars of Trollope's unspoken thesis. Lady Laura Standish is as close as Trollope ever comes to a tragic figure—a passionate, strong-minded woman whom George Eliot would have presented more sympathetically, one of those unhappy females who did not fit the molds of Victorian society. But her social maladjustment, though accurately indicated, does not interest Trollope. He could find no excuses in society for the individual's catastrophes. He is interested in Lady Laura's personal failure to adjust to the conditions created by her own choices. Because her great interest is politics and she needs money, she marries Mr. Kennedy, a rich, middle-aged MP, although she has been attracted to Phineas Finn, a handsome, penniless Irishman whose position in the House is far more precarious. (Members of Parliament were unpaid when Trollope wrote, an important element in many of his plots.) Mr. Kennedy turns out to be, not the cipher he seemed, but a dour and rigid Presbyterian who wishes his wife to remain in his lonely Scottish mansion and observe the Sabbath. His exactions are only increased by her frivolous and hostile reaction. She leaves him to return to her father in London, where she becomes increasingly absorbed in her passion for Finn; by this time he, like a sensible man, has put her out of his mind and finds her even less attractive when she throws herself in his way. Kennedy's pathetic madness, alone in one room of the great cold house, his attempt to murder the man he regards as his wife's lover, his death, and Lady Laura's exile in Dresden, are all implicit in the initial refusal to compromise in a situation which was freely chosen and at least as open to adjustment as that of the Pallisers.

Compromise precludes tragedy, of course. It is meant to. And tragedy today is at a premium. Because Lady Laura's marriage is a shambles and Lady Glencora's a success, we are tempted to credit the former with greater imaginative depth. Unhappiness has come to seem truer than happiness. Trollope's happy endings were indeed dictated by the market (there is, of course, one for *Phineas Redux,* to cover up the Lady Laura debacle; Finn solves his problems by marrying another Trollopian exemplar, Mme. Max Goesler, a rich widow whose social intelligence secures her a place at the top of London society even though she has been a duke's mistress and is by implication Jewish). But Trollope accepted, as Dickens never did, the responsibility for providing the prerequisites for happy endings, and that is why his are tolerable and even instructive. His *Autobiography* tells us that he tried to

> enjoy the excitements of pleasure, but to be free from its vices and ill-effects,—to have the sweet, and leave the bitter untasted. . . . The preachers tell us that this is impossible. It seems to me that hitherto I have succeeded pretty well.

He does not say how he managed this. It is in the novels already, their single subject: the *expertise* of living.

Although Trollope's concern with compromise is most obvious in his treatment of marriage, it informs all his work. Parliament and the Church provide the social framework for his society, and it is no surprise to find his pragmatic philosophy of adjustment and his distrust of abstraction illustrated in his treatment of both politics and religion.

Trollope's "Parliamentary Novels" are engrossed with personalities, not politics. Phineas Finn, Madame Max, and the rest merely work out their arrangements against a background more sophisticated than Barsetshire. Even when Palliser becomes Duke of Omnium and Prime Minister, his difficulties are rooted in people and not political issues. Trollope tells us he made the Duke a mouthpiece for his own convictions; these were deep but not numerous, and illustrate explicitly the commitment to compromise implicit in the novels. It is almost too pat to find him calling himself "an advanced Conservative-Liberal," and making the Duke head a coalition government.

Trollope's attitude toward abuses is always mild; toward reforms, equivocal. None of the many MPs among his characters ever initiates a reform, with the exception of Phineas Finn's minor measures for improving the lot of Irish tenants (the Duke's perennial scheme for decimal coinage is merely a comic invention). The occasional current issues that creep into his pages—secret ballot, Home Rule for Ireland, votes for women—even the most liberal of his characters uniformly oppose. In no novelist is the status quo more absolute. Yet any change is accepted as absolute in its turn. The Duke of Omnium is inflexible when it finally occurs to him that his own pocket borough is not immune from the provisions of the Reform Bill, and he never influences another election. But even here Trollope is ready with the other side, reminding us that this reform closed Parliament to many promising young men who could not afford an electoral contest and assured the permanent Conservatism of the Duke's rural but hitherto Liberal borough. Trollope himself espouses "I will not say equality, for the word is offensive, and presents to the imagination of men ideas of Communism, of ruin, and insane democracy,—but a tendency toward equality." The Duke on one occasion goes so far as to call equality "great, glorious, and godlike," but the Duke is Trollope's Don Quixote as well as his parfit gentil knight. This is a flight into cloudland, and is labeled as such.

Equality is part of "a millennium . . . so distant we need not even think of it as possible"; though "we can . . . do a little and a little to bring it nearer," it is "so little it won't touch Matching in our day." Matching Priory is the Duke's home, the most cherished among his estates (he owns half Barsetshire); he is admitting that his convictions would hardly bear "the test that has been attempted in other countries"—the redistribution of the land to those who work it.

It is characteristic that Trollope does not allow the Duke to be unaware of the threat to himself that equality contains. Trollope is complacent, but he is not a sentimentalist. He is not mild and reasonable because he is unconscious of social forces. In America the powerful myth of equality has come close to annihilating not only the reality but the idea of class differences. But Trollope knew how his world was put together, and that a rich aristocrat could not become egalitarian for nothing. Trollope may not have been interested in ideas, but he was aware that they have consequences, for which those who hold them are responsible. It is one of the reasons why he rarely gave any idea his unqualified support.

The Warden, his first successful novel, uncharacteristically makes a reform movement precipitate the whole action. But the situation is characteristically equivocal, based, as he says in the *Autobiography,* around "two opposite evils": "the possession by the Church of certain funds . . . intended for charitable purposes, but which had been allowed to become incomes for idle church dignitaries" and "the undeserved severity of the newspapers toward the recipients of such incomes." Trollope felt his attempt to treat both evils at once showed an "absence of all artistic judgment" and that he should have made a villain of his idle church dignitary, instead of creating in the Reverend Septimus Harding his only saint, a man of perfect sweetness and charity. But Trollope shows his customary critical blindness in condemning *The Warden* for its virtues. It is exactly this interweaving of good and evil that gives the book its moral complexity and makes it intellectually perhaps Trollope's most interesting work. The Warden is a mild man, but conscience makes him stronger than the strong. Like James's Strether (James thought *The Warden* had "exceeding beauty"), he must in middle age examine his way of life for the first time, and he accepts the results with steadfastness.

He becomes convinced that he has no right to his sinecure as Warden of Hiram's Hospital, the counselor and friend of the twelve old paupers specified by the ancient charity, and although the Church and his family oppose him with all their power, he astonishes them by carrying through his resignation. He gives up his fine house and his income and moves without complaint into lodgings, and it is clear that he has made the right choice. But what does his sacrifice accomplish? His post is left vacant, the income undistributed, the old men have no more money than before, and they have lost their gentle friend. The reformers have succeeded only in making them greedy and dissatisfied. The whole story illustrates the desolation caused by naked principle at work among human beings—and this even when the principle was one that Trollope supported. (It is significant that no one thinks of expending the income by taking in more superannuated workmen; in a later book the problem is solved by giving the post to a needy clergyman with twelve children. Trollope was not interested in the working classes.) Such an attitude by itself hardly produces constructive action, but the insistence that principle works no good unless tempered with humanity has made English reforms more durable even as it has slowed their pace. If England was transformed in the nineteenth century it was no thanks to Trollope, but he made his contribution nevertheless.

Mr. Harding's sainthood will not pass muster with the religious. He is a true Trollopian saint, saintly in action with no doctrine to sustain him or to make him savage. He has no opinions on Methodism or the Oxford movement. He does not expect to accomplish very much and he is not particularly intelligent. He is merely a perfectly good man.

Trollope was even less likely to bestow thought on religion than on politics, and his clergymen are as bare of ideas as his politicians. Some are dedicated, some are worldly, almost all do their best—but they do not think. In *Framly Parsonage* Trollope tells us why.

> I have written much of clergymen, but . . . I have endeavoured to portray them as they bear on our social life rather than to describe the working of their professional careers. Had I done the latter I could hardly have steered clear of subjects on which

> it has not been my intention to pronounce an opinion, and I
> should either have laden my fictions with sermons . . . or de-
> graded my sermons into fiction. Therefore I have said but little
> of this man's feeling or doings as a clergyman.

It is typical that he should consider ideas, as such, foreign to an account of "social life." So, in *Framly Parsonage,* that subtle victim of spiritual pride, the Reverend Mr. Crawley, a man nearly destroyed by his inability to come to terms with life, smarting under poverty and the neglect which his stiff-necked attitude makes inevitable, is lectured by his old friend Dean Arabin because he will not accept charity. The dean tells him to sacrifice his pride. Crawley replies that it is all he has left of manliness. They argue at some length; but these two clergymen, both among Trollope's rare portraits of intellectuals, have not a word for pride as a Christian problem with a Christian history. Even when verisimilitude would seem to demand ideas, Trollope is not willing to furnish them.

Yet his great inchoate thesis is there. He is, of course, the chronicler of the Anglican church, and he could never have accommodated himself to the more rigid requirements of Catholicism or Dissent. Anglicanism, like other English institutions, is a Trollopian phenomenon. Compromise is built into the Church of England; from its inception the creature not of principle but of human desires, at this very period it was successfully incorporating the extremes of high church and low, the one bordering on Rome and the other on unadorned evangelical protestantism. The English know how to deal with extremes. Dean Arabin, who himself has withstood the lure of the Oxford Movement, even has a good word for schism: "We are too much apt to look at schism in our church as an unmitigated evil. Moderate schism, if there may be such a thing, at any rate calls attention to the subject, draws in supporters who would otherwise have been inattentive to the matter, and teaches men to think upon religion." Even schism can be moderate. The enemy in religion, as in politics, will be, not any specific opinion, but the excessive zeal which makes coexistence (to borrow a relevant modern term) impossible. Among Trollope's clerical figures, he deals harshly only with the zealots. Mrs. Proudie is well known, and there are other figures who express his apprehension of the dangers of zeal. The priest in *The Way We Live Now*, though born an English gentleman, is a "pervert" to Catholicism, and when befriended in his poverty abuses the hospitality of his friends by running down their religion while they are both unprepared and unwilling to criticize his. Such issues Trollope believes must never be joined.

Of course compromise is easy if ideas do not interest you. It becomes hard to understand why all ideological differences cannot be submerged in a simple agreement not to mention them. And to one who has himself compromised very extensively, compromise is likely to appear as a moral imperative, particularly if it is already a psychological necessity. It is thus not surprising to find that Trollope himself took the same pride in conformity that natural rebels take in rebellion.

Summing up his career in the Post Office, which he tells us he had "thought very much more about" than his writing, he outlines his technique of dealing with an office disagreement: "How I loved, when I was contradicted . . . to do instantly as I was bid, and then to prove that what I was doing was fatuous, dishonest, expensive, and impractible!" Submission was to him a pleasure and a method. He expected his characters to triumph, if at all, by observing the rules. Again and again they resolve a situation, not by going outside it, but by a rigid observance of the limitations it sets. When Lucy Robarts is rejected by Lady Lufton as a wife for the young lord, this is her cue to cease seeing him altogether, to accept wholly the limitations of her position, and to see it altered not in spite of, but because of, her acquiescence. Yet she is not a passive person, nor is Lady Glencora, whose usual way of dealing with her husband's prohibitions is to observe them literally while disobeying their obvious intention. Madame Max Goesler, a foreigner and Jewish, overcomes all her handicaps by discreet conformity, and is rewarded by a place in the most brilliant society. We might recognize in this a specifically feminine reaction, the more pronounced in a society where women had many privileges but no rights, if we did not know it was the approach of the burly, choleric Trollope.

Surely no other author has been so proud of his submission to the mechanical limitations of publishing.

> The date fixed was the first of July . . . in accordance with the exigencies of the editor. . . . An author . . . is bound to suit himself to these exigencies, and can generally do so without personal loss or inconvenience if he will take time by the fore-lock. With all the pages I have written for magazines I have never been a day late, nor have I ever caused inconvenience by sending less or more matter than I had stipulated to supply.

This trivial achievement had an importance for Trollope out of all proportion. He returns to it again and again; he takes as much pride in it, or more, than he does in his real literary successes. Its com-pulsive quality is apparent in his insistence that all writers should be like himself—"the great need . . . that men engaged in literature should feel themselves to be bound to their industry as men know that they are bound in other callings." "Unmanly" is a terrible reproach for Trollope, and this is his word for his less systematic colleagues. It must have been a bitter thing—more bitter than he allowed himself to suspect—to know that, unmanly or not, they could do better work than he; he clings, therefore, to his own small distinction, which has the merit of allowing him to assure himself that he is working as hard as he can.

Trollope goes out of his way to humble his own achievement before George Eliot, but he will not accept the threat to himself implied in the realization that one could not write *Middlemarch* at the rate of 250 words the quarter-hour. Here, in the central compro-mise that made possible his enormous output and his double career, he could not afford to admit what he knew well enough, that those who compromise always give up something. The regularity of his industry was a cover for a deeper mental laziness, and his tidy habits were a justification of his inability (fundamentally a profound un-willingness) to put himself into competition with the novelists he really respected. Revision to him meant checking for grammar, and he of all people protested he could not cut. Mechanical indus-triousness protected him from the necessity for real labor or artistic growth. "But I think," he writes with asperity, "that no allowance should be given to claims for exemption from punctuality, made if not actually on the score still with the conviction of intellectual superiority."

He was equally sympathetic to less mechanical limitations, both the perennial limits of "what will sell" and the rigid Victorian exclusiveness in subject matter. His first novel, *The MacDermots of Ballycloran*, was set against an Irish background of land abuses and near famine, the heroine was seduced, and the hero hanged. He never made that mistake again. His next tries were random gropings in search of the market he found in *The Warden*. Having learned its requirements, he remained spiritually, morally, and mentally committed to them. The remarkable thing is that his vision of life actually altered to fit the market, so that his happy endings do not seem false or intrusive. Conformity and compromise worked so well for him that their success affected his whole outlook. Trollope, from childhood until at twenty-four he went to Ireland and first succeeded in a responsible job, was poor (sometimes literally penniless), dull at school and dirty too, rejected by his associates and to a large extent by his family. Writing presented itself as a way to conform to the family pattern that he had been considered too dull to fit—and as a way to win money and popularity. This meant a style that would be "popular," "good and lucid," "agreeable and easily intelligible"—his own adjectives. It meant a subject matter "both salutary and agreeable to my audience."

> I do believe that no girl has risen from the reading of my pages less modest than before. . . . I think that no youth has been taught that in falseness and flashness is to be found the road to manliness; but some may have learned from me that it is to be found in truth and a high but gentle spirit. Such are the lessons I have striven to teach.

We need not snicker at moral criteria in literature. That Trollope's subject matter is salutary is exactly what I am arguing; but the elementary sense in which he conceived the word is clear. He willingly submitted to the tabus of Victorian publishers: "at page 93 by all means put out 'foul breathing' and page 97 alter 'fat stomach' to 'deep chest,' if the printing will now allow it." It is true that he maintained to Thackeray, who had rejected a story for the *Cornhill*, that "squeamishness—in so far as it is squeamishness and not delicacy—should be disregarded by a writer," and the squeamishness of his audience should in justice not be underestimated. There were objections to Glencora's contemplated adultery, and Trollope had to write one clergyman that "ignorance is not innocence." But if he defended himself against literary censorship it was because he had precensored his work himself—editors found that the author who never submitted a word over or under was by no means so accommodating when asked to cut his work because of the editor's miscalculations. Even the mild rebellion of Lady Glencora remains curiously embarrassing to him—he apologizes continually for her very reality, for exactly those slight improprieties that his modern readers find such a relief. He interrupts to point out her indiscretion, her indelicacy (often unnoticeable to our crass perceptions), as if he were afraid of the power of what he knew to be his best work and felt that his audience could not be trusted to evaluate her unaided. She must regularly be accompanied by a sort of literary duenna, Alice Vavasour when Glencora is a young wife, Marie Goesler when she becomes Duchess, who by her faultless conduct keeps us constantly aware of Glencora's departures from the Victorian norm. Yet she accommodates herself to her world, like Trollope himself. His characters' successful adaptations are a fictional celebration of the means of his own conquest of poverty, squalor, and contempt. His autobiography celebrates it more baldly, and the triumphant listing that closes it—forty-six books in thirty-two years, their itemized earnings adding up to the proud sum of £68,939 17s. 5d.—is the intended proof. He had had his cake and eaten it. Temperance, industry, and good sense had won out, and the money was there to attest the victory.

It is true that compromise can be another name for conformity. And Trollope did conform, and counsel conformity, to the upper-middle-class social order he considered pleasant and good. He did apotheosize the bourgeois virtues: he celebrated Philistinism; he recoiled from any taint of aestheticism or intellectualism, at once deprecating his talent and emphasizing his ordinariness and common sense. He had had his fill of being different. But the Philistines are up for reevaluation. As Clement Greenberg says:

> It is no longer possible to rest a fruitful criticism of contemporary life on a total rejection of the kind of experience that gives

rise to Philistinism. We are better able today to appreciate the
benefits of a middle class confident enough in its Philistinism—
as the German middle classes were not—to insist that politics
be expedient rather than ideological.

"The kind of experience that gives rise to Philistinism"—what is
this but Trollope's experience? Convention, kindness, decency, safety, and money, an unanalyzable amalgam, supposing an uncritical
but not entirely unrealistic confidence that somehow they all go
together. Trollope speaks to the middle class, the novel's traditional
subject and audience. Today that limitation seems somehow shameful. Yet Trollope's province steadily enlarges. Recruits from above
and below swell the army of the Philistines, and to them Trollope
can offer basic training.

Conformity will take us far in this world—and conformity is a
modern bugaboo. But that is because we rightly fear the excessive
materialism to which we are expected to conform, which has nothing in common with the rigid shapes of social decency to which
Trollope counseled submission. We may feel that Trollope's characters would accommodate themselves to a straitjacket, but we must
admit that they manage as well as we do. And conformity is not the
whole; for compromise, the willingness to adjust oneself to a limited, nonideal world, involves the use of the will and the intelligence
to reconcile differences. Total submission, the denial of differences,
is a perversion.

Thus it is not only the safety of Trollope's world that draws us,
but his knowledge of how we may pluck safety from danger. It is
easy to deprecate his message. He himself wrote a novel (*The Prime
Minister*) to show that if agreement is always possible between gentlemen, not everybody is a gentleman. But in a world increasingly
barbaric by Trollope's standards we have today his choice—agree or
crack up. Fantastic that these obvious ideas should need new emphasis: to live within our limitations, to recognize, indoors and abroad,
the "ideal solution," not as our birthright but as an ignis fatuus that
will lure us to destruction. "'Have you never seen that Mama is not
happy here?' . . . 'I have seen it. . . . She has led a life of restraint;
but then how frequently is not restraint the necessity of such a life?'"
How frequently indeed, and how seldom recommended. The op-

posite virtues have had their spokesmen for fifty years and more. Now that we have learned to rebel, we may begin to suspect that total rebellion deprives us of the limits which alone give rebellion meaning.

From *The Massachusetts Review*, Spring 1962.

Henry Wilcox, Babbitt, and the
State of Britain

> "Has Mrs. Newsome money? . . . is there a business?"
> "Lord, yes . . . a great production, a great industry . . .
> well on the way to becoming a monopoly. It's a little thing they
> make—make better, it appears, than other people can, or than
> other people, at any rate, do."

I t is James's delicate joke that at no point in *The Ambassadors*
does he allow us to find out what this object is. "Vulgar," as
Strether tells us, but not "unmentionable," it is simply not a word to
be pronounced in the civilized European society upon which his
innocent American eyes have newly opened. The occupation of the
English hero of *The Spoils of Poynton* is similarly dismissed; he comes
and goes on "the business with which London so abundantly fur-
nished him." For three generations Britain has played at maintaining the fiction that one can have civilization without economics, as
the Victorians had ladies without legs. It is the attitude of the
gentry, familiar to us from Jane Austen and from our own American
South, that if money cannot come imperceptibly, we can at least
avoid talking about where it does come from. In displaying the
proper place of money and production in society, Henry James
merely shows the convert's excess of zeal.

Civilizations, like ladies, have substructures, of which we are
aware but from which we avert our eyes—not the less because we
are ironically aware of what we are doing. The superstructure must
seem to be all: beautiful things, refined perceptions, personal rela-

tions. And yet it is not all. Today Britain feels itself in trouble.* No
serious journal or periodical in England in the past six years is
without its agonizing reappraisal of The State of Britain. The words
recur so often that their capitals have become part of them. The tone
of clustered gloom was best rendered in the full issue of *Encounter*
devoted to the question "Suicide of a Nation?" The answer, given
entirely by Britons, might be summarized as "very likely."

The malaise diagnosed there seems to afflict both super- and
substructure alike. Shocked by their exclusion from the Common
Market, Englishmen have begun to think about "the little things
they make." When French importers tell visiting British busi-
nessmen, "You can't expect us to import bowler hats," the criticism
strikes home. It is now a common thing to read in the British press
that someone has said that "we need a Harvard." No one needs to
explain that he means the Business School.

E. M. Forster, taking up the novel where the nineteenth century
left it, might seem to be, like James, a celebrator of superstructure.
His people, like James's, operate at their leisure; at leisure his aristocracy of the sensitive and considerate struggles to add refinement of
the heart to refinement of manners and intellect. "Personal relations," says Helen Schlegel, "are the real life, forever and ever." Yet
Forster's Schlegels epitomize the growing impatience with Jamesian
gentility even among the gentle. *Howards End* appeared only seven
years after *The Ambassadors*. The Schlegels share James's world. But
the insights of the solitary old man who sat in the British Museum
Reading Room and wrote *Das Kapital* are already beginning their
slow penetration of England. Margaret Schlegel tells her surprised
aunt that "the very soul of the world" is economic; "We stand upon
money as upon islands." (Half-German, she can say out loud things
which proper English leave unspoken.) Later, she decides to marry a
businessman and remarks to her horrified sister, "More and more do
I refuse to draw my income and sneer at those who guarantee it."

In *Howards End* those who guarantee it are the Wilcoxes, the
public men, those who, in a recurring figure, "have their hands on

---

*"Today" was 1963.

the ropes of the world." The Wilcoxes, Margaret recognizes, make civilized life possible. They run the economy and the empire. To be sneered at by intellectuals is the normal lot of such people, and Forster is a hard man on the easy sneer. Basing an oeuvre on his perception of how cultural assumptions divide men, he saw in the split between businessman and intellectual as difficult a challenge to the reconciling power of personal relations as any divisions between Englishman and Indian. In England itself, thinkers and doers needed a Bridge Party. Forster began *Howards End* by trying to provide one. He failed, and his failure is instructive as a symbolic representation of what ails England today, the more striking because it was conceived so long before the symptoms began to show.

People have put the book down for good when they realized that Margaret Schlegel was actually going to marry Henry Wilcox. Yet that marriage is at the center of what Forster was trying to say. It is the symbol of his insistence that we come to terms with the public world, the "world of telegrams and anger," which, unregarded, underlies the reader's assumed world of sensitivity and leisure. The Schlegels, standing on islands of money, cultivate the mind and the spirit. But they are able to act as if the personal is all that matters because they can afford to, and they can afford to because the world of telegrams and anger supports them. The least (perhaps the most) they can do is to realize it, and this Forster makes them do.

Why, then, does Forster weave the ambiguities so thick? "How dare Schlegels despise Wilcoxes when it takes all sorts to make a world?" exclaims Margaret. But Forster created the Wilcoxes to be despised. It is as if he could not help himself. It is a powerful attitude indeed that can wrestle the mind of a writer into its own shape even as he frames a fable to challenge it.

It was Forster, after all, who made the Wilcoxes obtuse, insensitive, snobbish, and narrow—chill English Babbitts without Babbitt's enthusiasm or good nature. Why did he do it? If these are the qualifications for running a rubber company, would it not be better if the marriage of the two worlds did not take place? Forster plots a story to bring to our attention the incompleteness of our own civilized selves. Then, driven by an unexpected vindictiveness, he punishes the Wilcoxes for what he has made them, humbles Henry to Margaret, shows up his strength as a facade, even sends his son to prison for manslaughter. Against this kind of card-stacking the Wilcoxes haven't a chance. Margaret may be able, in some sort, to love them, but their creator tried and failed. "Panic and emptiness"—the phrase becomes a leitmotiv like "telegrams and anger." The bigger they are, the harder they fall.

The intellectual finds the rout of the Wilcoxes so satisfying that he can forget that the book set out to challenge the assumptions which its denouement reinforces. But to give *Howards End* its full power, the Wilcoxes must be seen with the eyes of 1910. Then, in England, the Wilcoxes seemed threatening and invincible. Deficient they might be in the kind of strength that matters, but in the world outside, surely, they carried everything their way. However the novelist might contrive their defeat, they would win anyway, and continue to do the indispensable dirty jobs for which their insensitivity fitted them. There is nothing in *Howards End* to prepare us for the real shocker: that in the actual contest between Schlegels and Wilcoxes for the piloting of England, the Wilcoxes lost.

They did not lose elsewhere. Their foreign counterparts still have their hands on the ropes of the world, making typewriters in Italy, sputniks in Russia, building a new plastic Europe out of the ruins, so that even the Leonard Basts, even the unimaginable hordes below, have something of a life for themselves. But not in England. Forster's picture of the Wilcoxes is deeply English, the product of a culture that has accepted the proposition that the sorts of things the Wilcoxes were good at were not the things a civilization ought to foster and admire. D. H. Lawrence reproved Forster for being too kind to Wilcoxes and reminded him, "Business is no good." He had missed the point. Setting out to bring the two worlds closer together, Forster had ended by arrogating most of the virtues and all the imagination to one of them.

Henry Wilcox seems pallid beside George Babbitt, who should be his counterpart. It is not a matter of art. They share most of their important characteristics—the confusion and incompleteness of their thought, the guilt-ridden incomprehension of their sexuality— but Lewis's picture is crude and simplistic where Forster is cunning and rich. The imagined action that brings Wilcox's deeper nature into play is far more adequate to Forster's conception than the unsatisfactory vignettes that pass for plot in *Babbitt*. Yet Wilcox lacks Babbitt's vigor, as human being and as symbol.

He lacks Babbitt's naive, invulnerable confidence in what he is doing, his romance with real estate and with Zenith, so much deeper for him than any possible romance with a woman. More of a gentleman than Babbitt, impeccable in grammar though limited in vocabulary, Henry Wilcox has the distaste for talking shop which can make British social occasions seem so arid to serious-minded Americans, who like to hear people talk about what is important to them. We learn a great deal from Babbitt about real estate. We learn nothing from Henry Wilcox about rubber. Rubber, as something that can occupy the mind—even a Wilcox's mind—is as inconceivable to Forster as to James. It is, in the proof, "a little thing they make"—no more. Though Forster could imagine Henry Wilcox as a human being, he could not imagine him *as a businessman*.

In the country which made the Industrial Revolution and abruptly lost faith in it, there was plenty of social support for the view that the outer world and those who operated in it were, in the Schlegels' words, "obviously horrid." The Philistines were only respectable to other Philistines. Disparate minds like Arnold, Ruskin, Marx, and Lawrence attacked them. They found few defenders. Unlike America, England did not need a Sinclair Lewis.

Babbitt was a powerful creation, not because he was a Dickensian "original," but because he represented a type admired and supported by his society. He was at home in a nation in which his contribution, though the reader might for a moment be cajoled into considering it ironically, was in large measure assessed as he would assess it. The booster was an acceptable apotheosis of the American, not only in contemptuous foreign eyes, but in American eyes as well. But English Babbitts—if indeed the concept is imaginable at all—lacked the self-confidence, and with it the crude fertility of the American type. The rewards English society afforded them were too narrow. The poor need more than bread, we know, and the rich need more than money. England withheld its ultimate rewards from the producer, the technologist, the engineer, let alone the tycoon and the booster. That was enough. There was no need to satirize them.

Ladies acquired legs after the First World War, but although in theory historians had set economics underneath civilization, in practice English society was still lurching along on superstructure. Gentlemen might occupy themselves in the City, for finance has always outranked production. But making things was not an occupation for Englishmen who wished to admire themselves.

> "Every intelligent person knows that Zenith manufactures more condensed milk and evaporated cream, more paper boxes, and more lighting fixtures, than any other city in the United States, if not in the world. But it is not so universally known that we also stand second in the manufacture of package-butter, sixth in the giant realm of motors and automobiles, and somewhere about third in cheese, leather findings, tar roofing, breakfast food, and overalls!"

In England "top people" did not put their minds to the making of paper boxes and lighting fixtures, whereas in America there were thousands of blinkered but influential citizens to whom Babbitt's euphoric catalogue was not intrinsically funny.

It is thus no inconsistency that an essay on English attitudes begins with an American, averting his eyes from the crudities of the industrial object. James, and Eliot after him, had this reason among all the others for choosing England—not only tradition and the deep-rootedness of history, but an atmosphere friendly to the kind of mind which wanted to ignore the realities that supported it.

And today? It seems a long way from Jamesian delicacy to the general acceptance among intellectuals of the proposition that art, culture, national vitality depend, like national survival, on economic abstractions like the growth rate, and on the making and marketing of large quantities of tangible objects. But how much has really changed? How much of Britain's intellectual vitality is made use of in the substructure of her civilization?

There is in England a series of books for boys, presenting, in terms of simple success stories, the facts on job possibilities for boys leaving school. Deliberately conventional, they are useful sources for contemporary British attitudes; and none is more illuminating than

Ken Jones, Electrical Engineer, by D. O. Summers, which tells in story form what kind of boy, in England, becomes an engineer.

Ken is about to graduate from a "secondary modern" school, to complete, at sixteen, the third-rate education that the greater part of England still deems appropriate for the 80 percent of its children who do not, at ten and a half, pass the qualifying examination called the Eleven Plus.* Ken's abilities have thus already been rated low by the standards of his society. His school offers no physics, but the careers master has nevertheless spotted his interest in radio and suggests to his father that he might become an engineer. Mr. Jones replies, "Oh yes, he's always playing around with electrics or radio or something . . . but it's not the sort of work I'd want him to do for a living."

The careers master is surprised. The American reader is astonished. The boy has failed the big test already; surely engineering training would give him a chance at professional status that does not come often to the secondary-modern boy. But dad, who has a desk in an insurance office, doesn't see it that way. He doesn't want his son to spend his life mending wireless sets, and has to have it explained that the primary meaning of the word *engineer* is not "radio-repairman." (How many American fathers need to be told that an engineer only rarely drives a train?) Straightened out, he still feels "sure that his mother wouldn't want him to go into a factory." Unconventional viewpoints are seldom portrayed in books for fifteen-year-old school-leavers; what Mr. Jones says is good evidence of the public attitude toward the profession whose inventiveness affects so directly the gross national product. The "brain drain" has grown no less severe in the years since Lord Hailsham charged in Parliament that America was living parasitically off British scientific intelligence. Britons might fight it more effectively if they heeded the less widely publicized remarks of Viscount Stoneham in the same debate. In the antiseptic indirect discourse of the *Times:*

> It used to be said that engineers were not the sort of people who joined one's club. He would put it the other way: 'Unfor-

---

*It seems only fair to note that the Eleven Plus is no longer in use.

tunately the people who join my club are not engineers.' . . .
There were plenty of brains in the public schools. Why were
not more of them employed in technology and engineering?
When the headmaster of Eton was an eminent scientist, science
would have arrived.

Yet the arrival of science, surely, in the country of Clerk Maxwell
and Brunel, is independent of the identity of the headmaster of
Eton. The visitor from overseas takes some time to realize that the
viscount knows more about England than he does. No matter how
many English books an American has read before he gets to England, he is unprepared for the fact that the English class system
really is a system. Months go by before he really takes it in. He reads
Zuleika Dobson, curiosity wilting before ennui as the antique romp
uncurls. He moves on to *Decline and Fall,* all set for something
slashing, and finds a bit of trivial fun. Bewildered, he wonders where
the reputations come from. Finally, he catches on: it's not trivial if
you live here. Gibes at public schools, satires on Oxford and Cambridge, are important because Oxbridge and public schools are
important. It matters if engineers do not find their way into the
right clubs, because clubs matter. It matters if public schools do not
emphasize science, because public schools matter, in a way that Ex-
eter and Andover never will. At Harvard teachers of Classics do not
far outnumber professors of physics, as they do at Oxford; but even
though Harvard is Harvard, it would not matter if they did.

A profession's self-image and a society's image of it are relevant
to what the profession can accomplish. Britain's industrial revolution, as James Morris has pointed out, was made by "half-educated,
vigorous, bullying, irrepressible men of ambition," too far outside
the Establishment to care what it thought of them. As they made
money, the Establishment, always adaptable, absorbed and changed
them. Only, of course, it was not them it absorbed, but their sons
and grandsons who, once processed through public schools and
Oxbridge, could hardly be expected to keep their zeal for a better
mousetrap. Babbitt in England? He had already lost half his virtue
when he became a Wilcox.

Viscount Stoneham's club lacks engineers and Ken Jones's dad doesn't want his son to work in a factory. It is clear that over a wide section of society engineers don't make it. The social attitudes responsible for this state of affairs are implicit, but they are paralleled by one that is both explicit and widespread—an intellectual rejection of the idea of technology itself.

It is common, of course, to put technics on a lower level than pure knowledge. Better, if you have a choice, to invent the Pythagorean theorem than the wheel. The low rating of applied science has become a twentieth-century academic cliché, although it was not natural to previous great ages of science and would have been inexplicable to as recent and as great a physicist as Lord Kelvin. It is not, however, peculiar to England. There is another, more sinister element in the British rejection of technology—an overt, conscious hostility that surfaced for a nation's inspection in F. R. Leavis's savage attack on Sir Charles Snow.

When one actually hears Dr. Leavis, one cannot help feeling that there is much that is pathetic about this aging paranoid, reliving old glories and repeating old strictures against the world of telegrams and anger. But it is ominous, not pathetic, to know that he is taken seriously, that columns of the young form behind him to defend the cause of humane studies. For this cause which Leavis believes to be foundering in what he calls "the Snow world" has for fifty years in England carried everything its own way.

The fact is, the Wilcoxes lost. They could not reproduce themselves. Perhaps Forster was right in portraying them as without imagination, even business imagination. It may have been gone already. Certainly it was hard to sustain in a culture that afforded it so little emotional support.

For social indifference and intellectual hostility are intensified in England by emotional rejection of the fruits of technology. The optimistic enthusiasm for things made better than other people made them, symbolized by Prince Albert's Great Exhibition, had already begun to seem naive twenty years later. Partly it was because technology, coming first to Britain, blasted it so thoroughly with soot and ugliness. But beneath the revulsion of Morris and Ruskin lay something deeper—the unexpected British puritanism.

Unexpected only to an American, who has learned that he is the

Puritan, and that England in her genius for moderation rejected that Calvinistic chill. He has heard that British food is monotonous, that British houses are cold. But again, it has not sunk in that they are cold because the British want them that way. He is nonplussed when he encounters the concept of "background" heating, in which radiators are actually designed to be incapable of heating a room above 55 degrees in winter. It is, perhaps, that English winters normally are not severe? But he visits Florence in December and finds that if an Italian does decide to convert his fifteenth-century farmhouse from charcoal braziers to central heat, he puts in radiators with a surface area quadruple that of an English one because he plans to throw the braziers away. The British householder, shivering among the radiators, has no intention of abandoning his electric fires or his chilblain cream.

In short, the transatlantic visitor discovers what many Englishmen could have told him—that there is a positive value set on discomfort and inconvenience. Things that merely make life easier— from supermarkets to cereal packages that don't have to be torn open with the teeth—are regarded with distrust, indifference, or contempt. Even so staunch an enemy of the Establishment as J. B. Priestley gets in his digs at "the consumer role," and writes feelingly of the restless young, "unable to find ecstasy among the toothpastes, chocs, and after-shave lotion." Yet is it the voice of Babbitt or of reason which objects that the consumer civilization is more fairly symbolized by the hire-purchase washing-machine? Its design may be primitive, since no one has thought about it, but it does wash clothes. It has done as much as the welfare state to give the working-class mum a pleasanter life. Perhaps it is the housewife who must at length speak up for technology: the enemies of materialism, on both sides of the Atlantic, are men. Easy cleanliness is peripheral to Priestley's life, or Leavis's; it is central to hers.

There is much to be said for cheerful endurance, of inconvenience, discomfort, and dirt. America, in these years, might find it a usable virtue. England will not. Discomfort may have built the kind of character that salvaged from the debacle of Dunkirk Britain's finest hour, but it will not help Britain meet her current challenge, which pervasive voices in Britain compare to another Dunkirk. For

the growth-rate measures growth in amenities, in comfort, in civilization—in no Greek sense but in the crass Roman sense of hot
baths and hypocausts—unless, of course, you prefer to take your
growth in missiles. Make no mistake about it, it is the American
materialistic ideal, the civilization that mastered plumbing and went
on to striped toothpaste and fiberglass boats. Repellent it may be if it
goes no further; but it is potentially liberating too, as the society
based on the labor of servants was, for a few, potentially liberating.
Civilization still stands on islands of money. Britain cannot compete
in any market, Common or world, by manufacturing products it
doesn't believe in and doesn't think people ought to have. The
products don't come out good enough. The British consumer magazine *Which?* (it is significant that this pale copy of our *Consumer
Reports* was only started in the late fifties) reported as recently as
1963 that the best British dishwasher required the user to rewash
five dishes in an average load, and remarked that since one of the
best was rated "relatively poor" by American testers, "we conclude
that we have yet to see a first-class machine in this country."

How do you get good minds to designing dishwashers? Ken
Jones, in his school for third-raters, could take Latin but not physics.
He passed it, too. Being fictional, he could be lucky. Real boys are
less so. W. Allen, Principal of the School of Architecture, remarked
in a letter to the *Times:* "Creative capacity [in invention and design]
is often unrelated to scholastic ability and by giving the latter such
exclusive esteem . . . we have damaged our national capacity for
action." It seems likely that there are gifted designers among those
who are not selected to go on for education at all. And of those who
are, few choose engineering. The Principal of Manchester College of
Science and Technology, Dr. Bowden, sums up a survey of the attitudes of English sixth-form boys toward engineering and science:

> Nearly all the ablest boys in our science sixth forms want to do
> pure science; only mediocre students want to study engineer-
> ing or read for diplomas in technology. Few boys know that it
> is possible to study engineering in universities. They think that
> technologists go to secondary schools and learn to use their
> hands, whereas scientists come from grammar schools and learn
> to use their brains.

In America, too, bright boys reject engineering. But in a culture whose mandarins are not yet dominant, it doesn't yet matter. Boys who like science, in American high schools, are as often as not counseled into engineering by guidance officers who themselves may have no idea of a distinction between pure and applied science. These students arrive at college set on being aeronautical engineers, with all a small boy's model-airplane romanticism. If they are really good, the pure scientists fall on them, nudging them out of engineering into physics or mathematics. Each time it seems a victory for the free life of the intellect. But it can be a victory only in a society in which important forces are still working on the other side, in which a majority of "top people" still have enough of Babbitt in them to take for granted that making things better than other people do is a worthwhile occupation for anybody.

American intellectuals can afford to see themselves as Schlegels beleaguered by armies of up-to-date, personally adequate Wilcoxes. Operating from warm and convenient houses, our clothes and dishes washed by efficient and constantly improving machines, we are free to look on students rescued from engineering—or business school—as souls won for the faith. It is by one of those major transvaluations which are the shocks and rewards of travel that we realize that the balance of society would be upset if Babbitt lost confidence in himself. Ford and Edison are narrow culture-heroes, and nobody can debunk them better than an American intellectual. But in the end, how dare Schlegels despise Wilcoxes when it takes all sorts to make a world? Forster gave us the question and muddled the answer—as all answers, perhaps, deserve to be muddled. But he did invent some sort of marriage, and some sort of marriage there must be. Like other marriages that work, it must be based on mutual respect. Both partners are indispensable. But for the next twenty-five years, in Britain, Wilcoxes are more indispensable than Schlegels, and in desperately short supply.

From *The Berkshire Review*, Spring 1968.

Recuperating Jane

Jane went to Paradise;
   That was only fair.
Good Sir Walter met her first
   And led her up the stair.
Henry and Tobias,
   And Miguel of Spain,
Stood with Shakespeare at the top
   To welcome Jane.

Kipling accompanies his homage to Jane Austen by a story as far as possible from anything we are likely to associate with a gentlewoman's quiet life in Bath and Hampshire, or with six novels which, as the main narrator of "The Janeites" explains, aren't "adventurous, nor smutty, nor what you'd call even interestin'—all about girls o' seventeen . . . not certain 'oom they'd like to marry; an' their dances and card-parties an' picnics, and their young blokes goin' off to London on 'orseback for 'aircuts and shaves."

The linguistic disparity strikes hard. It is meant to. The Austen critic just quoted is a London hairdresser (hence his alertness to the details of Frank Churchill's barbershop excursion) and a returned soldier. The time is 1920, the place a Masonic Lodge, one of the few peacetime settings where it could be imagined that the masses and the classes could share experience, as for four years they had shared experience in the trenches of France. Ever the virtuoso, Kipling has found out a way to wrench Jane Austen into the Great War, as his Cockney recalls for a lodge brother how it was in the dugout where officers and men of an artillery unit shortly to be blown to bits shared in-group allusions to Austen's novels while the men served, and the officers drank, the postprandial port that was the sign of their class and their privilege.

The story, as I have just sketched it, can only appear preposterous. Jane Austen in the trenches? Yet she did not appear there by accident; she is there so that Kipling may confront head-on issues that were already troubling him in 1920, and that trouble us increasingly as we head toward the end of our common century: the issues of readership and class. Who reads Jane Austen? And how? (We know, of course, that nobody reads Kipling, but that, as he would say, is another story.) How can we assimilate into our wider world personages and concerns as narrowly class-bound—we would add, gender-bound—as those of these six pellucid novels?

Kipling shows the difficulties; he chose them. To make the implausible plausible is the virtuoso's work. Since common soldiers did not routinely read Jane Austen in the trenches or anywhere else, Kipling frames a fable. He makes one of the soldiers "a toff by birth," though it only shows when he's drunk, who amid the gas and the shelling of the 1918 German offensive hits upon the idea of initiating his fellow soldier into a secret Society of Janeites. He models it upon the Masons, to which they both belong, and the Cockney finds that the privileges of membership are worth the price of admission. A soldier can contradict his superior officer, as long as it's about Jane, and the current password (*Tilniz an' trapdoors*) pays off in Turkish cigarettes from the officers' stores—and in a saving intellectual distraction for men who knew they "couldn't expect to av'rage more than six weeks longer apiece." So the Cockney works his way up through the "'igher Degrees, includin' the Charges" ("Every dam' thing about Jane is remarkable to a pukka Janeite") and turns out to be no mean critic. His summation, in fact, would fit nicely into any of the books I'm reviewing seventy years later: "They're all on the make," he says, "in a quiet way, in Jane."

But there's more to the story than talk. Kipling knew how to make a plot do its job. The only survivor when his unit is blown apart, the half-dead Cockney is overheard likening a garrulous nurse to Miss Bates. Jane is indeed a password to privilege; she gets him onto a hospital train where there was "no room for a louse," and he lives to tell his Masonic brethren, "You take it from me. . . . There's no one to touch Jane when you're in a tight place."

Of course it's dismissible—and perhaps we should dismiss it— as a war idyll, a sentimental assertion of the sharing of a culture inherently unshareable, the dream of a toff who needed to convince himself that in the crucible of war, at least, England had been not two nations but one. Who can prescribe the uses of literature, personal and public? We need to think, though, that it has uses; although it is exactly the complaint of Kipling's Cockney that "her characters was no *use*," being "only just like people you run across every day," the story knows that's just the point. Miss Bates *is* just like his Auntie ("good as gold—but *you* know"), and Kipling works it so that it's exactly that perception that saves him.

Unlike his younger contemporary Virginia Woolf, Kipling was not repelled by the reality of class. Born to heteroglossia, he had grown up hearing and valuing the voices of the multiworld of India, and he could hear and value the various voices of England. But he needed very much to believe what Virginia Woolf, for all that Fabian involvement, gave no sign of believing—that "the Colonel's lady and Judy O'Grady are sisters under the skin." Which, however implausible, is what you have to believe if you are to believe that Jane Austen is there for everybody, for everybody to make use of.

Yet facts are facts. When I taught *Emma* in a community college, students who had been content, even absorbed, in reading *Paradise Lost* asked "Why are we reading this?" My failure? Theirs? Hers? All three? Kipling knew Jane's class limits; why else should his Cockney quote his toff's insistence that her "lawful issue" was "'Enery James," another writer for whom the lower classes didn't properly exist? Yet by placing "England's Jane" at the top with good Sir Walter and Fielding and Smollett and Cervantes and Shakespeare, Kipling staked for her claims he wouldn't have staked for 'Enery— the old-fashioned claims of scope, universality, the immortality of the classic. And now, with the very idea of the classic under assault as yet another fortress of elitism, what can we claim for Jane Austen? Is this even a question we need to answer, when we can take her over for the Academy, swathe her in reams of papyrus, and preserve her, corpsed, for future generations of graduate students?

For James Thompson as for Kipling, Jane Austen is part of "The Great Tradition," though it is with no friendly hand that he capitalizes the phrase.* Novels "continually in print and continually read since 1811" are "simply too familiar"; "we have never had to rediscover or recuperate her work, nor has there been any systematic reassessment of it." "We," naturally, means critics. "Far too often," he complains, "what has passed for criticism . . . is really appreciation." For "if we approach Austen's novels with the aim of showing how good they are, there is little chance that we will ever begin to understand them, because we begin by sharing their assumptions." Thompson cites Fredric Jameson on the "class homogeneity" of those assumptions, and the "restricted class of readers" who share them; such agreement "is not brought back into the world by fiat." So much for Kipling's Masonic idyll.

And so much, too, for appreciation. It is activity of which no one will be able to accuse Mr. Thompson, though he does concede that of "those many novels from the 1790's, Austen's are the best remembered and perhaps even the best." Janeite outrage, however, should not distract us from an important issue. "No criticism can proceed adequately until it stands outside the unexamined, unrecognized, a priori assumptions within which the work was first conceived."

And really, doesn't that sound as if it had to be true? "We will never see Austen's work clearly if we accept her fiction as right or correct or natural: Rather, we need to see it as explicitly time-bound and historical, not the product of right or truth or nature or even a powerful morality." In short, if you mean to understand a work, get outside it.

C. S. Lewis saw it differently. "The first demand a work of art makes upon us is surrender. Look. Listen. Receive. Get yourself out of the way. (There is no use asking first if the work before you

---

*James Thompson, *Between Self and World: The Novels of Jane Austen* (University Park: Pennsylvania State University Press, 1988).

deserves such surrender, because until you have surrendered you cannot possibly find out.)"

"Surrender" is a big demand; to get yourself out of the way, bigger yet. The demand is made upon "us," a considerably larger company than Thompson's "we." Coming from *An Experiment in Criticism,* Lewis's advice certainly includes critics. But it includes the ordinary reader as well. It rests, in fact, on the archaic assumption that there shouldn't be that much difference between them—or us—our common interest being in understanding, from which appreciation may, though it need not, follow. For although self-surrender is essential for Lewis, it is the first demand a work makes upon us, not the only one. If you mean to understand a work, get inside it. To get inside it, of course, we must see the work as time-bound, as historical, because we must surrender to its history, bind ourselves in its time, not our own. Surrender, however, does not enforce acceptance. Afterward, considering "whether the work . . . deserves such surrender," we are free to "recuperate" it by refusing its notions of nature, right, or truth. But surrender must come first.

For is it really self-evident that coming to a novel from outside is the way to see it clearly? That's how Virginia Woolf came to *Ulysses.* The way she saw it is notorious: "an illiterate underbred book, . . . the book of a self-taught working man, and we all know how distressing they are, how egotistic, insistent, raw, striking, and ultimately nauseating." Kipling may condescend to his Cockney, and sentimentalize class differences by easy erasure. But he would never have written that. Thompson's outside is larger than Bloomsbury's. But as a locus from which to pursue understanding it seems to have served him no better. There may be something to be said for appreciation after all.

The contrast between Austen's voice and Thompson's is more jarringly hetero- than any glossia of Kipling's. What Jane Austen's representation of character does, Thompson tells us, is to "enact bourgeois ideology of the individual subject within a high capitalist, consumer society." From *Northanger Abbey* to *Persuasion,* he sees her novels illustrating, progressively, relentlessly, the "privatization" and "alienation" Georg Lukács found inherent in the "objectification of social relations under capital." Austen's antidote for this is love, "intimacy, morally corrective union," which "functions to efface the ideological contradiction between social responsibility and private withdrawal," and "serves as the private 'solution' to alienation and the objectification of social relations." Yet since "romance and re-ification are two sides of the same coin," love isn't much use. The continuing appeal of the novels, Thompson suggests, is due, not to any pleasure they might afford us, still less to any assent we might give their notions of nature or truth, but to "our implicit awareness that hers is the first recognizable formulation of modern personal relations." Alienated, isolated, Jane Austen points to the way we live now. No less time-bound than she, we stand outside her a priori assumptions only to recuperate her into our own.

Evidently, Thompson's book is bleak reading. Fresh from re-visiting the novels, few readers will be convinced that Emma's socia-ble Hartfield "is a type of Crusoe's island," and Emma herself an-other Crusoe, an "isolated consciousness," Lukács's "individual, egotistic bourgeois isolated artificially by capitalism." One suspects that Lukács somehow did not have that particular Emma in mind. Highbury is not Yonville; Mr. Knightly is not Charles Bovary. Are we to believe there will be no more balls, no more picnics, no more parties when Emma is married? Will Mr. Knightly and his wife cease to interest themselves in the affairs of their neighbors? Apparently. "Objectification is cured . . . by a process of exclusion"; "private withdrawal succeeds social responsibility." So Thompson ends his book with a vision of "Captain Wentworth and Anne Elliot at their reunion, lost amid the public crowd in Bath, as two individual 'souls dancing in private rapture.'" Austen ends *Persuasion* rather differ-ently, with the inclusion of the previously excluded Mrs. Smith, now explicitly identified as Anne's friend *and* her husband's, in the wider society, as Anne glories in being the wife of a sailor, a member of "that profession which is, if possible, more distinguished in its domestic virtues than in its national importance." Alienation is where you find it.

And if you're looking for it, Freud is, as Thompson says, "help-ful." Doubly helpful, in fact. "His clinical vocabulary helps to demystify what Austen calls love," while "the terms of transference provide us with a model" for a heroine's attitudes toward the men in her life. "To analyze such matters, Freud is our most ready guide because our understanding of psychology is formed by the assumptions of psychoanalysis." Never mind the difficulty of finding a university psychology department where those assumptions are now generally accepted. "We" are not psychologists but literary critics. Readers will judge for themselves the degree of illumination afforded by diagnosing "all six of Austen's heroines" as examples of the "two basic manifestations of narcissism," "mirror transference" (Emma, Elizabeth, Elinor) and "idealizing transference" (Anne, Fanny, Catherine). Austen herself is endowed, in a flutter of biographical ifs and must-haves, with a "narcissistic personality structure" and an unrequited family romance to explain it, as her "personal neurosis" reinforces her condition under capitalism to recuperate for the late-twentieth-century reader a body of work sufficient to satisfy the gloomiest outsider, and to arouse an ahistorical wonderment that anybody could read it for pleasure—in the trenches or anywhere else.

From one extreme to the other: Park Honan's biography* comes at Jane Austen so thoroughly from inside that he seems to forget there's any place else. Honan doesn't theorize about history and psychology, but he knows so much about Jane Austen and about the years in which she lived her life and her father and mother and aunts and brothers and sisters and cousins and nieces and nephews and great-nieces and great-nephews lived theirs that you scarcely feel the lack. He knows about the British navy, in which two of her brothers, as well as Captain Wentworth, found their careers; he knows about the Battle of Trafalgar that Frank Austen missed out on; he knows about the trial of Warren Hastings and what the Austens thought of it; he knows about Jane Austen's cousin Eliza Hancock, who may have been Hastings's daughter and whose husband was guillotined under the Terror and who acted in suggestive amateur theatricals in the Austens' barn, just like in *Mansfield Park*. There couldn't be a cosier refuge for a pukka Janeite reeling from an

---

*Park Honan, *Jane Austen: Her Life* (New York: St. Martin's Press, 1987).

encounter with Thompson's book. There are no less than four gene-
alogical charts. (That of Jane's mother, containing a baron, two
knights, and a duke, handily disposes of Thompson's suggestion
that her family was only "pseudo-gentry.") Honan has unearthed a
great deal of new material—for example, the sixty-odd numbers of
the periodical the Austen brothers put out while they were at Oxford, which may have influenced (and been influenced by) their
fourteen-year-old sister, and witty verses by Jane Austen's mother,
who turns out to have been a spunky lady not given to repining at
the transition from her aristocratic background to her hard-working
life as the wife of a country parson in a house with "a cellar that
regularly flooded and a patchwork of cracked and exposed rafters."
She is an attractive figure among her cows (six) and chickens and
ducks and children (eight), and I was disappointed when Honan,
like Thompson, used Freud and the novels to argue that Jane didn't
like her. But we needn't be bound by Honan's conclusions; from his
extraordinary richness of detail, we can draw our own. This must be,
from now on, the standard biography.

You do, though, have to be a pukka Janeite to read it. Every
dam' thing about Jane is remarkable to Honan. Nobody is likely to
come closer to reconstructing Jane Austen's world and the people
and places in it. But after twenty chapters crammed with such sentences as "As likely as not Mrs. Penelope Lutley Sclater came bus-
tling over from Tangier Park," one may well feel trapped in a Jane
Austen novel written at Tolstoyan length by a Miss Bates with total
recall.

Happily, Claudia Johnson's book provides a middle way.* Like
Honan, she has been able to inhabit the novels, like them, enjoy
them, come at them from inside. Yet she is no mere appreciator, still
less a Procrustean theoretician, still less a pointilliste of facts. She is
the best kind of scholar-critic. Rather than standing outside Austen's
assumptions, she asks us (the inclusive us, scholars, critics, and readers who may be neither) to discover with her what those assumptions really were. We might have thought, after reading Honan, that

---

*Claudia Johnson, *Jane Austen: Women, Politics, and the Novel* (Chicago: University of Chicago Press, 1988).

our knowledge of them was complete. But Johnson takes us into Austen's mind as well as her life and times. She has examined, not her brothers' juvenilia, but works we know she read and valued as an adult, the vast and popular literature written by her female contemporaries. "'Only a novel!'" she wrote in *Northanger Abbey.* "In short, only some work in which the greatest powers of the mind are displayed . . . in the best chosen language." Reading the forgotten novels of these largely forgotten women with a consciousness of the turbulent times in which they wrote, Johnson finds in Maria Edgeworth, Elizabeth Inchbald, Hannah More, Sophia King, Amelia Opie, Mary Hays, Charlotte Smith, Frances Burney (who did not just write *Evelina*) an unexplored fund of ideas with which Austen's work is in dialogue. From novels with titles like *Belinda* and *Cecilia,* Johnson recreates for us a complex political discourse. "A consciousness of how the private is political, and a sensitivity to the problems women writers encounter living and writing in a male-dominated culture" will show that "few ostensibly 'historical' truths are as stubbornly persistent and as entirely *a*historical as the belief that with the exception of a few unseemly radicals, Austen and her ladylike contemporaries were not . . . concerned with the moral implications of gender distinctions, and that, as a sensible woman, Austen never mixed with the political debates of her time." Novelists in the years following the French Revolution had dealt explicitly with "politically charged" material; Johnson shows us how, in a time of "anti-Jacobin" reaction—Jane Austen's years—they found ways to use it "in an exploratory and interrogative, rather than hortatory and prescriptive manner." If primogeniture, the inadequacy or tyranny of fathers, the unreliability of brothers, the dependency of daughters, regularly animate the plots of Austen's novels, perhaps we should pay attention. *Mansfield Park*'s skepticism of the patriarchal family is no passing shadow; it was there in *Sense and Sensibility* and will be there in *Persuasion.* The new readings that emerge from Johnson's impeccably researched, judicious book show us that the familiar novels of England's Jane, that national treasure, do at least as much to challenge the status quo as to affirm it.

Claudia Johnson's study should persuade us to open the annals of intellectual history to novels that few of us have read and that

virtually no one has taken seriously. With a quiet felicity of style and
a welcome avoidance of overstatement, Johnson not only identifies
concerns and responses invisible to us, but convinces us that these
are not scholarly illusions, but living facts that modify conclusively
our understanding of texts we thought we knew. She pries open our
assumptions with another telling quotation from *Northanger Abbey:*
"To come with a well-informed mind is to come with an inability of
ministering to the vanity of others, which a sensible person would
always wish to avoid. A woman especially, if she have the misfortune
of knowing anything, should conceal it as well as she can." How well
Austen concealed her well-informed mind is shown by the pervasive
condescension that has accompanied two centuries of critical praise.
If "dear Aunt Jane," as one Victorian critic called her, made it into
the canon, it was "on terms which cast doubt on her qualifications
for entry and which ensure that her continued presence there be
regarded as an act of gallantry." She told her talentless nephew that
she worked on two inches of ivory; we believed her. R. W. Chapman
certainly did; glossing her work with appendices full of fashions and
Regency accoutrements, leaving allusions to London riots or the
Antigua slave trade unexplored, his standard edition "created the
author [it] presumed." The Austen Claudia Johnson creates is very
different. Yet she is no alienated late-twentieth-century stranger, but
a woman of sense and sensibility whom the admiring Janeite will
find entirely recognizable as she responds ironically, moderately, ju-
diciously, and discreetly to the issues of her day.

Such an Austen is far from Honan's High Tory, equally far from
Thompson's neurotic isolated by the twin juggernauts of historical
and psychic determinism. Having read Johnson's book, I think now
I would have a better answer if a student from outside the pale of
privilege asked me, "Why are we reading this?" The urge of education is the urge to share what we value. Is it an urge we should
honor? Indulge? Repudiate as a mechanism of class domination?
Johnson has helped me to recuperate Kipling's answer from the
mists of sentiment. We are reading this, perhaps, to discover how
much a brilliant and not wholly fortunate woman can teach us about
how to live within bounds, how to recognize them, even display
them as bounds, and still not find them a prison, and still do one's

serious, amused, responsible best to live well inside them and stretch them a little for those who come after. Whatever your class, whichever your gender, I can't think history or psychology will render that lesson obsolete. Unswathe the papyrus. Start in on *Northanger Abbey* and read right through to the end of *Persuasion*. Limits straiten us all. And there's no one to touch Jane when you're in a tight place.

From *The Hudson Review*, Winter 1990.

Crippled Laughter: Toward Understanding Flannery O'Connor

O nce upon a time a grandmother, her son, his wife, and three children were driving to Florida through a locality where a dangerous criminal had escaped from prison. After their car was disabled on a lonely road they encountered the criminal, known as the Misfit, and two henchmen. When the grandmother allowed him to see that he had been recognized, he ordered the entire family to be shot except for the old lady. A brief conversation ensued between them, in which the Misfit showed himself to be a man of fastidious manners, deep feeling, and highly developed religious consciousness. The grandmother expressed her sympathy for his evident pain; he then shot her in the chest.

Once there was a girl with a Ph.D. in philosophy, a weak heart, and an artificial leg, who because of frail health lived with her goodhearted but conventional mother on a back-country road, compensating for her dependence and isolation by making herself as unattractive as possible and asserting her intellectual superiority as unpleasantly as she knew how. She had fantasies of seducing a young Bible salesman, the first man who had ever seemed attracted to her, but his attraction was in fact to her wooden leg, which he made off with, leaving her humiliated and desolate, marooned in a hay-loft.

"I am certainly glad you like the stories," wrote Flannery O'Connor to Robie Macauley soon after the publication of *A Good Man Is Hard to Find*, "because now I feel it's not so bad that I like them so much. The truth is I like them better than anybody and I read them over and over and laugh and laugh." Let us begin with that laughter; it is the most obvious way into the thicket of paradoxes that is O'Connor's writing.

Master of a prose whose directness and precision give almost physical pleasure, unusually aware of her relationship to her readers, Flannery O'Connor was consciously committed to communication. "One never writes for a subtle reader," she wrote to a friend. "Or if you do, you shouldn't." "Unless the novelist has gone completely out of his mind," she told a Georgia audience, "his aim is still communication, and communication suggests talking inside a community." Yet she submitted her readers to tests they failed repeatedly, which indeed they were bound to fail. She was committed to a Southern fiction. Yet her stories left Southern readers indifferent, while feeding every Northern stereotype of Southern degeneracy and fanatacism. She was committed to a Catholic fiction. Yet Catholic readers could not recognize sainthood in the backwoods Protestants she put forward as prophets, or the operation of grace in the violence she thought necessary to counter the sentimentality of the religious—nor could Catholic or Protestant understand, in the harsh universe she presented as Christian, the invisibility of hope. She was committed to the standards of the sophisticated Northern literary establishment which made her reputation and to which she sold her stories. Yet its secular liberalism could be depended on to reverse good guys and bad, and to see nihilism and absurdity in fictions expressly framed to deny them; "The Misfits, Shiftlets, Manley Pointers," one critic wrote, "are O'Connor's God." She embraced the neocritical orthodoxy of the self-sufficiency of the work. Yet in letters, lectures, and public readings she was indefatigable in supplying friends and strangers with the explanations the stories were to have made unnecessary.

The inability to laugh as loud as the author is only the first indication of the reader's failure. The stories invite us to misevaluate character and event as grossly as any freshman encountering, in the introductory anthology, the obligatory O'Connor story. Her own critical writings, collected as *Mystery and Manners,* are substantially concerned with setting the reader straight, and misunderstanding is a continuing theme of the extraordinary letters collected by Sally Fitzgerald as *The Habit of Being.* Throughout O'Connor's career, expert readers, writers, and friends missed the point—or, worse, mistook it. In 1955 she wrote:

> I spent the weekend in Connecticut with Caroline [Mrs. Allen Tate]. . . . The chief guests were dear old Malcolm Cowley and dear old Van Wyke Brooks [*sic*]. Dear old Van Wyke insisted that I read a story. . . . I read "A Good Man Is Hard to Find," and Mr. Brooks later remarked . . . that it was a shame someone with so much talent should look upon life as a horror story. Malcolm was very polite and asked me if I had a wooden leg.

Three years later she complains to another correspondent:

> All my stories are about the action of grace on a character who is not very willing to support it, but most people think of these stories as hard, hopeless, brutal, etc.

And in 1963, a few months before her death:

> I heard from C. Carver [for years her preferred editor]. . . . She thought ["Revelation"] one of my most powerful stories and probably my *blackest.* Found Ruby evil. . . . I've really been battling this problem all my writing days.

When stories so artfully crafted (and assiduously revised) consistently require the ministrations of their author, something has gone wrong. We who have been trained to luxuriate in ambiguity will scarcely reject a fiction of paradox. The Comic and the Terrible can be opposite sides of the same coin, as O'Connor claimed they were, and that "grace comes somehow violent" has been the burden of tragedy since the *Agamemnon.* But we must distinguish between the paradoxes that express real complexities, the mysteries of this world or another, and those unresolved discords that announce the artist's and the reader's linked failure.

It is not that the explanations O'Connor provided to so many audiences and correspondents are unconvincing. On the contrary, they are extraordinarily successful in saving the fictional phenomena. The cannily placed Christian symbols become transparent in their strong light, and black hats so readily distinguishable from white that we wonder how we ever confused them. Once we have read the letters, it is no longer possible to make the Misfit into a Christ symbol or the grandmother into a witch (as Andrew Lytle did) or to recoil from the bloodstained prophets of *Wise Blood* and *The Violent Bear It Away*. Characters are saved, or identified as devilish; and when we return to the stories, we must agree that the clues are there.

Yet the explanations, in the very elegance of their economy, expose a central miscalculation. Fiction, O'Connor cautioned, has no instant answers: it should leave us, "like Job, with a renewed sense of mystery." But this is exactly what the explanations do not do. Instead of renewing mystery, they relocate it, transferring it from the characters and events of the story to the realm of theology. Perhaps this is the proper place for it. Yet the stories seem to shrink under these anagogical readings—a word she does not hesitate to borrow from Saint Thomas. What remains after explication is not the rich tangle of human reality but clear exemplars of the central Christian mystery of redemption through the acceptance of violence and pain. Again a paradox: no author warns more explicitly against "the tendency . . . towards the abstract, and therefore toward allegory, thinness." "When you can state the theme of a story, when you can separate it from the story itself, then you can be sure the story is not a very good one. The meaning of a story has to be embodied in it . . . not abstract meaning but experienced meaning." Yet her explanations *require* us to allegorize, and once we learn to bridge the gap between the midcentury modernity of her fictional method and her Catholic value system, mystery flies heavenward. As incursions of grace through arson and through murder and through sudden stroke become familiar to the point of predictability, all moral ambiguity evaporates, leaving the stories that puzzled us all too clear.

Certainly O'Connor was not well served by her literary mentors. Her letters are laced with references to the rules of the neocritical classicism she learned in Paul Engle's class at Iowa. Caroline Tate never let her forget them, and for all her originality, she was not ready to let them go, as if, in her isolation, they were a lifeline to the world outside. They sustained her literary practice as her Catholic orthodoxy sustained her moral life, guiding revision after revision, digested again and again for the young writers to whom she was so generous with encouragement. Careful about that omniscient narrator. Watch out for the point of view. "If you violate the point of view you destroy the sense of reality and louse yourself up generally." "The omniscient narrator is not supposed to use colloquial expressions." "When you present a situation you have to let it speak entirely for itself." "A story is not an essay." "Show these things and you don't have to say them." But sometimes you do. In stories stiff with craft, the readers still went wrong. Principles elicited from Joyce and James were not adequate to carry a burden of conviction more like Dostoevsky's. O'Connor was out for bigger epiphanies, and both her readers and her art might have been better served by fictions looser and more baggy, by some of the explicitness, adaptiveness, and stylistic generosity of her letters. She herself perceived it; there was not much that she did not perceive. "I did fail myself," she wrote of "The Displaced Person." "Understatement is not enough."

Taught by Brooks and Warren, she placed a heavy burden on symbols. "Read 'The Dead,'" she advised. "See how he makes the snow work in that story." In "The Enduring Chill" a young know-it-all returning home near death from a disease he refuses to have treated is humbled when it is identified as merely undulant fever; the "shock of self-knowledge" that ensues, she explains, "clears the way for the Holy Ghost." The operation of the third person of the Trinity is to be recognized not in any change that takes place in the boy, but in a bird-shaped water stain on his bedroom ceiling. The wooden leg of poor Hulga who has rejected Joy and embraced ugliness of body and spirit symbolizes "a wooden part of her soul": "When the Bible salesman steals it, the reader realizes that he has taken away part of the girl's personality and has revealed her deeper

affliction to her for the first time." O'Connor maintains a double
standard of symbolism that takes some getting used to. She laughs
loud and often at readers who "try to make everything a symbol."
The questioner who hankered to know "the significance of the Misfit's hat" was told it was to cover his head. Freudian symbolism is
impatiently dismissed; church steeples are emphatically *not* phallic,
and Oedipus is visible in the bushes only to Northern sophisticates.
"The Freudian techniques can be applied to anything at all with
equally ridiculous results," she wrote to William Sessions. "Lord,
Billy, recover your simplicity. You ain't in Manhattan." Religious
symbols, however, lurk in the most realistic imagery. In "A View of
the Woods," "the woods, if anything, are the Christ symbol. They
are bathed in a red light, and they in the end escape the old man's
vision and march off over the hills." It is not by accident that to Joy-
Hulga's nearsighted vision the departing Bible salesman appears to
be walking on water.

By the time we have read a few more such explications (and
there is one for almost every story), we have learned our lesson: "to
be on the lookout for such things as the action of grace in the
Grandmother's soul, and not for the dead bodies." But as O'Connor
told an audience of writers, "a story is good when you continue to
see more and more in it." If we allow such explanations to carry full
conviction, we are in danger of seeing less and less.

Nevertheless, we go on reading the stories, as inadequately,
most of us, as most readers have read them in the more than quarter-
century since they first began to appear, horrified still when we
should laugh, dissatisfied alike with our readings and with explanations which, for all their elegance, fail to resolve the dissonances that
assault us. "John Hawkes has a theory that my fiction is the voice of
the devil," O'Connor wrote Cecil Dawkins the year before she died,
conceding that for one story at least ("The Lame Shall Enter First")
it was "a good insight." It is a stunning concession, and an unset-
tling one. We can trust neither the tale nor the teller. For most
readers, the stories do not and cannot resolve as she would have
them, but retain the murky hostility and anger out of which they
grew.

Our task as readers would be easier if her explanations had

remained inaccessible. Without the preservation of print, authorial intentions known by hearsay, if at all, could conveniently be forgotten. But the explanations are there, in all the clarity of their exposition and the intensity of their conviction. And discordant as they are with the actual experience of the fiction, they draw us beyond it into a lived experience in which we see not less and less but more and more. The value of the occasional writings, and above all of the letters, is not that they unlock the stories—although they do that—but that they introduce us to the extraordinary human being whose darker voice the stories were. For the richest discordancy of all is left to us to resolve—that between the luminous warmth of the letters and the fiction's merciless laughter.

For the letters shine. They are a cornucopia of pleasure, a day-by-day encounter not only with a surpassing intelligence, but with a resilient and humorous virtue that converted intelligence into a premature and touching wisdom. They call upon us for that rarest of modern emotions, admiration, simple and overflowing, for the human being who wrote them, whose heroism—no weaker word will serve—burns all the stronger because every line communicates that she would no sooner lay claim to heroism than she would to sainthood. The facts of her life are now well known: that her mortal illness struck her when she was scarcely into adulthood; that, separating her from her contemporaries and her intellectual peers, it brought her home to live with her mother on a dairy farm four miles outside a small town in Georgia; that it took fifteen more years to kill her. From these years the nearly six hundred pages of published letters are only a selection; she wrote many more. She wrote to friend and stranger; she made strangers friends. The letters poured through the Milledgeville post office, scarcely a day without one. Out of the airless isolation of a small Southern town, out of weakness, pain, and loss, out of progressive crippling and disfigurement, the voice reaches, amazing us by the strength with which she says what is hers to say and the delicacy with which she fashions it to the interests, the needs, the emotional and intellectual and spiritual readiness of each correspondent, reaching out to the life from which she had been excluded in a daily manifestation of the Christian charity she could not practice directly. They can be read in, read through, read again. Trivial and profound, they envelop us in an atmosphere of responsiveness, encouragement, and affection. "If you believe in the divinity of Christ," she writes, "you have to cherish the world at the same time as you struggle to endure it." The world, in the fiction, is scarcely endurable; we who cannot laugh at its dark mayhem enter it armored and withdraw as soon as we can. It is in the letters that she cherished it.

O'Connor's letters are too rooted in the lives of sender and recipient for successful excerpting, but here are samples. To a student who had written because he was too shy to approach her after a reading, she responded with a gentle respect that must have astonished him:

> As a freshman in college you are bombarded with new ideas, or rather pieces of ideas, new frames of reference, an activation of the intellectual life which is only beginning, but which is already running ahead of your lived experience. After a year of this, you think you cannot believe. . . . About the only way we know whether we believe or not is by what we do, and I think from your letter that you will not take the path of least resistance in this matter and simply decide that you have lost your faith and that there is nothing you can do about it.

To an old friend, with a realism humorous, tough, and just self-deprecating enough to be acceptable:

> . . . let me give you the advice of an old and world-weary customer. Myself. This thing of demanding honesty in people is in the upper reaches of extreme Innocence. The only people of whom you can demand honesty are those you pay to get it from. When you ask [someone] to be honest with you, you are asking him to act like God, whom he is not, but whom he makes some attempt to be like in giving you what you want, and it doesn't make him show up too well, of course. Never, above all things, ask your *family* to be honest with you. This is putting a strain on the human frame it can't bear. . . . To love people you have to ignore a good deal of what they say while they are being honest, because you are not living in the Garden of Eden any longer. . . . Enough from the Sage.

At that writing the Sage was thirty-three years old.

To another friend, she relaxes into the comfortable comedy of shared values:

> . . . the Methodist-Universalist . . . left in the middle of my talk. I don't think it was a protest gesture, I just think he thought he could live a useful life without it. I told them that when Emerson decided in 1832 that he could no longer celebrate the Lord's supper unless the bread and wine were removed that an important step in the vaporization of religion in America had taken place. It was somewhere after that I think he left. . . . Have you read about the lady in Texas who is having a chapel built in the shape of John Glenn's capsule?

But the letters frustrate quotation: One never wants to break off. These we *can* "read over and laugh and laugh," at the one-legged peacocks and one-eyed swans, at the unwieldy packaging of the books that were always passing between her and her friends in the mail, at the customs of the natives ("My standard is, When in Rome, do as you done in Milledgeville"), at her illness. About that she joked continually, lest by any chance she should invite what she least wanted, could least afford to accept: that pity which threatened as nothing else could her Stoic fortitude and her Christian patience.

These jokes tell us more about the stories than any explication. "The only way you can help a person on crutches is going down the steps to hold on to her belt in the back. Then if she falls, you got her. For my part I am always glad to have the door held open, that's all." Such hard-won equilibrium was rewon daily:

> An old lady got on the elevator behind me and as soon as I turned around she fixed me with a moist gleaming eye and said in a loud voice, "Bless you, darling!" I felt exactly like the Misfit and I gave her a weakly lethal look, whereupon greatly encouraged, she grabbed my arm and whispered (very loud) in my ear, "Remember what they said to John at the gate, darling!" It was not my floor but I got off and I suppose the old lady was astounded at how quick I could get away on crutches. I have a one-legged friend and I asked her what they said to John at the gate. She said she reckoned they said, "The lame shall enter first." This may be because the lame will be able to knock everybody else aside with their crutches.

If that passage reflects back on "A Good Man Is Hard to Find," it also looks forward to "The Lame Shall Enter First," in which the lame character is a devil of cruelty and resentment, and the one who offers sympathy a fool. At the close of "A Good Man," the Misfit remarks of the murdered grandmother that "she would of been a good woman if it had been somebody there to shoot her every minute of her life." The Misfit took on the job for the grandmother, but it is the author who takes care of the reader. Anytime we begin to feel sympathy, she shoots us.

Only to the two correspondents to whom she was closest, Maryat Lee and the anonymous "A.," both fellow southerners, both working at writing, did she, at rare intervals, risk speaking of what illness and exile meant to her, and then only after she had managed to wring out the necessary acceptance. To A.:

> I have never been anywhere but sick. In a sense sickness is a place, more instructive than a long trip to Europe, and it's always a place where there's no company, where nobody can follow. Sickness before death is a very appropriate thing and I think those who don't have it miss one of God's mercies.
>
> Needing people badly and not getting them may turn you in a creative direction. [My father] wanted them and got them. I wanted them and didn't. We are all rather blessed in our deprivations if we let ourselves be, I suppose.

To Maryat Lee, who was considering leaving New York:

> So it may be the South. You get no condolences from me. This is a Return I have faced and when I faced it I was roped and tied and resigned the way it is necessary to be resigned to death, and largely because I thought it would be the end of any creation, any writing, any work from me. And as I told you by the fence, it was only the beginning.

Roped and tied and resigned as to death, no condolences asked or given. "In my own stories I have found that violence is strangely capable of returning my characters to reality and preparing them to accept their moment of grace. Their heads are so hard that almost nothing else will do the work." Dear old Malcolm was not without perspicacity when he asked if she had a wooden leg. To her, too, violence had been done.

To profit fully from the immense body of writing that Flannery O'Connor produced in her years in the country of the sick we must put the letters first. I do not mean merely to read them first, although there is every reason not to postpone the pleasure, but to *put* them first. To understand the whole that is more than the sum of its parts, let us take the letters as primary and the fiction as a gloss upon them, the black repository of all that the letters do not say, of the rebellion and disappointment and anger which the letters show so thoroughly surmounted that we might almost believe they were never felt.

Such a reading will show why O'Connor could give pity no place even in a Christian fiction, why she jeered even at compassion, its more expansive synonym. "It's considered an absolute necessity these days for writers to have compassion. Compassion is a word that sounds good in anybody's mouth and which no book jacket can do without." Within pity lay self-pity, everywhere in ambush.

Her gift, she was sure, was for the grotesque, for freakish characters maimed in body and soul, though "not . . . any more freakish than ordinary fallen man is." Sternly she told her audiences how to read: "When the grotesque is used in a legitimate way, the intellectual and moral judgments implicit in it will have the ascendancy over feeling." She embraced her limitations with excruciating self-knowledge: "The writer cannot choose what he is able to make live, and as far as he is concerned, a living deformed character is acceptable and a dead one is not." She could tell A. what was none of Malcolm Cowley's business: "My disposition is a combination of Nelson's [in "The Artificial Nigger"] and Hulga's." Presented with the emotional detachment that for her was "legitimate," her grotesques require from the readers an answering detachment—not compassion, but acquiescence in her own authorial judgment, even if it calls upon us to join in the immemorial laughter elicited by kicking a cripple. Though our bemused emotions may refuse to respond to her comic exigencies, we realize that the author has a right to laugh; Jews laugh at Jewish jokes and even originate them. "His prophet-freak is an image of himself."

Of us too, perhaps. We are all freaks, we say easily, and (as she wrote in another letter) we are all the poor. But it is an elevated perspective indeed from which some are not poorer than ourselves, and entitled to our compassion; few of us have earned it, and secular liberals need not apologize for their halting practice of what is, after all, a Christian virtue. In any case, as we read the letters and stories together—what she typed out in ease and intimacy and what she crafted with cunning—we open ourselves to something tougher and more challenging than that "hazy compassion" she contemptuously dismissed as a threat to judgment, to understanding and admiration of a choice that, while it fatally weakened the art she pursued in the only pride she allowed herself, exalted the meaning of that for which she took no credit, the life she lived. If we are to understand what she meant by grace, we need both stories and letters, both tale and teller, for it is in the letters, not the fiction, that grace is enacted.

Such a deliberate confusing of life and work, certainly, makes the experience of fiction—the most impure of the arts, O'Connor called it, and the most human—more impure and more human still. Characteristically, she tried to fend off such a reading, writing A. that "of course I have thrown you off . . . by informing you that Hulga is like me. . . . You cannot read a story from what you get out of a letter. Nor, I repeat, can you . . . read the author by the story. You may but you shouldn't—read T. S. Eliot." By her harsh standards she was right. For if we read like this, intellectual and moral judgments lose their ascendance, elbowed out of the way by feeling, and we find ourselves gripped by emotions not often elicited by the printed text, by love for its author, and gratitude not for what she created but for what she was. In a final paradox, it may be just such sloppy, intrusive emotions that transport us back to the cool realms of criticism and allow us to grope our way further into the literary puzzle we began with: how so accomplished an artist consistently failed to convey to her fallen readers the meanings she intended.

The reader who makes his way beyond horror and blind pity is most likely to perceive the pervasive theme of O'Connor's fiction not as the operation of grace but as the humiliation of the proud. The old man of "The Artificial Nigger" sets out to teach his cocky grandson a lesson; he gets a devastating comeuppance. More commonly the pattern of pride is a middle-aged woman; usually she runs a dairy farm like the woman Flannery O'Connor knew best. Strong and narrow, widowed or dominating a weak husband, Mrs. McIntyre of "The Displaced Person," Mrs. May of "Greenleaf," and Ruby Turpin of "Revelation" are complacently sure of their superiority and competence. Violently these are wrenched from them, by death or the next thing to it. It is a revealing pattern, the more so as we read the letters and see how the stories have darkened foibles treated in the letters as materials for comedy and not for horror.

But still more revealing is the complementary pattern of pride that occurs first alongside the other, then gradually takes over, the festering pride of that train of grown-up children living in sullen dependence on mothers now seen through their conventionality as hardworking and loyal patterns of unthanked love. The children are called girls and boys even into their thirties, not merely by their mothers, but by that omniscient narrator; even, in her letters and lectures, by O'Connor herself. The theme becomes obsessive; Joy-Hulga is joined in the second collection not only by Asbury but by Tom in "The Comforts of Home," Mary Grace in "Revelation," Julian in the title story, "Everything That Rises Must Converge." In "The Partridge Festival" there are two of them. Sore, hostile, and condescending, they are literally and figuratively ugly, ugly in the particular sense that every Southern child learns as soon as it can speak. "How come you be so ugly sometimes?" asks the cook in one of the few stories where the child actually is a child, "A Temple of the Holy Ghost." "God could strike you deaf dumb and blind . . . and then you wouldn't be as smart as you is." The child replies, "I would still be smarter than some." The black hired hands ask the same question about Asbury: "How come he talks so ugly about his ma?" Hulga has embraced ugliness as Asbury embraces illness, compounding pride and despair, deadliest sins of all, as she stumps around in a grotesque sweatshirt and insists that her mother must take her "LIKE I AM." The letters here tell us more than we have any business knowing; it is with a sense of unpardonable eavesdropping that we read Flannery's account to A. of her own shirt, embossed with a bulldog "with the word GEORGIA over him," which she wore "all the time, it being my policy in life at that time to create an unfavorable impression." We learn from Robert Giroux that she chose to paint her self-portrait at her ugliest, face swollen from cortisone and hair fallen out from fever. The pain we feel as we look at the jacket photo for *The Habit of Being* is less for a young woman's crutches and disfigured face than for the gallant self-discipline behind the prim smile, the neat dark dress, the pearls, the pumps she had learned to wear to please her mother. "A Temple of the Holy Ghost" is a story more positive than most; in it the child, listening to the "Tantum ergo" in the school chapel, is freed for a time from her "ugly thoughts," and prays "Hep me not to be so mean," "Hep me not to talk like I do." That prayer, too, is not easy to overhear. It is the prayer of a fiction that asserts grace but enacts pride, ugliness, and rebellion in order to castigate them—a penitential fiction. The prophet of *Wise Blood* bound his body with barbed wire and blinded himself with lye.

Is this, as Josephine Hendin claims, "an art as emotionally flat as Robbe-Grillet"? As we have seen, O'Connor asks us not to sympathize but to judge. So sparely conceived a fiction might indeed seem preventive of the sentimentality she found so inimical personally and artistically. But although the buttoned-down techniques of the Joycean short story may enforce more objectivity than we wish to feel, the problem lies beyond technique, in a definition of sentimentality that seems to widen to include feeling itself. "I come from a family," she wrote to A., "where the only emotion respectable to show is irritation. In some this tendency produces hives, in others literature, in me both." Feeling was suspect in religion, too. When a friend who accompanied her to mass said afterward that "he hadn't felt any warmth in it," she wrote her longtime correspondent, Father McCown, "They look for that and we never think about it." When A. left the church, it only confirmed O'Connor's sense of the fragility of a faith which "must always be emotionally involved." Faith, she wrote to another friend, is not "a big electric blanket." But the readers and reviewers who wanted something "more affirmative" were not necessarily looking for an emotional bath in "pious pap," "that large body of pious trash for which we [Catholics] have long been famous." What is in question is not the right she defended to

A., the artist's right "to select a negative aspect of the world to portray." She was not a Céline or a Genet; her subject matter was not theirs. When what is to be communicated is a vision of grace, a little affirmation may be in order. That suffering can hammer understanding into hard heads is not a controversial discovery but a common experience, and one not limited to Christians. But grace is not only violent; even in the Christian exemplar the violence of crucifixion is preceded, as it is followed, by demonstrations of love.

"You can safely ignore the reader's taste, but you can't ignore his nature. . . . Your problem is going to be difficult in direct proportion as your beliefs depart from his." Indeed. She persuaded herself that she wrote violently because "violent literary means" were needed to communicate her vision to a "hostile audience" that "does not believe in evil": the discordancies and distortions of the grotesque, she claimed, were what would make people see. "When you can assume that your audience holds the same beliefs you do, . . . you can use normal means of talking to it; when you have to assume it does not, then you have to make your vision apparent by shock—to the hard of hearing you shout, and for the almost blind you draw large and startling figures."

But the means she chose to bridge the gap between her readers and herself only made it wider. It was to A. that she identified the real question: "not is this negative or positive, but is it believable." The repetitive mayhem of her fiction does not invite belief but parody.

O'Connor was on stronger ground when she argued, not from her readers' limitations, but from her own. The negative she knew she could make live: "Anybody who has survived his childhood has enough information about life to last him the rest of his days." She doubted her capacity to vivify the positive; she was only beginning to try. "The meaning of a story has to be embodied in it." When a writer is, as she said, "only really interested in a fiction of miracles," the miracles must be credible; they must be enacted within the fiction. The reader needs more than a water stain in the shape of the Holy Ghost to make us believe in sullen Asbury's redemption. We may, conceivably, be saved through sacraments, but not through literary symbols.

II

> Asbury's train stopped so that he would get off exactly where
> his mother was standing. . . . Her thin spectacled face below
> him was bright with a wide smile that disappeared as she
> caught sight of him bracing himself behind the conductor. The
> smile vanished so suddenly, the shocked look that replaced it
> was so complete, that he realized for the first time that he must
> look as ill as he was.

"The meaning of a story is not abstract meaning but experienced meaning." It was hard experience that had taught O'Connor that violence can "return . . . characters to reality and prepare them to accept their moment of grace," that it can prepare them to forgive the ugliness of others and combat their own. Such experience was hinted to a few but confided to none; it existed in a privacy as complete as that in which poor Hulga cherished the stump of the leg she had seen blown off at ten years old. Roped and tied and resigned in the way it is necessary to be resigned to death, Flannery O'Connor had experienced the change that comes to Asbury, that is in preparation for Hulga—accepted and enacted the inner turning that is the root meaning of the word *conversion*. She could put it into symbols, but as yet she could not acknowledge the pain and loss and open it to compassion; even in her fiction she was not ready to share it. She would take her ugly characters up to the moment of grace— even, on occasion, allow them a vision. But she herself had gone beyond symbols into a world of believable, daily action. The stories never carry us there.

So little love shows in them that it is easy to conclude that she does not care about her characters. Those who knew her knew better. She loved her grotesques, though she refused them her pity; perhaps she refused it because she loved them. "Maryat's niece asked her why I had made Mary Grace so ugly. 'Because Flannery loves her,' said Maryat. Very perceptive girl." The letters show her thinking about her characters long after they had reached what is for most authors the remoteness of print, inventing new adventures for Enoch of *Wise Blood*, weighing the possibilities of salvation for the Misfit, sketching a Christian future for Asbury or the young prophet of *The Violent Bear It Away*. We learn to know them better there than in the stories themselves, where we never enter their minds in full sympathy, and at crucial points do not enter them at all. "Who do you think you understand?" she challenged A. "If anybody, you delude yourself. I love many people, understand none of them." We may take this as a statement of humility—or, like her other procla-mations of limitation, of pride. "LIKE I AM." Whichever it is, it is a dangerous claim for a novelist. If grace operates at all, it operates inwardly. To make her chosen subject believable, she would have had to dare her way into more understanding than she was yet ready to admit, and find the artistic means to carry her readers with her. Without it, it is the violence she made live, and not the kingdom of heaven she believed it could bear away.

"I know nothing harder than making good people believable," she wrote to her editor, Denver Lindley. And a year before her death she wrote to a friend she never met: "I know what you mean by light. There are a few people I can identify it in but I can never describe it." Acquiescing in the talent for the grotesque that she saw as both a limitation and a strength, she did not often try. Yet we may wonder if her limitation was as absolute as she maintained. The old priest in "The Displaced Person" is a convincing embodiment not only of charity but of another disposition she rarely portrayed, re-sponsiveness to beauty. We all know O'Connor raised peacocks, but from the many references in her letters, we could not guess that they were anything more to her than an occasion for laughter at the grotesque contrast between their plumage and their habits. Laugh-ter, we know by now, was one of her chief ways of cherishing the world. But there were others:

> The cock stopped suddenly and curving his neck backwards, he raised his tail and spread it with a shimmering timbrous noise. Tiers of small pregnant suns floated in a green-gold haze over his head. The priest stood transfixed, his jaw slack. . . . Christ will come like that, he said in a loud gay voice.

"If I set myself to write about the essence of Christianity, I would have to quit writing fiction or become another person." Per-haps she was right; she understood herself well. But she was moving forward. "I appreciate your prayers. I've been writing 18 years and I've reached the point where I can't do again what I know I can do well, and the larger things I need to do now, I doubt my capacity for doing." Already, four years before her death she had written to Andrew Lytle:

> I have got to the point now where I keep thinking more and more about the presentation of love and charity, or better call it grace, as love suggests tenderness, whereas grace can be violent or would have to be to compete with the kind of evil I can make concrete. At the same time, I keep seeing Elias in the cave, waiting to hear the voice of the Lord in the thunder and lightning and wind, and only hearing it finally in the gentle breeze, and I feel I'll have to be able to do that sooner or later, or anyway keep trying.

She was not given enough time.

From *The American Scholar*, Spring 1982.

Merrill's *Divine Comedies*

My office mate, fresh from the university; his developing dissertation, which has to do with Pound; the things he says, which I don't understand. Semiotics? Phenomenology? Husserl? To ferry us to shallower waters I pose as idle a question as comes to mind. Do people read Pound for pleasure these days? I expect one of two answers: He'll say they certainly do, and his enthusiasm will strengthen me for one more try. Or he'll say they don't. But he says neither. Instead: "That," reflectively, "is a very interesting question."

I can find no reply. *Interesting?* In a first-class Ph.D. program, with a first-class fellowship and a first-class mind, he has spent two years of life on Pound. He'll spend another before he's done. Surely he cannot find the question of whether people get pleasure from reading the poems he thinks worth writing about unfamiliar enough to be interesting?

> Fed
>
> Up so long and variously by
> Our age's fancy narrative concoctions,

> I yearned for the kind of unseasoned telling found
> In legends, fairy tales, a tone licked clean
> Over the centuries by mild old tongues,
> Grandam to cub, serene, anonymous.
> Lacking that voice, the in its fashion brilliant
> Nouveau roman (even the one I wrote)
> Struck me as an orphaned form, whose followers
> Suckled by Woolf not Mann, had stories told them
> In childhood, if at all, by adults whom
> They could not love or honor.

So James Merrill, trying out the voices for the tale he had to tell in *The Book of Ephraim*, the pièce de résistance of his seventh book of poems, *Divine Comedies*. He abandoned his original idea of a novel and settled on a telling not in prose but in verse. It is a verse not orphaned but fully parented in the flesh and the spirit, suckled, if not by Woolf, by a crowd of others. Yeats and Stevens, Kafka, Proust, Auden, Dinesen, Brünhilde, Tadzio, Miss Malin Natog-Dag—past presences, real and fictional, pervade his poetry. Highly seasoned and anything but anonymous, it is in some important sense serene, with the serenity of those who can still experience history, personal and public, as properly occasioning love and honor.

We may wonder how Merrill's rainbow narrative of the holiness of the heart's affections amid passing time will fare among a generation most of whom have had poems read them in childhood not at all. The reviews give hope the pleasure principle's not yet dead. For their keynote is enjoyment. Helen Vendler hopes the story's not yet finished. Harold Bloom says he's read "The Book of Ephraim" a dozen times. A *dozen?* I believe him; I'm catching up. It's a heady feeling after all these years, a kind of incredulous satisfaction. One hundred and thirty-six pages of poetry, eighty-nine of them in *Ephraim* alone, not latter-day pages compounded of white space and print in a ratio of twenty to one, but most-for-your-money pages solid with iambic pentameter, and I'm reading them *fast* because I want to see what comes next, and then again slow because I want to figure out how it fits in. I'm reading them for fun, and then poring over them for profit and delight.

Fun, of course, is to be expected from comedies, but who today expects to realize expectations? Dante (the celestial mechanics of whose tour of the spheres Merrill will casually explain) certainly did not promise fun. Nevertheless, the parallel Merrill's title asserts has more than the customary ironic validity. Dante is the most personal of poets, relying on those he had loved and honored to guide him through the universe, memorializing in rich human particularity the history, poetry, philosophy, the politics, the geography of his public and private world. Merrill's *Comedies* are similarly rooted. Like Dante, like Yeats too, Merrill makes his poetry out of events and people whose primary significance is that they have happened to him or that he has cared about them. It is a significance which, if the poet is good enough, is sufficient for us all. The furnace that broke down in Athens in the cold rain of winter 1964, the one that broke down in Stonington ten years later at the year's end, the irresistible meal consumed at a Venetian *trattoria* ("melon with ham, risotto with shellfish, / Cervello fritto spitting fire at us, / Black cherries' pit-deep sweetness . . . Strega and espresso,")—food, music, pictures, plants, animals, lovers, family, friends, the rooms and landscapes they inhabit, are named and suffused with meaning. Taking place over nearly twenty years (1955–74, Eisenhower to Watergate), the poem compasses the poet's own maturing and binds the generations. The huge cast of characters includes babies and adolescents as well as the youngish, the aging, the old, the dying, and the dead. Like Dante, Merrill secures his events in time. Dates are placed where we can find them, for it's by the calendar that we grasp time's passage. For reasons we'll discover, each of the twenty-six sections of the "Book of Ephraim" begins with a letter of the alphabet; D, Dramatis Personae, provides essential orientation, dates of birth and (particularly) of death. For Dante and Yeats personal experience leads beyond itself to—literally—another world, and Merrill's testimony, like theirs, is that that world is inherently personal. And for Merrill too the praise and interest of the other world is tempered by his unregenerate attachment to the things of this one.

What kinds of pleasure did people use to get from poetry, in the olden days when poets could make a living by writing it? We've forgotten. Even in school we don't read Scott or Browning any more. Our adolescents do their own traveling, or get their exotic backgrounds from film and the *National Geographic*. Merrill offers "Market, mackerel, minaret, / Simmering mulligatawny of the real"—persons and places and events perceived through the affections and rendered in orders and textures of language that affirm their value for the poet, and so for us. In this, as in other ways, Merrill has chosen to honor tradition. Until literature's yesterday, poets mostly told stories. The memory of that has been dimmed for us. Just as well. The combination of "our age's fancy narrative concoctions" with the unabashed privatism of this tone-deaf century's lyric voice would be enough to break the patience even of the docile readers it has trained and fed. Fed, as Merrill says, Up.

The reader's attention to verse narrative required faith—faith that prolonged attention would pay off, that a tale would emerge which was intelligible, exciting, and significant. Dante, like all the great narrative poets, lets us know clearly where he starts from, whom he proceeds with, what goes on—basic clarities that sustain us to attempt the incidental riddles and enjoy them. Merrill, though he's no more than Dante an easy poet, gives us all the clues we need to follow him through a poem of many riddles and many settings. Dante named every river in Italy. Merrill gives us Kandy, Kyoto, Kew, Geneva, Santa Fe, Venice, the papyrus swamps of the Nile, the South African veldt and, as exotic as any, Purgatory, Oklahoma, where young Temerlin's educated chimp-child, Miranda, makes Merrill the sign for "happy" and charms him with a great open-jawed kiss. "Who can doubt / She's one of us? . . . / Weren't we still groping, like Miranda, toward / Some higher level?" Merrill, like Yeats and unlike Dante, has had to make his own myth. No wonder his narrative holds the attention; it's about reincarnation and communion with the cherished dead.

Merrill is on his last life; a dear friend gone before has intervened for him (as Plato did for Wallace Stevens). His companion David Jackson will have two, at most three, more. Can this be *serious?* The humor is disarming enough. Merrill's father dies and gets through to his son, plainly undimmed:

> Are we in India? Some goddam fool
> Hindoo is sending him to Sunday School
> He loved his wives, his other children, me,

> Looks forward to his next life. Would not be
> Weeping in my shoes. An offhand salute and gone!

Born again, we learn, to a greengrocer in Kew. Some are reborn, some, like Auden, BYRON PAVLOVA BILLY SUNDAY JOB OTTO & GENGHIZ KHAN MME CURIE, are moving upward and need not return. "Wallace Stevens . . . / Reads us jottings from his slate of cloud." Mozart, however, preferring live music to the humdrum spheres, is now a black rock star. Like Yeats and Dante, Merrill tells us what we most long to hear, and from someone so much smarter and more sophisticated we might just manage the required suspension of disbelief—to hope that personality survives death.

So JM and DJ and assorted friends, assembled in the flame-red dining room at Stonington, submit to the guidance of—or do they guide?—a ten-cent-store teacup among the letters and numerals, simple materials of

> The Book of a Thousand and One Evenings Spent
> With David Jackson at the Ouija Board
> In Touch with Ephraim Our Familiar Spirit.

Ephraim? Greek Jew, A.D. 8–36, a favorite of TIBERIUS and a lover of CALIGULA—the caps of the ouija messages. Ephraim is gay in every sense, not least in Yeats's dead serious one, of gaiety transfiguring dread. Continuously witty, he fills them in on Heaven and the NINE STAGES of an afterlife that allows for growth but not punishment. Dante, Merrill tells us, had to invent his Hell and Purgatory to fit the prevailing dogma, working "from footage / Too dim and private to expose";

> His Heaven, though as one cannot but sense,
> Tercet by tercet, is pure Show and Tell.

Ephraim is at STAGE 6 (with GBS):

> Here on Earth—huge tracts of information
> Have gone into these capsules flavorless
> And rhymed for easy swallowing—on Earth

> We're each the REPRESENTATIVE of a PATRON. . . .
> These secular guardian angels fume and fuss
> For what must seem eternity over us.
> It is forbidden them to INTERVENE
> Save, as it were, in the entr'acte between
> One incarnation and another.

DJ's and JM's patrons (JM's an editor of Pope, whence all these couplets) are fusty souls who disapprove of their representatives' life-style; we hear much more about E and his cherished representative, who, thanks to the poet's unauthorized intervention, comes to life behind the silk bangs and serene blue eyes of Wendell Pincus, born to JM's niece Betsy. Uncle James will meet him in Venice in a Dantean encounter eighteen years later. JM and DJ think an unexpected lot about babies: JM's ex-shrink, consulted in panic after their meddling brings transcendental sanctions and (temporary) silence, is ready with the twentieth-century explanation: "what you and David do / We call folie à deux." JM gets the picture:

> Somewhere a Father-Figure shakes his rod
> At sons who have not sired a child?
> Through our own spirit we can both proclaim
> And shuffle off the blame
> For how we live. . . .

Plausible. Yet "FREUD / We learned that evening DESPAIRS / OF HIS DISCIPLES," and "the question / Of who or what we took Ephraim to be / and of what truths (if any) we considered / Him spokesman" is explicitly begged. Too clever not to hedge this bet, Merrill concedes he may be "a projection / Of what already burned, at some obscure / Level or other, in our skulls." Yet experience is stranger than fiction; the experience of Ephraim is "a strangeness that was us," but also "was not." The point's not to check out his stories (which they conspicuously do not do) but

> Never to forego, in favor of
> Plain dull proof, the marvelous nightly pudding.

Frivolous? Ephraim reports Pope loves the poem, but JM fears

Stevens will think it "mere bric-a-brac," as Auden, who read parts while still alive, thought it "folderol," secure in "*his* dogma, rooted like a social tooth." When Ephraim in the face of one death emits a truly ghastly pun, he shocks even his interlocutors into asking, "Must everything be witty?" His answer, in a weighted Alexandrine, ends a section:

> AH MY DEARS
> I AM NOT LAUGHING   I WILL SIMPLY NOT SHED TEARS

There is much more than puns and games in this poem about "the test of time that all things pass." Crippled and blinded by stroke, Maya, patroness of their love and the most vividly established personage in the poem, dies as they watch.

> The blind, sunset-invaded
> Eyeball. Lucent spittle overbrimming
> Lips wiped of all pretense. And in the ward's
> Gloom the gleam of tongs, clean stench of gauzes.
> What light there was fell sideways from a mind
> Half dark. We stood and tried to bear
> The stroke for Maya. . . .

They couldn't. Destroyed and gone, like so many other friends "never held in high enough esteem." How sorely welcome, then, her message:

> DAVID   JIMMY   I AM YOUNG AT LAST
> WHO ALL THESE YEARS TRIED TO APPEAR SO
> MY HAIR IS TRULY RED

Wholly enwebbed in their context, Merrill's lines frustrate quotation. We need all he has already told us about Maya to feel the joyous urgency of these trochees, the opening, of all things, of a sonnet, as we need the full section (it is R) to see that its sharp rhythms and strict, astringent assonances avert all threat of sentimentality.

Merrill's *Comedies* are well named. Where death is not accepted as final it is hard to sustain a sense of tragedy. But euphoria, too, passes. By the end of the poem Ephraim no longer comes, or the aging companions no longer summon him. *Tempora mutantur.* So do we. For all the frivolity, Merrill announced his theme at once in A: "the incarnation and withdrawal of a god."

> We've modulated. Keys ever remoter
> Lock our friend among the golden things that go
> Without saying, the loves no longer called up
> Or named.

Keys of music, keys that secure treasure—the play of language is for pleasure. But these persistent puns are more—they are the poet's testimony to an ancient faith, the faith in the profound significances handed us by the adventitious and the random. It is not merely incidental that Merrill reveals himself as a virtuoso of trope and form, blank verse his common speech, developing sonnets as casually as the rest of us stammer, sliding imperceptibly into couplets, "loose talk tightening into verse." He can toss off a whole narrative section in sonnets; he casts his meeting with WENDELL P in supple terza rima, even ending, as Dante ended his canticles, with the word "stars." "The twinklings of insight," Merrill tells us, require a "metrical lens" to focus them, and "kismet" is "veiled as a stern rhyme sound."

That the exigencies of rhyme and meter bestow insights that the wildest freedoms withhold is known to anyone who ever managed a double dactyl. But Merrill's faith is even more profoundly traditional: the faith that appearances and chance connections are upheld by correspondences no earthly poet has created. If our varied "languages"—his quotation marks—"bird-flight, / Hallucinogen, chorale, and horoscope" are all "facets of the universal gem," randomness is only apparent. Dante, whose terza rima mirrored the Trinity, would have found the idea wholly familiar; Renaissance cabalists would have seen nothing singular in making the letters of the alphabet an organizing principle. Merrill's virtuosity, while offering us all the traditional pleasures, remains a means, not an end. The end— even more profoundly traditional—is to mirror experienced truth.

But what is to be made of the experience now that Ephraim no longer comes, and the companions have "grown autumnal, mild"?

Always previously invoked among the heavens, Ephraim at last sinks "back underground," one more god whose grave guarantees returning spring. Yet over Strega and espresso Uncle James can still speak of the self's "great, great glory" to counter young Wendell's rejection of "doomed, sick, selfish, dumb mankind," and "DJ's old-fashioned / Trust in nature, human and divine" is underwritten no less in the end than in the beginning. In the cold house in Stonington at the story's end (yet "Has it ended?" Merrill asks) JM and DJ, still together, consider burning the carton of dusty messages. But they don't do it. "Too much / Already, here below, has met its match." Ambiguous enough. But the only kind of hero the poet can be is a hero of our time. Merrill presents his affirmations in the acceptable modern mode, through a shimmer of qualifications and concessions, shadowed forth in other voices, other tongues. But the poem's epigraph, from the *Paradiso,* is *Tu credi 'l vero*—You believe truly.

In Q, a prose section of personally significant Quotations, Merrill for once transmits Ephraim's message raw and unversified: & NOW ABOUT DEVOTION   IT IS I AM FORCED TO BELIEVE THE MAIN IMPETUS. Indeed; as Dante learned, it moves the sun and the other stars. Or, in Merrill's own exquisite image, what ties us to the dust is "the tough tendril / Of unquestioning love alone." We owe him our gratitude for risking his credentials as a modernist to show us that poetry still offers its old-fashioned pleasures. These poems, in language we can remember and possess, are testimony to an achieved web of values both transcendent and human.

II

First, in 1976, came *Divine Comedies,* containing "The Book of Ephraim." In strong pentameter, James Merrill at once made clear what it was: not at all the usual thing in form or content, but the "Book of a Thousand and One Evenings Spent / With David Jackson at the Ouija Board / In Touch with Ephraim Our Familiar Spirit." The poem's material would be the carton of messages spelled out over twenty years to Merrill and his friend at their house in Stonington, Connecticut, by the dime-store cup that pointed to the board's twenty-six letters. Spelled out to them or by them? Do they follow the cup or guide it? Questions of which Merrill is never unaware, and to which he himself can give no final answer. Imperceptibly, however, they recede in importance as the poetry takes over; by the end of "Ephraim" disbelief has long been suspended.

"Ephraim" was followed two years later by *Mirabell: Books of Number.* JM and DJ (as the board's capitals identify them) were still at it. The letters now spelled out, rather than messages from departed friends and the gay revelations of Ephraim, giddy Greek, more difficult lessons, imparted by a crew of red-eyed, red-hot bats who identified themselves by number. They "describe themselves now as fallen angels, now as volatile subatomic particles; the scale, accordingly, wobbles throughout, from vast to microscopic." (The authoritative explanatory prose quoted is Merrill's own, not part of the poem, but prefaced to an excerpt published in the *Kenyon Review* of Summer 1979). The new familiar is 741; JM and DJ become as fond of him as they did of Ephraim, so that everyone is delighted when he metamorphoses into a peacock and changes his numerical designation for the name they give him, Mirabell—M's having, for Merrill, multiple mana. Mirabell's realm is the complex of mathematical formulas that frame? support? explain? express? the macro- and microcosm of physical and human nature. He speaks often of GOD B—Biology.

Mirabell's "main fields," writes Merrill, "are History and Science, often much mythologized."

> Thus we are told of an Arcadian Atlantis whose immortal denizens resembled centaurs and themselves created the bat-angels to serve them. It didn't work. Two rival worlds—one electrically, one atomically powered—ended in mutual destruction. It would be for Man to reconcile those opposites. . . . [Mirabell's] visits prepare us for a seminar with the Angels—whose 25 lessons are in fact the marrow of the third volume.

Merrill lets the ouija board itself set the poems' structure. *Ephraim*'s reveals itself gradually: twenty-six sections, beginning with successive letters of the alphabet. *Mirabell*'s is immediately apparent, as befits what the bat-angels asked Merrill to provide, POEMS

OF SCIENCE: ten parts, each subdivided in ten, and numbered from 0 to 9.9. After letters and numbers, there remained on the board YES, NO and the ampersand—the manifest of the reconciliation of opposites assigned to Man.

Man, God and the cosmos. High talk. How softly and seductively *Ephraim* began, then, we only now realize. That was the kindergarten, Merrill tells us, for the school of *Mirabell*, and for the Angels' seminar of these final *Scripts for the Pageant*. YES & NO. White and Black, Matter and Antimatter, Life and Death, two scripts for a future performance. Between them we, as readers and as human beings, are left to choose. JM wants that perfectly clear; he asks, and is answered in capitals. "We do the judging? Everyone? INDEED."

Tentative in title, cannily ambiguous in structure and content, these *Scripts* are no more ambiguous in spirit, no less committedly affirmative, than the *Paradiso* to which they are already being compared. And as the reviews appear, the comparisons accumulate: *Ulysses*, *The Waste Land*, Proust. Sober critics, some themselves poets, reach for the sky: Blake's Prophetic Books, *Paradise Lost* and *Regained*, the *Comedy* itself. Recalling these in scope, however, the trilogy is like none of them in manner. And the manner is the matter, Merrill being a supreme mannerist.

Yet the matter is no less substantial for that. To have the poem now completed* is like the reception of an immense, unhoped-for present: the long poem that it's been proved a hundred times over we can't expect in this age of anxiety, privatism, fragmentation, and the loss of the confidence and will to speak any public language. In "Ephraim" Merrill had already brought off something miraculous enough—eighty-nine pages of solid poetry. So we thought, not yet able to glimpse the grand design (though it was there). *Mirabell*, transitional, was longer still (182 pages); the bard suspended our hopes but did not disappoint them. Now *Scripts* is nearly half as long again. At its completion Merrill, like Prospero, breaks the mirror

---

*It wasn't, quite. When the trilogy's three parts were finally printed together as *The Changing Light at Sandover* (Atheneum, 1982), Merrill added a Coda, "The Higher Keys."

that has been since "Ephraim" the symbol of his poetic field, as well as what it was in actuality, the central focus of the room where his spirits gathered. He does not drown his book, however, but leaves it for us to read and live with.

"James Merrill has created a poem as central to our generation as *The Waste Land* was to the one before us"—so writes Phoebe Pettingell in *The New Leader*. If so, our generation is in luck. Might Eliot's long legacy at last be spent? The trilogy is sufficiently unlike the literature of the last sixty years, the best and the worst, that we need have no trouble recognizing its differences. In the midst of fragmentation, it unifies—science and poetry, past and present, public and private, cosmic and domestic, the dead and the living—as epic used to, as no short poem can. In the midst of literature (and lives) made out of heartsick discontinuities, it is continuous, with the continuity not only of reason—purposeful narrative, tightly connected event—but of the heart—loyalty, friendship, of love that so yearns for continuity that it seeks it beyond even that black discontinuity that JM and DJ refuse to take as final. In the midst of personal and linguistic privatism, it manifests for the reader an affectionate concern that we'd forgotten could exist in serious literature, and a shining faith in the power of language to render shareable our grandest imaginings and our most personal experience, to make the private public.

Public, not popular. These Divine Comedies will not be that. But they will reach that same enduring public that learned its way to sharing Dante's experience—not the credulous, the Castaneda-freaks and horoscope-watchers to whom its apparatus initially might seem to appeal, but all those who care enough about the pleasures and responsibilities of life and language to do the work (and play) of reading a poem extraordinary enough that its author well might think—as Dante and Milton thought—that in some decisive way it came from Somewhere Else. And if it didn't, Merrill's flipped coin still comes up heads. What a piece of work is a man, out of whose hot and busy brain heaven, purgatory, and paradise can spin themselves?

YES & NO. This is the final message. *Scripts* is both the gayest and the darkest of the three volumes. SUDDEN FIREWORKS OF PLEA-

SURE, spells one of the calm Angels, thinking about man's life and not quite understanding it. He might have been talking about the experience of reading these poems. Certainly the language here dazzles against the dark. It also, as appropriate, glitters, glistens, glimmers, glints, or glows, as well as bringing off a great many other special effects I lack alliterative verbs for. The lines are crammed with jokes and puns, Olympian *jeux d'artifice* in several foreign tongues plus dialects of English. Examples? Hopeless to quote; it is in context that the words light up. Perhaps these lines (from *Mirabell*, 9.9) on Hell? Hell is

> (a syllable identified
> In childhood as the German word for *bright*
> —so that my father's cheerful "Go to Hell,"
> Long unheard, and Vaughan's unbeatable
> "They are all gone into a world of light"
> Come, even now at times, to the same thing).

Certainly the gleam is gone. Yet this casual parenthesis, thrown into the midst of a sentence on its way to somewhere else, which I picked out merely because it was self-contained and illustrated a pun, demonstrates how inseparable Merrill's wordplay is from his highest seriousness; only as I write do I perceive that it manages to embody what the whole poem is about: brightness and death, the loved human being and the flashing revelations of language.

And the verse! "Make it new!" Merrill can do anything with these old forms we've been told so often are outworn. This poem should reinstate the study of prosody in the English curriculum. Sonnets crystallize so effortlessly out of his narrative pentameter that we often don't realize we're reading them. Like "Ephraim" and *Mirabell*, *Scripts* has its terza rima canto ending, for a flourish, with Dante's key word, "stars." Each order of creature speaks in its appropriate meter. Throughout *Mirabell*, the bat-angels manifest their numerical nature in the tuneless syllabic fourteeners they speak in. But when Mirabell himself sweeps into the splendid farewell fete of *Scripts* in full peacock fig, transfigured into "blue, green, gold, a comet-streak," his fourteen syllables have been transfigured too; now divided into eight and six, his lines are rhyming tetrameter and trimeter. Mortals, dead and living, speak in pentameter. The Angels' verse is free and ample. The unicorn from Atlantis, four-footed, speaks in the four-beat alliterative line of *Beowulf,* as befits an early creature, but rhymed and speeded up to match his light canter.

Like the peacock, the unicorn is enchanting—one of the many delights and surprises of this last book. But the magician, the poet-Prospero, controls all meanings; the flying bats, the pterodactyls of the early world, it turns out, are a metaphor for THE BLACK VOLATILE HALF of the atom, followed, MINUTES ONLY AFTER THE BIG BANG by THE FIRST NUCLEI OF HELIUM, which are stable, DEPENDABLE, . . . FOURFOOTED—like the unicorn creature of Atlantis. The enchanting creatures have been transformed—into the irrefutability of metaphor.

And yet, JM asks,

> if it's all a fable,
> Involving, oh, the stable and unstable
> Particles, mustn't we at last wipe clean
> The blackboard of these creatures and their talk,
> To render in a hieroglyph of chalk
> The formulas they stood for?

The answer comes from W. H. Auden in the spirit world. He speaks for all poets:

> WHY MAKE A JOYLESS THING
> OF IT THROUGH SUCH REDUCTIVE REASONING?

Merrill has not done so. The celestial elevator swoops up and down through all the levels of meaning. But Merrill knows the trick—or truth—of Dante's allegory: that all the levels must be founded on the literal, in which we live. The poem's ultimate gaiety is the most serious of all—the daily life and affection of DJ and JM over twenty-five years, celebrated in this volume with a silver anniversary party, and of their families and friends, beloved beyond death.

YES & NO. The text of YES is naturally affirmative, propounded by God's favorite, Michael, Angel of Light and the Air which makes light visible: THE MOST INNOCENT OF IDEAS IS THE IDEA THAT

INNOCENCE IS DESTROYED BY IDEAS. Paradise is gained, not lost, by the work of intelligence. Yet in the last of these ten lessons of light a new, strange voice is heard. God's voice is lost in darkness. The mirror-field is "bitter-black and vast." The god who set life's cosmic enterprise going is signaling to unknown brother gods in the galactic emptiness a song even the angels cannot hear. But humans can; its lonely, persistent permutations are the song of life.

> I AND MINE HOLD IT BACK BROTHERS I AND
> MINE SURVIVE BROTHERS HEAR ME SIGNAL ME . . .
> ALONE IN MY NIGHT BROTHERS I AND MINE
> SURVIVE BROTHERS DO YOU WELL I ALONE
> IN MY NIGHT I HOLD IT BACK I AND MINE
> SURVIVE BROTHERS SIGNAL ME IN MY NIGHT
> I AND MINE HOLD IT BACK AND WE SURVIVE

"Song of the blue whale," asks JM, "alone is space?" Or (in an exquisite lyric moment) God seen in all the vulnerability of the human. From *Tristan*, Act I,

> ONE SAILOR'S CLEAR
> YOUNG TENOR FILLS THE HOUSE, HOMESICK, HEARTSICK—

God himself in need of comfort.

After that, the five lessons of &, the central section, connect (of course) and relax. A dazzling sestina is at once a hymn to the four elements of the four Archangels—Earth, Air, Water, Fire—and the chronicle of DJ's and JM's perfectly real trip from Athens to Samos. It introduces the arrival in the beyond of dear friends whose death the poem has already prepared for. George Kotsiás, doctor and scientist, is a specialist in cell biology. Robert Morse is a gifted amateur from Stonington, from whose wrists (*Mirabell*, 8.8) "fugue by fugue Bach's honeycomb / Drips . . . then whoops! the Dolly Suite." Fire is GK's element; it is he who explains about helium and stable and unstable particles. Light-minded TINY BOB, his element Air, slips disconcertingly in and out of E. F. Benson baby-talk, but he is one of those whose joking, like JM's own, is a way to cope with

the dark without denying it. "Barbarity," JM will say later, "To serve
uncooked one's bloody tranche de vie." Grownups do not ask for
sympathy. Grace under pressure, if you like, though that's the phrase
of a shade Merrill does *not* call up. "Style" is Merrill's word for it,
which can turn, "in mid-sentence . . . iron to sunlight."

Now Merrill's four main human contacts with the universe are
in place, one for each element; RM and GK have joined Auden and
Maria Mitsotaki (Earth and Water), known already from "Ephraim"
and *Mirabell*. It is they who, with JM, junior poet, and DJ, the
faithful Hand on the cup, hear what's inaudible even to angels. And
WHA voices the message of these middle lessons: EQUIVOCAL
NEWS of mankind trembling ON A CRUST SO FRAGILE / IT NEEDS
GOD'S CONSTANT VIGIL TO KEEP US AFLOAT. It is a measure of the
power of Merrill's elegantly established light-mindedness that he
can make WHA ask the big, simple question straight out, rendered
no whit less serious by the poet's pun:

> THEREFORE I SAY OF THIS OUR FRAGILE EARTH:
> IS IT DOOMED? IF SO, WILL OUR LINEAGE, OUR LINES
> MEAN MUCH, LOST IN A POLLIWOG SEA OF ATOMS?

But as the lessons of YES contained NO, so NO makes room for
YES. The negative text to Michael's affirmative is proposed by
Gabriel, Angel of Death, his element Fire and the atom's own dark
power, if not black antimatter itself. This text, too, is equivocal: OF
ALL DESTRUCTIVE IDEAS THE MOST DESTRUCTIVE IS THE IDEA OF
DESTRUCTION. Do we ignore in death and destruction their con-
structive function? Ideas indeed destroyed the Garden, but were we
meant to stay there? Maria, plant-lover, water-nature, nurturant
Muse and Mother, pleads eloquently for Man: WE COME, WE MOR-
TALS, FROM AN AVID WEED / CALLED CURIOSITY. God and Nature in
all they do have shown that they WANT THESE SECRETS OUT, so that
WE, MANKIND, may DO IMMORTAL WORK, to save the future and
perfect it. And if EARTH BECOMES PARADISE, greedy mankind, OUR
RACE OF THIEVES, will be justified, like Prometheus, who stole
heaven's fire for man's good.

So the poem proceeds, a succession of songs of creation and

destruction—individuals and species and civilizations destroyed, buried, but over them (and this in the lessons of NO) A WREATH OF GREEN STRONGER THAN ANY BLACK. GOD B sings all alone, and his words close the poem:

> . . . I ALONE IN MY NIGHT
> HOLD IT BACK HEAR ME BROTHERS I AND MINE

But the permutations are new, and they take on new meaning in this final context. God's eerie decasyllabics subside to mortal pentameter; we realize that the lonely song of survival is our own. It is MAN who MUST PROVIDE and, in the poem's recurring phrase, MAKE SENSE OF IT.

And the sense we make is anchored in the personal life that takes place daily on this fragile earth on which, past all believing, the cosmic mystery has placed us. Jimmy and Dave and their manifold affections—their friends, their cat, their wallpaper, their carpet, their mirror—have sustained the whole cosmic pageant, as if (strike that—why hedge?) to affirm the truth: that the cosmic imperatives, LOVE, SURVIVE, rise out of our own "undestroyed heartscape," and that if they have no roots in our personal experience they have no roots at all. YES or NO? When JM, at sunset in the house in Athens, the spirits dispersed, the whole incredible enterprise over, leans over the balustrade to look down at the three-story drop and feel the urge that is so simply gratified, we know what must HOLD BACK the night if anything can, when DJ comes wordlessly to take his place beside him.

From *The Nation,* February 12, 1977; May 3, 1980.

Talking Back to the Speaker

Let's suppose I have something to say. And I fool around with it, and write it again, and try it another way, and another, because even though it's saying what I want it to, it's not saying it right. And suppose it finally comes to me that the trouble is the *voice:* that I'm writing it for *The Hudson Review* when it should be for *PMLA*. Or vice versa. So I rewrite it one more time and send it in. If it's published, and if (just suppose) it's talked about, its theses, its illustrations, its attitudes, its arguments, will not be attributed to a speaker. They will be attributed to me.

I have, of course, a number of voices. I want to juggle two of them here: one loose, a bit anecdotal, appropriate to personal history; the other appropriate to the chase through texts. The texts will show how small can be the beginnings of a major change in the conditions of literary perception, and how inconspicuously it can achieve authority. I'll use the other voice to insinuate what I think.

"It has become traditional," explains J. Paul Hunter in the poetry volume of *The Norton Introduction to Literature,*

> to distinguish between the person who wrote the poem and

the person who speaks in a poem, for an author often chooses
to speak through a character quite different from his or her real
self.

Traditional: what everybody knows, without knowing how we
know it; the universal practice which has come to seem right. Hunter, with his "often," is a pretty low-key expositor of the tradition,
willingly conceding that "in many poems the speaker is very like the
author, or [there's a catch] very like what the author wishes to think
he or she is like," and that "between the speaker who is a fully
distinct character and the author speaking honestly and directly, are
many degrees of detachment." Written not for freshmen but for us,
M. H. Abrams's *Glossary of Literary Terms* is considerably more
categorical:

> In recent literary discussion "persona" is often applied to the
> first-person narrator, the "I," of a narrative poem or novel, or
> the lyric speaker whose voice we listen to in a lyric poem.
> Examples of personae are . . . the first-person narrator of
> Milton's *Paradise Lost* (who in the opening passages of various
> books discourses at some length about himself); the Gulliver
> who tells us about his misadventures in *Gulliver's Trav-
> els;* . . . the speaker who talks first to himself, then to his sister,
> in Wordsworth's "Tintern Abbey"; the speaker who utters
> Keats's "Ode to a Nightingale" . . . ; and the Duke who tells
> the emissary about his former wife in Browning's "My Last
> Duchess." By calling these speakers "personae" . . . we stress
> the fact that they are all part of the fiction, characters invented
> for a particular artistic purpose. That the "I" in each of these
> works is not the author as he exists in his everyday life is
> obvious enough in the case of Swift's Gulliver and Browning's
> Duke, less obvious in the case of Milton . . . , and does not
> seem obvious at all to an unsophisticated reader of the lyric
> poems of Wordsworth and Keats.

For "recent literary discussion" Hunter's "degrees of detachment"
are only a function of the reader's naiveté. That every literary "I" is
fictional is "a fact." "We stress" it. It takes only a single pronoun to
embody a tradition.

Now an anecdote. I've told it elsewhere so I'll keep it short.

It's twenty-five years ago. You can tell, because I'm teaching Great Books, and in a community college, and to pretty much everyone who comes in off the street. We're reading the *Inferno;* a student, not one of the smart ones, raises his hand. He hasn't spoken before, but now he has a question. "We've read what Homer says about the afterlife, and what Plato says, and now we're reading what Dante says, and they're all different. Mrs. Park. *Which of them is true?*"

The good students rustle and smirk; already they know (how?) that this isn't a question you ask in English class. A bit of irony will reinforce them and solace me; they're on my side, I need them, teaching isn't easy. Or I can drop irony for sympathetic explanation, summon I. A. Richards out of the air in which he is unquestionably hovering, and say something to the effect that "the statements which appear in the poetry are there for the sake of their effects upon feelings, not for their own sake," and that "to question whether they deserve serious attention as *statements claiming truth* is to mistake their function." I catch myself just in time. Who is closer to Plato and Dante, I and my little band of sophisticates, or this earnest questioner? Which of us is reading as they expected to be read?

That happened long ago. Today we have a more elaborate armamentarium against the profound demands of naiveté. Today I could explain to my student that Plato told his myths of the afterlife through a speaker who, though called Socrates, was only a fiction invented for a particular artistic purpose. I could involve him in distinctions between Dante the narrator and Dante the poet. I could invoke specters, an "implied author," a ghostly "authorial presence." I could raise wall after glass wall between him and these vanished human voices he had come to think had something to say directly to him. If I really worked at it, I could bring even such a student to believe what my smart students of a generation ago already suspected; that in English class, what's relevant is what's complicated, not what, if anything, is true.

Actually, I don't get many students like that any more. I'm teaching in a different place, and time, too, alters curriculum and consumers. Great Books aren't being taught much these days: teachers have doubts about "the canon"; students' interests in literature seldom reach back past 1900. Not that they're not smart. Most of the students in my sections of Introduction to Literature don't need Hunter's explanation; some wouldn't even be surprised by Abrams's. The preppies and the kids from suburban high schools already know what you are supposed to do when you talk about a poem; the others will find out the first week that you say "the speaker" and not "Frost says," that it's not Shakespeare who's worried he's growing old, not Donne who's saying good-bye to his lover, not Keats who talks to a vase. Soon the locution of detachment will become second nature. A class on *Channel Firing* will clue in the laggards, since the others have already had *My Last Duchess*. Next step "The Turn of the Screw," or if that's too familiar, *The Good Soldier*. That'll learn 'em who to trust.

The speaker. The narrator. I want here to trace something of the history of this innocent locution, since there was within living memory a time when it wasn't traditional, when the distinction between "the person who writes" and "the person who speaks" went unmade, except, of course, when poems like Browning's enforced it. Did reading feel different then? If language conditions experience— and certainly to think *that* has become traditional—so pervasive a change in the way we talk about poems and stories must matter; must affect as well as reflect the way they are taught and encountered—not to say written. Does critical and pedagogic practice enact an idea of progress, of gain uncompensated by loss? What should we conclude about a time when professors and critics were more unsophisticated than today's freshmen, when everybody said "the poet says," or "Milton," or "Keats" as if it was the most natural thing in the world? For memory informs me, and my coevals confirm, that it was possible as recently as the 1940s to take courses from the likes of Austin Warren and F. O. Matthiessen and emerge innocent of the distinction. Back then, when Yeats wrote that his heart was driven wild, we assumed that—masks or no masks—he meant it.

It happened that between the forties and the sixties I was out of the academic world, and when I got back into it, the tradition was in place. My colleagues taught *My Last Duchess* and *Channel Firing;* they said "the speaker"; they talked about voice and tone. One likes to do the done thing; soon I was doing it too. I do it to this day, off and on, at least when I'm teaching Introduction to Literature. But because I didn't grow up with it, because I encountered the ideas not as an exciting corrective but as a fact accomplished, I still view it as an outsider. It is as an outsider that I interrogate the nagging discomfort I feel when I hear the words, or read them, or say them. It's small, but in twenty-five years it hasn't gone away. It is out of that discomfort that I chase down the history of the phrase and ponder its implications.

If I can remember a time before the speaker, I can remember too how we read poetry in the olden days. By the time I was eighteen, I had read hundreds of poems, thousands of lines, hitting the high spots, sieving out phrases that fitted my sense of life, ignoring the rest; drunk on eloquence, sometimes merely on sound, on Abanah and Pharphar, on silken Samarcand and cedared Lebanon—reading like a child, if that conveys any meaning today when it's a rare child that grows up on poetry. We were still reading like that in college; the word *impressionistic* was made for us. We didn't know you *could* analyze a poem. I remember the exams—marvelous, expansive essay topics, tempered by "spot questions," previously unseen passages whose period and author we must identify merely by style, by the way the words went. We got quite good at this, so we must have learned something, but nevertheless it was a revelation to take Matthiessen's course and pay *attention* to poems, to watch meaning emerge from the scrutiny of syntax and symbol and structure. Imagine it, you could write a whole paper on one poem. Unbeknownst, we were being introduced to "close reading," to the New Criticism, as yet hardly christened. But not to "the speaker."

People had written about poetry (if we begin with Plato) for more than two millennia without feeling the need for such a phrase. Where should I start my chase? Not with Johnson; champion of the common reader, his sense of the poet's relation to his utterance would be as direct as Sidney's a century and a half before. Shelley wouldn't use it, nor Wordsworth, nor Arnold. Though Chambers's Victorian *Cyclopedia* recognized the "mysterious, misanthropic personage who tells the story of Tennyson's *Maud*," or the possibility that some of Shakespeare's sonnets were "written in a feigned char-

acter," there was no word of a speaker. Maybe Eliot? For our generation of readers, everything started with him.

How the years telescope our past! Revisited, Eliot sounded a lot
closer to Arnold than to Cleanth Brooks; he didn't do close reading,
found it "very tiring" when other people did, had, apparently, no
need for "the speaker." I. A. Richards? That seemed more likely. He
had given us poetry as pseudostatement, and one good distancing
mechanism deserves another. I took out *Practical Criticism*.

Cambridge students in the twenties, apparently, read no better
than our freshmen do today. (But how much better they wrote!
How wide their vocabularies! How complex their sentence structure! How much they seemed to know about prosody, about literary
history, even though it only seemed to get in their way!) They read,
in fact, much as I had twenty years later, and Richards had found out
what to do about it. By the simple but original expedient of presenting them with unattributed poems, he deprived them of their hard-
learned stereotypes and, sentence by sentence, insisted that they
attend to what the poet was saying. In 1943, I hadn't really thought
that poems came in sentences, like prose; I'd thought they were a
different kind of thing altogether.

Since Richards had literally eliminated the poet from his students' experience of reading, I was ready momentarily to encounter
the poet's surrogate, the speaker. And I did, first in a trivial example
(quoted from a rather obtuse student who had evidently reached for
the phrase lacking the poet's name), then used by Richards himself.

> Furthermore, the speaker . . . chooses or arranges his words
> differentially as his audience varies. . . . Finally, apart from
> what he says (Sense), his attitude to what he's talking about
> (Feeling), and his attitude to his listener (Tone) there is the
> speaker's intention, his aim, . . . the effect he is endeavouring
> to promote.

Had I already located the *ur*-persona? Not so fast. The book was half
over. Richards had considered thirteen poems without mentioning
a speaker; he was now embarking on a general discussion, not of
poetry, but of "human utterances," of speech itself. Naturally speech
implied a speaker. This one, like most others, had aims and inten-

tions, endeavoured to promote effects; "we speak," Richards informed us, "to say something." His *we* was inclusive. Here was no mask, no "voice," no Duke of Ferrara, not even necessarily a writer. Richards's speaker was only ourselves talking. I kept on reading, but in 185 more pages the speaker did not reappear.

Might he show up in Richards's star pupil? William Empson's *Seven Types of Ambiguity* appeared in 1930, the year after *Practical Criticism*. It gave us a word we couldn't do without, and taught us, more than any other single book, how much could be teased out of a poem. (Eliot was later to refer to "the lemon-squeezer school of criticism.") But it did not distinguish poet and speaker. The single time Empson used the term was to make clear, in discussing Herbert's *The Sacrifice,* that "the speaker is Jesus." The term was available at need, but normal usage remained, to use Abrams's word, "unsophisticated." It did not occur to Empson to render anonymous that "speaker who talks first to himself, then to his sister" in *Tintern Abbey* or to attenuate Wordsworth's relation to what, in Empson's straightforward words, "he wants to make a statement about."

> Wordsworth seems to have believed in his own doctrines and wanted people to know what they were. It is reasonable, then, to try to extract from this passage definite opinions on the relations of God, man, and nature.
>
> Wordsworth may . . . have *felt a something far more deeply infused* than the *presence* that *disturbed* him.
>
> He talks as if he owned a creed.

When Empson writes of Shelley's "Skylark" that "the poet is rapt into an ecstasy which purifies itself into nescience," it might be Matthew Arnold.

Five years later, in R. P. Blackmur's *The Double Agent,* the speaker's voice is still inaudible, even in the chapter on "The Masks of Ezra Pound," where Blackmur explains, for readers to whom it is evidently unfamiliar, a term that neither Richards nor Empson had used:

> *Persona,* etymologically, was something through which sounds were heard, and thus a mask. . . . Mr. Pound's work has been to

make *personae,* to become . . . in this special sense . . . a person
through which what has most interested him . . . might be
given voice.

Yet Blackmur talking about poets was no more sophisticated than
Empson. For him, too, poets spoke to say something, and in general
the poem was what they said: "An apple, Mr. Stevens says [in *Le
Monocle de Mon Oncle*], is as good as any skull to read." It might be
"says," or something stronger: "For Keats, the Nightingale . . . let
him pour himself forth." In any case, Keats uttered the ode, not a
speaker.

By 1935, then, speaker and persona had made their appearance,
but separately and very inconspicuously. Clearly, they had not yet
made their way into critical practice, let alone theory.

It wasn't until I rounded up an old copy of Brooks and Warren
that I found what I was looking for. I should have looked there first.
Here were the terms I had found in place in the mid-sixties: Richards's *tone* and, with it, the speaker as we have come to know him.
For the first time? Who can say? Literary critics have not as yet
earned a concordance, and the teacher, as someone once remarked,
sculpts in snow.

Cleanth Brooks and Robert Penn Warren's *Understanding Poetry*
was first published in 1938, and its fourth edition is in print today—an astonishing record of pedagogical influence. Brooks and
Warren brought the principles of neocritical reading within the
compass of teachers in every college, then in every high school.
Revisiting it today, it's hard to appreciate the originality of this
modestly titled "Anthology for College Students." The poems were
accompanied by the explanations, questions, and exercises of a conventional textbook. Certainly the selection was new; metaphysical
and modern poems were generously interspersed among the nineteenth-century favorites. But it was their arrangement that most
plainly proclaimed a new agenda. They were not in chronological
order, nor were they grouped by author nor by theme. A long
"Letter to the Teacher" made the priorities clear: "Study of biographical and historical materials," served by chronological and authorial ordering, and "inspirational and didactic interpretation,"

invited by thematic grouping, were mere substitutes for the proper "object for study," "the poem in itself."

The poem in itself was now inherently dramatic (as Blackmur had said it sometimes, but not always, was). As a little drama, it had acquired a speaker. "What does section four [of *Ode to the West Wind*] tell us about the speaker? Does the poem sufficiently present his situation? Or do you need to consult a life of Shelley in order for the passage to gain full significance?" The answer was not far to seek.

Though Richards had not doubted that a poet, like other human utterers, had aims and intentions, he had denied him the truth-value of what he said. Poetry was different from philosophy, from all expository prose; it made pseudostatements. (Eliot concurred, then demurred when he became a Christian.) Brooks and Warren made the application clear: there should be no "confusion between scientific and poetic communication." Poetry's pleasure and profit should be sought, not as of old in particular beauties or isolable *sententiae,* but in the poem as "an organic system of relationships," "object for study," objet d'art. In his *Principles,* Richards had named "message hunting." Brooks and Warren introduced the term to a generation of teachers and students—and poets—who learned from it not only how poetry should not be read but what it should not be.

And how does "the speaker" function to deter message-hunting? *Mrs. Park, which of them is true?* Why should the speaker speak truly? The Duke of Ferrara did not. Once the poet was dissolved in the persona, his poems scattered under new rubrics like "tone" and "imagery," a student was no longer in a position to ask questions about the attitudes and convictions of a single human being. *We* speak to say something; "the speaker" might say something different in every poem. And though the poet-as-speaker might retain his aims and intentions, the student must experience them with some loss of urgency. The danger of "inspirational or didactic interpretation" is markedly reduced when the unacknowledged legislators of mankind speak at one remove. Only a fool trusts a man in a mask.

Yet again, not so fast. If any such implications existed, they were still in embryo. Brooks and Warren might say "the speaker," but they were far from saying it consistently. And they certainly did not think of their new phrase as a possible focus of critical or pedagogic attention. Their Glossary contained no entry for "speaker" or "persona," and in their single explanatory sentence the poet came first. "Every poem implies a speaker of the poem, either the poet writing in his own person or someone into whose mouth the poem is put." The authors themselves shifted between speaker and poet almost at random.

> [Of *A Slumber Did My Spirit Seal*] Is it the speaker saying that his loved one seemed so thoroughly immortal that he simply was asleep to the possibility that she could ever die?
>
> [Of *The Scholar Gypsy*] The poet says that his own age is confused by doubts.

There is, of course, a distinction to be made between the poet insofar as he speaks to say something, and the poet *qua* poet, shaping, ordering, choosing, and now and then the authors seemed to have it in mind: "Does the poet succeed in dramatizing the suggestion that the daffodils accept the speaker as a companion?" But the distinction collapses in practice. Back to the *Nightingale:* "This poem is obviously a reverie induced by the poet's listening to the song of the nightingale," not the poet as craftsman, but "the poet . . . just sinking into the reverie," the poet who "wishes for a dissolution of himself," and "breaks out of his reverie" in the last stanza. "Poet" melts imperceptibly into "speaker" as the discussion progresses, the total number of occurrences of each holding equal at eleven. In the books as a whole the usage is almost entirely fluid: if "the speaker" of the *Nightingale* has an "attitude toward death," it's "the poet" who has an "attitude toward fate" in Marvell's *The Definition of Love.* Sometimes the likely distinction is actually reversed: for *Among School Children* it's "the speaker himself and . . . the woman he loves," yet for *Two Songs from a Play,* so much less personal and circumstantial, it's "Yeats believes." Brooks and Warren are not yet committed to the speaker. "Is Johnson actually pointing a moral?" they ask of *The Vanity of Human Wishes;* when push comes to shove, as it generally does with the Doctor, it's back to the poet. Even an inspirational or didactic interpretation may get by if you agree with it: for *Shine, Perishing Republic,* the questions are "Does this poet hate America? Is he trying to admonish his country?"

Brooks was no more consistent when writing alone and for grown-ups, and only slightly more conscious. In *Modern Poetry and the Tradition* (1939), written, presumably, while he was working on *Understanding Poetry,* we hear much more from poets than from speakers: "Marvell . . . compares himself and his mistress to parallel lines"; "Donne may argue as in 'The Nocturnal on St. Lucy's Day' that he is nothing." Speaker and poet comfortably coexist: of *Ode to the Confederate Dead:* "The world which the dead soldiers possessed is not available to the speaker of the poem. . . . Moreover, the poet is honest: the leaves for him, are merely leaves." Eight years later, in *The Well Wrought Urn,* the smokeless air over Westminster Bridge still "reveals a city the poet did not know existed," and it is "the poet" who begins the Immortality Ode "by saying he has lost something." By the next page, however, there has been a silent metamorphosis into "what the speaker has lost," and soon the usage is hopelessly confused: "Wordsworth says that the rainbow and the rose are beautiful": "the moon is treated as if she were the speaker himself"; "the poet cannot see the gleam." Practice has not yet hardened into consistency, still less into precept. Elton's *Glossary of the New Criticism,* published the next year, glossed "tone" and "irony," but not "persona."

Brooks came closest to making the distinction explicit in the chapter on Gray's Elegy, where he reproved Empson for failing to realize that "we are not dealing with Gray's political ideas," but with "what the Elegy says," with "the *speaker's* choice." The emphasis is Brooks's own; we can imagine him underlining the word. The issue resurfaced only in an appendix, where Donald Stauffer was criticized for confounding "the protagonist of the poem with the poet, and the experience of the poem as an aesthetic situation with the author's personal opinion." But Brooks was only working toward such aesthetic purity; in the body of the book he had not yet attained it. Old simplicities die hard.

It was not until 1951, in Reuben Brower's *The Fields of Light,* that we were told straight out that a poem is not merely a drama, but "a dramatic fiction," and that "its speaker, like a character in a play, is no less a creation of the words on the printed page." Brower's first chapter is titled "The Speaking Voice"; its first heading is "The Speaker." It is indeed an *ur*-text for persona, cited as such in Abrams's bibliography. Here the space allotted to "the poet writing in his own person" has visibly contracted; Brower is considerably farther along the road to the Universal Speaker:

> The voice we hear in a lyric, however piercingly real, is not Keats's or Shakespeare's; or if it seems to be . . . we are embarrassed and thrown off as if an actor had stopped and spoken to the audience in his own person.

Description hardens into prescription. Poets may seem to speak in their own voices, perhaps they even do so in fact, but they shouldn't. Brower can accept it when Shelley, in *Ode to the West Wind,* comes on in "his familiar character of priest-prophet," but with "I fall upon the thorns of life! I bleed!," "the dramatic fiction slips disturbingly: the allegory refers us too directly to Shelley's biography," though Brower concedes that it is "only after the poem's high commotion is past that we feel the lapse." But however compelling the theatrical metaphor, those of us who remember how entirely, in the forties, we had learned to condescend to Shelley may suspect that it was less the slippage of the mask that embarrassed than the sentiment. There seems no reason, after all, why a priest-prophet in his familiar character can't feel sorry for himself. The unobtrusiveness of the human author has become a criterion, in poetry and in the novel as well; Brower reproves E. M. Forster for "somewhat portentous observations" which "in their unironic solemnity . . . are not altogether in character for the narrator of *A Passage to India.*"

James would have committed no such gaffe. Four years later, Brooks and Wimsatt would identify the novelist's "problem of securing an impersonality for his art," and ask, "How does the narrator avoid introducing himself into the work?" How? He does so by joining the speaker on stage. There sock and buskin conveniently separate him from authorial temptations to say what he thinks or feels, and readerly temptations to experience his statements unprotected by irony. Mechanisms of detachment tend to cluster.

Yet actual critical practice continues to resist such aesthetic austerity. In Brower's verbs, poets still speak for themselves. As he compares sonnets by Donne and Hopkins, "Hopkins calls directly on God for help"; "Donne . . . for all his queries, [is] certain of his close and passionate relation to Christ," while "Hopkins [is] tortured at the very center of his faith." There are no apologies for this near-lapse into biography. Although Brower asserts a distinction between speaker and poet, he makes it only when need compels, as it does in its discussion of *Love III,* where his use of "story-teller," "narrator," "sinner," and "guest" (not, however, "speaker") only underlines the difference between Herbert's dramatized and universalized encounter with divinity and Donne's and Hopkins's direct and personal address.

Brower was far too good a reader to sacrifice that difference to a theory; writing naturally of "the intimacy of Donne's prayer" in Holy Sonnet 10, he reserved "the speaker" for the overtly dramatized situation of *The Ecstasie.* In fact, Brower seldom used the term. It appears in a discussion of the *Essay on Riches,* to be immediately canceled by a reference to "Pope's ridicule." It is notably missing in the extended treatments of *Absalom and Achitophel,* of Yeats's *Two Songs,* even of *Surprised by Joy,* though a footnote is there to admonish us that "a biographical reading, which the usual footnote to the poem invites, is altogether misleading and singularly unprofitable." Brower's transitional location between past naiveté and future rigor is marked by the doubled noun with which he concludes his discussion of the speaking voice: "The poet-speaker."

T. S. Eliot's "The Three Voices of Poetry," first published in 1953, is also cited as an *ur*-text for persona. Actually to consult it, however, is to experience the retroactive power of an idea to compel us to misunderstand a text, indeed to reverse its meaning. Eliot in 1953 was writing plays, and far from making the dramatic voice the type of all poetic speaking, he was particularly concerned to distinguish it. He explicitly restricts the poet as persona to the third of his three voices, that actually to be heard on a stage. In the first voice, "the voice of private meditation," the poet is "talking to himself—or to nobody"; in the second, he is "talking to other people." Only in the third does the poet create "a dramatic character

speaking in verse." Devotees of the universal persona may be startled to realize that by this Eliot does not mean dramatic monologue
but actual drama, in which the poet is "saying . . . only what he can
say within the limits of one imaginary character addressing another
imaginary character," characters who have "equal claims" upon him,
and whom, therefore, "he cannot wholly identify . . . with himself."
In dramatic monologue, however, "it is surely the second voice, the
voice of the poet talking to other people, that is dominant." Though
metaphorically "he has put on costume and makeup," he hasn't
really:

> Dramatic monologue cannot create a character. When we listen
> to a play by Shakespeare, we listen not to Shakespeare but to
> his characters; when we read a dramatic monologue by Brown-
> ing, we cannot suppose we are listening to any other voice than
> that of Browning himself.

To the author of *Prufrock* it couldn't be clearer: "What we normally
hear . . . in the dramatic monologue is the voice of the poet." Even
in the play *The Rock,* the chorus was "speaking directly for me,"
speaking, moreover, in the second voice, the voice that Brooks and
Brower found so off-putting but which Eliot here claimed as his
own: "The voice heard in all poetry that has a conscious social
purpose—poetry intended to amuse or instruct, poetry that
preaches or points a moral"—that invites a reader, among other
things, to consider whether what it says might be true. No wonder
Eliot didn't say "the speaker."

But for all his influence, Eliot was not teaching English in
American colleges. Brooks and Warren were; it is from their second
edition, published in 1950, that I have quoted, and the memories of
fifties graduates confirm that it was in that decade that the speaker
permeated the diction of the English class. And as the decade progressed, critics became more aware of what they were doing; for
their 1960 edition, Brooks and Warren revised their Nightingale
section to eliminate those eleven occurrences of "the poet." They
were less aware of why they were doing it. Though the invocation of
"the speaker" harmonized with New Critical deemphasis of biogra-

phy and "conscious social purpose," the association was never explicit. Even in 1960 Brooks and Warren did not completely banish the poet; though Keats was speakerized, Marvell and Yeats were left alone.

Poems vary, however, in the insistence with which they solicit interest in their poet. Shakespeare's sonnets are notorious for inveigling critics into biographical lapses, and their treatment in what, for convenience, I shall call the Brooks and Warren years demonstrates how consistently the use of "the speaker" correlates with the critic's biographical stance.

When Empson wrote in *Seven Types* that "Shakespeare is being abandoned by Mr. W. H. and stiffly apologizing for not having been servile to him," he was only continuing a tradition already well established when Wordsworth, or someone very like him, said that "with this key / Shakespeare unlocked his heart." (Naturally, it was Browning who replied, "If so, the less Shakespeare he.") Even in 1941, in *The New Criticism* itself, John Crowe Ransom, trying to cool down Empson's "overreading" of Sonnet 73, was quite comfortable writing things like "At this stage in the sequence, Shakespeare is melancholy. He finds the world evil and would like to die. His health is probably bad, for he refers to the likelihood of death." Ten years later, Edward Hubler and Wilson Knight were still reading the sonnets as the expression of Shakespeare's personal concerns; neither used "the speaker." But by 1963 the speaker was claiming an authority critics could not ignore, though they varied in how consciously they recognized it. In Hilton Landry's *Interpretation in Shakespeare's Sonnets,* the speaker takes over, imperceptibly to the author, but before the reader's eyes.

As to biography, Landry is a fence-sitter. Though he applauds critical "efforts to dispose of the biographical school of sonnet criticism," he "cannot agree . . . that the poet's interests are not deeply involved," especially in view of Sonnets 40 and 41. And for the first half of his book the ancient locution comes naturally, as he writes of "Shakespeare asking the handsome youth, 'What is your substance, whereof are you made?'" "The sonnets which open the sequence urge the patron repeatedly to marry . . . but that was before Shakespeare's own dark lady seduced the patron." On page 63, however, the speaker makes a silent entrance; Sonnets 40, 41, and 42 now become "a trio of poems in which the speaker comments on aspects of a sexual triangle." For some ten pages thereafter poet and speaker coexist freely, in relation to the same poems and sometimes in the same paragraph. Then the balance tips. References to "the poet" and "Shakespeare" diminish, then disappear. By the end of Landry's book the speaker commands the field, with 27 instances in 24 pages. There has been no discussion of voice or persona, but the poet has slipped away.

The next year, when Murray Krieger came to the Sonnets, he not only said "speaker" but could be explicit about it: "Shakespeare presents us with a true lover . . . as his poet-persona." Poet-persona, lover, and Shakespeare are distinguishable, though still close; both Shakespeare and the speaker are poets, after all, so "the poet" can be written with something of the old ease. They may even both be lovers; once Krieger even slips into writing not that the speaker but "Shakespeare calls upon his friend" to accept "the blessing of parenthood." But for the rest his usage is both consistent and aware. How satisfyingly—and unexpectedly—the textual chase confirms personal history! It must have been just about 1964 that I got the news that poems were now to be talked about in a new way.

By 1968, the avowal of biographical interest has taken on a distinctly defensive coloration. Brent Stirling must confess on the first page of *The Shakespeare Sonnet Order* that, "unlike some readers," he "would like to have some of the answers to the biographical mysteries." Stirling still feels easy saying "Shakespeare." So does Barbara Herrnstein Smith in her 1969 teaching edition: "The nature of Shakespeare's relation to the young man is addressed in many of the sonnets." James Winny, however, whose *The Master-Mistress* was published the same year, uses every argument he can think of to exclude a biographical reading, including the moral one (Shakespeare wouldn't have confessed anything so discreditable), and except when such references as "eternal lines" and "black ink" validate "the poet," he is careful to say "speaker."

In his 1969 *Essay on Shakespeare's Sonnets* and his 1977 edition of the poems, Stephen Booth has achieved full theoretical and practical consistency. Cooler than Winny, he jokes away any lingering biographical impurities. "Shakespeare was almost certainly homosexual, bisexual, or heterosexual. The sonnets provide no evidence on the matter." Since Booth's interest is in linguistic rather than human events, he does not often refer to whoever it is that utters the poems, but when he does, as in the discussion of Sonnet 35, the entity who "blames himself" is "the speaker."

Hallett Smith's 1981 book on the sonnets is perhaps the best illustration of the newly traditional diction of detachment. He too thinks he hears Eliot's Voices; he begins *The Tension of the Lyre* by quoting the first one, "the poet talking to himself." Invisibly and immediately, however, it is transmogrified, paraphrased into "poems in which the poet seems to be talking to himself." That "seems" sums up the speaker's forty-year progress toward universal imperium. For Smith, "the focus is on the feeling of the speaker," "the speaker's love is like a fever": "there is little evidence in the first seventeen sonnets that the speaker feels love for the person addressed." And it's not only the speaker who's grown dim in the aesthetic distance, he's taken his friend with him, "the audience of the poem, fictional though it probably is." Pluralized, fictionalized, reduced to an It—what a fate for "the person addressed"! When at length Smith "must now consider the character of the poet (or speaker)," the parenthetical addition must disinfect so intimate a contact, and we are at once admonished to restrict our interest. "The 'I' of the sonnets . . . may or may not bear a close resemblance to William Shakespeare, but he is a *persona* with identifiable traits." We can guess which we are to prefer. Art's impersonality is more manageable than the untidy spectacle of poets who claim to look into their hearts and write. When Smith is momentarily brought "very close to the conclusion that the speaker in the Dark Lady sonnets is a man named Will, and that we are to take that person as William Shakespeare," his only recourse is to change the subject.

Poets tend to view things differently. Eliot had insisted that his verse spoke for him. John Berryman added his own emphasis: "One thing that critics not themselves writers of poetry occasionally forget is that poetry is composed by actual human beings. . . . When Shakespeare wrote, 'Two loves I have,' reader, he was *not kidding*." A qualification followed—it was 1962, and the tradition was hardening: "Of course the speaker can never be the actual writer, who is a person with an address" and other impedimenta he can't carry into the poem. Distinguishing person and persona, Berryman quoted Ransom's phrase, "the highly compounded authorial 'I.'" But all he seemed to mean was that a poet (he was talking about Lowell's highly personal *Skunk Hour*) may speak for others besides himself. It may even be the persona that makes the speaking possible: in a few years, Berryman would be writing the *Dream Songs*. When Robert Pinsky, poet as well as critic, identified the distancing persona as one of modern poetry's "strategies for retaining or recovering . . . the tones of the forbidden language of Arnold or Tennyson," Berryman was his premier example of how a poet through a persona "can use the style which annoys or embarrasses him, but which for some purposes he needs—needs more or less for its original, affirmative purposes." Needs as we all do; driven, we use irony to bypass irony. Reader, Henry was *not kidding*.

Only occasionally did critics join poets to retard the speaker's progress. Irvin Ehrenpreis resisted his invasion of eighteenth-century studies; in 1963 (the year of Landry's silent shift) his brief essay "Personae" insisted on what had never before required insistence, that the fictive work is written by "the real person," and "if he tells a story, we must ask what he (not his emanation) means by the story." But common sense appearing in an obscure festschrift and limiting its examples to Swift and Pope was not about to stop the tradition. Pinsky noted (in the mid-seventies) that speaking through a persona might "to a seventeenth-century reader . . . seem a bizarre way of writing poems of personal feeling"; he might have added that it might seem a bizarre way of talking about them. Indeed, C. L. Barber, reviewing in 1978 Booth's books on the Sonnets, demurred briefly but explicitly from "those manuals of New Criticism" that "neatly separat[e] a 'speaker,' a dramatized presence, from the poet who mimes him," and argued gently that the "formalism" of Booth's interpretation ignored "human motives," "human gestures in the poems . . . that must reflect actual, . . . if somewhat obscure, personal relationships." Barber offered alternative interpretations that not only used the old locutions—as in "the poet's relation to the young man"—but depended on them.

But these critical voices, eminent as they were, did not carry far. By 1981, the speaker's hegemony was so complete that John Reichert was impelled to ask, in a little read but trenchant essay, "Do Poets Ever Mean What They Say?"

And it was in 1981 that my chase started, with the unyielding explanation of "Persona" I have quoted from the fourth edition of Abrams's *Glossary*—carried over unchanged, I was to find, from the third edition of ten years before. I had to take it as Abrams's own view; other entries made it clear enough when he disagreed with the ideas he summarized. Yet doubt nagged; could the critic I remembered really practice the antiseptic sophistication he seemed to mandate? I must find out how Abrams himself had been talking in the years when critics were learning to say "the speaker." Textual chases never end, but every chase at last must have a stop. Mine would stop here.

By now dates had become evidence; I did not expect to find a speaker in *The Mirror and the Lamp*. That marvelous book was published in 1953 and begun much earlier; I had read it as an unpublished doctoral dissertation in 1944. I checked: in it, Young, Boileau, and Pope (for a sample) came right out and "said" what they said in their poems; MacLeish made "a poetic statement"; Cowley even "sang," as poets were erstwhile wont to do. And so it was even in 1963; in the essay "Romanticism and the Spirit of the Age," Abrams regularly introduced poetic quotations by the simple "says" (Collins, Coleridge); Blake "complained to the Muses"; and Wordsworth not only said and described, but insisted, dismissed, claimed and proclaimed, plainly pointed out, and bade farewell. Not for long, however. I could almost have predicted the date; if 1963 was for Landry the year of the speaker, for Abrams it was 1965. In "Structure and Style in the Greater Romantic Lyric" we hear for the first time of "a determinate speaker . . . whom we overhear as he carries on . . . a sustained colloquy, sometimes with himself or with the outer scene, but more frequently with a silent human auditor, present or absent."

The verbs are now all the speaker's—it is he who "achieves an insight, faces up to a tragic loss, comes to a moral decision, or resolves an emotional problem." In *Frost at Midnight,* the Coleridge who said things so readily only two years before has become "the meditative mind," "the solitary and wakeful speaker"; to the speaker, too, is attributed the childhood under review. Abrams's account of the *Ode on a Distant Prospect of Eton College* is equally fastidious: the poem "evokes in memory the lost self of the speaker's youth," and not Gray but the speaker "watches the heedless schoolboys at their games." When it's not the speaker who gets the verb, it's, by a common alternate strategy, the poem itself, as "Keats's first long poem of consequence . . . represents what he saw, then thought, while he 'stood tiptoe upon a little hill.'" And no sooner has Abrams quoted William Lisle Bowes's clear statement that his sonnets "describe his personal feelings," then he rephrases it with the familiar dubiety; the sonnets "present a determinate speaker, whom we are invited to identify with the author himself." The word *persona* makes its expected appearance two pages later. The tradition is, it would seem, firmly in place.

And yet within the year Abrams's own speaker had returned to the limbo whence he came. In the 1966 essay, "Coleridge, Baudelaire, and Modernist Poetics," Wordsworth (in *The Prelude*) is describing, and without intermediary, "how, 'inspired by the sweet breath of heaven,' he assumed the prophet's sacred mission," and "calling on his follow poet, Coleridge . . . to carry on with him 'as joint labourers in the work.'" Coleridge himself has reclaimed the right to say; the essay closes with him talking. "'Joy,' he says . . . 'is the spirit and the power, / Which, wedding Nature to us, gives in dower, / A new Earth and new Heaven.'"

Although his *Glossary* explanation appeared for the first time in 1971, by 1972 Abrams's own poets had got back all their verbs. In *Natural Supernaturalism,* Shelley remarks and diagnoses; Coleridge dismisses, reveals, and reviews his life; Arnold asks; Eliot remarks; Auden makes a wry comment; Plath testifies; and Stevens enquires, rejects, and says—all in verse, and all *in propria,* as we used to say *persona.* Wordsworth himself explains, announces (repeatedly), says, goes on to say, goes on to *pray,* puts it, feels, proclaims, and cries. Though Abrams of course recognizes when his poet speaks "through the medium of an invented character," and though he more than once discusses *Tintern Abbey,* there is no word of "the speaker who talks first to himself, then to his sister." When his sister is mentioned, in fact, the "his" refers directly to an antecedent "Wordsworth." Nor should we be surprised that Abrams couldn't keep his distance; that speaker is hardly consonant with the rich and humane contextuality of a critic the entire tenor of whose work opposes what he identified in 1966 as "an aesthetic of an other-wordly, self-sufficient poem." It is characteristic, though odd, that when Abrams returned briefly to the idea of persona (in "Two Roads to Wordsworth," published, like *Natural Supernaturalism,* in 1972), it was to praise it as an antidote to too much New Criticism, a concept that can "rehumanize poetry by viewing the poet, in Wordsworth's phrase, 'as a man speaking to men.'" But the reference to persona, though appreciative, is momentary. As with Brower, subject and verb tell the story, and through the seventies Abrams's speaker does not revive. Abrams's own *Norton Anthology* briskly returns to Coleridge the childhood he lost in 1965, as businesslike notes to *Frost at Midnight* inform the student that "The scene is Coleridge's cottage at Nether Stowey," "The infant in line 7 is his son Hartley," "The 'stern preceptor' . . . the Reverend James Boyer," and the "sister beloved" his sister Ann. And in an essay written as recently as 1983, Coleridge says, Wordsworth proclaims, and, to provide the grand coda, "Shelley announced that

> The world's great age begins anew,
> The golden years return.

And they yet may, if common sense keeps breaking in. But it's a long road back to innocence. I don't teach Great Books anymore, worse luck, but sometimes I teach Dante. This year, in a paper entitled "Textual Cocktails," I read that "the interplay of Dante-as-poet (as opposed to Dante-as-pilgrim, both poetic constructs of Dante-as-author), textualizes the *Inferno.*" The young man who wrote that is a marvelous student and a marvelous person, brilliant, excitable, and excited about ideas. But I fear he has almost lost the capacity to ask naive questions. I miss my community college students. Though they weren't used to literature, they were, some of them, perhaps for that very reason, ready to take it into their lives with an astonishing, hungry directness. I learned from them what I won't forget. Newly born Renaissance readers, they were coming into their heritage, reading for the reasons Horace and Sidney knew, for profit and delight. For them art could still hold the mirror up to nature. I learned to value that prelapsarian trust, to doubt that any paradise I could promise within The Poem Itself would be happier far. Could I sniff, farther down the road, an even newer criticism, one in which author, history, truth, meaning itself would dissolve, an insubstantial pageant faded? Subversion, as an activity, is overrated; the community college showed me that I did not want, and do not want, to undermine the assumption of very young people that great authors speak great words, and that great words proffer wisdom. Abrams would be the last to disagree that although we should not hunt messages, we should be willing to recognize and honor them when they are found.

Of course the speaker is often a useful concept, sometimes a necessary one. The pervasive attention to voice has increased the subtlety with which we are able to read literary texts as well as the length at which we can write about them, articulating nuances before undiscussed, if not therefore unapprehended or unfelt. But let's be sensible. Here, for example, is a new book attributing to Emily Dickinson "a voice, which though it is surely not hers, is so intimately defined by her habits of mind that it encourages friendship, familiarity, even affection." I'm told it's not hers, but I'm never told why. I'm supposed to know. Well, I don't know. Of course, as Abrams explained in the *Glossary*, "the I . . . is not the author as he exists in his everyday life," and "in each of the major lyricists the nature of the persona alters, sometimes subtly and sometimes radically, from one of his lyrics to the next." But do we really need to be told that the poet in everyday life never tasted a liquor never brewed, or wandered where the Muses haunt, especially since in the latter case the poet actually *was* with darkness and with dangers compass round? Our gain in subtlety is a loss in human community if we succeed in detaching the utterance from the uttering tongue and mind and heart, not occasionally and provisionally but as a matter of course. For we are all utterers—teachers, critics, poets, people—and at issue is the fullness of human commitment not merely to literature but to language, and language's commitment to what as human beings we think and believe and want and need to say. As to altering from one utterance to the next, everybody does that all the time, as any collection of letters—Flannery O'Connor's, say—will confirm. You'd have to be pretty unsophisticated to believe that "the speaker who utters Keats's *Ode to a Nightingale*" is the author as he exists in his everyday life, but you'd have to be more sophisticated than I care to be to believe that he's not Keats at all. I would prefer my students to recognize that poets are just like folks, arted up a bit, perhaps, but still doing for the most part the same sort of thing their teachers do when they write an article, that they themselves do when, without thinking, they alter their tone for a parent or an employer or a friend. And although it is certainly possible to draw therefrom the conclusion that every voice is fictional, I do not care to press the point. It seems unnecessary for students to question the coherence of their own personalities because they write differently for the college newspaper and for me. Unleashed, the idea of the speaker takes on a terrifying applicability.

From that speaker it is only a step to the "novelistic, irretrievable, irresponsible figure" conjured up by Roland Barthes, "the Author himself—that somewhat decrepit deity of the old criticism," who plays at seeing himself "as a being on paper and his life as a *biography* . . . a writing without referent," "a text like any other." Or Foucault: "It would be as false to seek the author in relation to the actual writer as to the fictional narrator; the 'author function' arises out of their scission—in the division and distance of the two." So quotation marks break out all over, as Derrida tells us that "it would be frivolous to think that 'Descartes,' 'Leibniz,' 'Rousseau,' 'Hegel,' etc. are the names of authors," and adds that the "indicative value" he attributes to them is only "the name of a problem." A problem indeed; a problem at once frivolous and dire, an intellectual heresy, a *trahison des clercs*. A concept that can assimilate the Milton who in darkness implored celestial light to shine inward to Lemuel Gulliver is a concept that devalues human personhood and human pain.

My voice has slipped; these notes have changed too much to tragic. Critics still use the names of poets naturally. Heartening inconsistencies still challenge critical rigor. Biography is back, albeit too often tricked out in such psychometaphysical garments as to obscure the human form divine rather than reveal it. If poets should reclaim the right (I quote Pinsky) "to make an interesting remark or speak of profundities, with all the liberty given to the newspaper editorial, a conversation, a philosopher, or any speaker whatever," even the inspirational and didactic may return: a recent issue of *The Hudson Review* contains an article on "the moral authority of poetry." And students, thank God, are ever virgin; each generation must be taught anew the mechanisms of detachment, or, as I'm told it's now called, distantiation. Left alone, it is no more possible to distance them from the human statement, from what Archibald MacLeish called "the human voice humanly speaking," than Brecht's epic gimmicks could insulate his audiences from Mother Courage.

Reading, rightly understood, is a relationship; we read, Auden said, "to break bread with the dead." "All methods of criticism and teaching are bad," wrote Northrop Frye, "if they encourage the persistent separation of student and literary work"; our job as teachers is to try our best to "weaken those tendencies within criticism which keep the literary work objective and separated from the reader." I would rather have students too naive than not naive enough. Distrust exacts a price, as when children are taught to refuse rides from strangers. We pay it as criticism metastasizes, as we read more and more cleverly, first looking behind masks, then discerning masks where no masks are, then persuading ourselves that the eyeholes are empty. Cleverness excludes, and distrust privatizes. Distrust of the text opens the way to elaborated and idiosyncratic readings, and to a criticism that legitimizes them, even as it delegitimizes the common and accessible experience it stigmatizes as naive. I want my students to hear voices, to recognize ambiguities—even, in moderation, ironies. I want them to experience the literary work as a thing well wrought. Yet I am conscious of the price. The "object for study" all too easily becomes "objective" in Frye's sense, a problem to be solved, not an utterance like our own.

In this objectifying process, I believe the speaker has played an unobtrusive but influential part. I have for my last years as a teacher my own project of subversion, my target the sophistication that compasses me round. Fortunately it's not impossible, if you're confi-

dently old-fashioned enough, to reactivate a nineteen-year-old's
naïveté. Dante, as ever, is a great help, Dante all tangled in biography and history, Dante the author, Dante the pilgrim, Dante the
poet of many voices, who in canto 20 of the *Inferno* uses his own to
tell us how to read a poem:

> Se Dio ti lasci, lettor, prender frutto
> di tua lezione, or pensa per te stesso
> com'io potea tener lo viso asciutto. . . .

"Reader, so may God grant you to gather fruit of your reading,
think now for yourself how I could keep my cheeks dry. . . ." Do we
think it was only the poet's emanation that wept? Think of the poet's
emotion, reader, so you can share it. If you want to gather the fruit
of your reading, take care how you interpose with poetic constructs,
especially those you yourself have constructed. Listen very carefully
to what Dante is saying. Consider, even, that it might be in some
sense true.

From *The Hudson Review,* Spring 1989.

Author! Author! Reconstructing Roland Barthes

When the Author died in France in 1968, it was Roland Barthes who, with his essay "La mort de l'auteur," administered the coup de grâce. Jacques Derrida had already warned, in *Of Grammatology,* of the frivolity of thinking that "'Descartes,' 'Leibniz,' 'Rousseau,' 'Hegel,' are names of authors," since they indicated "neither identities nor causes," but rather "the name of a problem." Michel Foucault would later record an "author-function" arising out of the "scission" between "the author" and "the actual writer." The subtext for all three shimmered in the Parisian spring, in the great year of academic revolution, when the students took to the streets and even the sacred *baccalauréat* felt the tremor. Barthes's way of putting it was somewhat more inspiriting than the transmogrification of authors into functions or problems: "We know now that a text is not a line of words releasing a single 'theological' meaning (the 'message' of the Author-God) but a multi-dimensional space, in which a variety of writings, none of them original, blend and clash." What Barthes was celebrating, in language permeated with the rhetoric of liberation, was release from the very idea of an

206

origin; it was nothing less than that staple of the 1960s, the death of God.

Barthes made sure his language told the story. The Author is "believed in"; his image is to be "desacralized," and with it his theological meaning. He is the God, "the origin, the authority, the Father" (as Barthes would write two years later), and not a very nice one. Literature is centered on him "tyrannically"; his "sway" is "powerful"; the new literature, now to be renamed *writing*, "liberates"; the Author is a myth it is "necessary to overthrow." Criticism, as Barthes would tell *L'Express* in 1970, could participate in "a kind of collective action." (Asked what it did, he answered, "It destroys.") The text, and the reader, are prisoners in the Bastille. With the erasure of the Author-God, the text, escaped from its Great Original, is revealed as an infinite regress of prior traces, of language, of ideas, of societal memories and assumptions. For "to give a text an Author is to impose a limit on that text, to furnish it with a final signified, to close the writing," and the reading with it. To dissolve the Author is to inaugurate that exhilaratingly "anti-theological activity," the conversion of literature to *écriture*, which "ceaselessly posits meaning ceaselessly to evaporate it." It is "an activity that is truly revolutionary since to refuse to fix meaning is, in the end, to refuse God and his hypostases—reason, science, law."

To the reader coming in late, and from over the water, the excitement may be somewhat hard to understand. Certainly revolutionaries of the word are easier to live with (and to embrace) than the other kind. But what is all the verbal shooting about? Is this Author-God, this Freudian Father ("a somewhat decrepit deity," Barthes would later call him) anybody we know?

Sixty years ago, like many American children, I had a game of Authors. It was geared to seven-year-olds, about the simplest game there was to play, on a level with Go Fish—a pack of cards with four suits, headed by Henry Wadsworth Longfellow, John Greenleaf Whittier, Edgar Allan Poe, and Oliver Wendell Holmes. (Not Melville back then, not Whitman, not Dickinson or Thoreau—an early lesson in the temporality of canons.) From the cards we learned such truths as that Longfellow wrote *Evangeline* and

Holmes *The Autocrat of the Breakfast Table*. Naturally, we did not
learn to think of the Author as God, Father, or even (*Whittier?*) as
an Authority. And even had we been English children, with a deck
displaying Shelley, Keats, Tennyson, and Browning, we wouldn't
have learned it either. To be able to associate authors with God, let
alone with his institutional hypostases, you have to be French.

In 1635, in a book significantly entitled *De l'Esclaircissement des
temps,* a portrait appeared of the powerful politician who the year
before had founded the Académie Française, Armand Jean du
Plessis, duc de Richelieu. From the cardinal's head, as if prefiguring
that Sun-King whose effulgence his policies prepared, shone forty
rays of light. Each of those rays bore the name of an Academician—
an Author.

Shall we try to imagine an analogous representation in an English-speaking context? No English prime minister has ever exercised Richelieu's absolute power. Had he done so, it remains inconceivable that the most sycophantic artist could ever have rayed forth
from his head the names, say, of Milton, Dryden, Shadwell, and
thirty-seven more, to Enlighten the Times with their harmonious
and even brightness. Nor can we conceive of an English prime minister—still less an American president—concerning himself to
create, as Richelieu did, an institution to regularize the national
language, guard its purity, and impose upon its primary public literature, the drama, binding rules of literary practice. We are likely to
imagine that a chief of state, even if he is not a cardinal, has more
important things to do. But that too is to think an English-speaking
thought. Long before Barthes, before Derrida, before Foucault,
Richelieu had made the connection between Authors and Authority,
between language and power. The relation of the dramatic Unities
to monarchical unity, of literary Decorum to political and social
conformity, was neither coincidental nor the expression of a vague
French Zeitgeist, an Esprit des Temps. As David Kramer has recently shown, the Academy and its projects were a deliberate response to the exigencies of an absolutism emerging from a century
of fragmentation and religious war. The Rules, literary and linguistic, imposed by Richelieu's Academy expressed the absolute

vision of what was to be Le Grand Siècle while helping to bring it into being.

It was Richelieu's Academy indeed. Perceiving their potential usefulness—or danger—he had by fiat institutionalized the cheerfully intellectual discussions of a group of literary friends, who were something less than enthusiastic to see their informal gatherings transmuted into an assembly of forty so-called Immortals. Some wished to decline the honor, but since Richelieu had forbidden unlicensed assemblies they thought better of it. "The Academy's statutes," Kramer reminds us, "were drawn up, not by a poet or a playwright, but by a *Conseiller d'Etat.*" The Immortals, when not raying directly from Richelieu's head, were in his pocket. He awarded pensions at will. "No one could be so much as proposed for election unless he was 'agréable au protecteur.'" All projects and decisions had to be likewise agreeable; many of them were directly suggested by the protector. The Academy's first and continuing project, the codification and purification of French, was initially undertaken so that the conquering tongue could be more readily learned by those the Cardinal's military campaigns were to subject to the glory of the crown. This was the original impetus for the great French Dictionary. Language was a means of control; French was to spread French *civilisation* abroad, as Latin had. It would equally set limits on what could be written—and thought—at home. We may, if we like, imagine a world in which Dr. Johnson composed his Dictionary, not to make the money he told Boswell every sane man wrote for, but to enhance the glory of the Hanoverian monarchy. That done, we have to imagine him thinking of himself as one of forty immortals and not laughing. It isn't easy.

It was, then, more than the afflatus of the 1960s that impelled Barthes to kill the Author, and rebel against "a language political in its origin . . . born at the moment when the upper classes wished . . . to convert the particularity of their writing into a universal language." Though there were contemporary reasons to proclaim liberation from the heavy rod of the Father-God, Barthes's sense of urgency, of need, of triumph was rooted deep in the historic soil of France. Only in France would it be possible to claim, as Barthes already had in "Authors and Writers" (1960), that "for the entire classical capitalist period, i.e. from the sixteenth to the nineteenth century . . . the uncontested owners of the language, and they alone, were authors"; that "no one else spoke." *No one else spoke.* The outrageousness of the hyperbole bespeaks its urgency. For when Barthes describes a "literary discourse subjected to rules of use, genre, and composition more or less immutable from Marot to Verlaine, from Montaigne to Gide," it is not hyperbole, but a truism of French literary history. "The certitudes of language . . . the imperatives of the structure of the genre"—these are not Barthes's own dismissive sarcasms, but the words of Professor Raymond Picard, a critic sufficiently infuriated by the originality of Barthes's criticism to call his "Nouvelle Critique" a "Nouvelle Imposture." Outside France, his essay *On Racine* wouldn't have raised an eyebrow. But in France those certitudes and imperatives *exist,* for everything from drama to orthography; one challenges them at one's peril. The walls of the prisonhouse of language are far thicker in France.

What rayed forth from Richelieu's head was exactly that clarity later to be called Cartesian, the absolute and simple brightness of the "clear and distinct ideas" that Descartes thought he could find in his own mind and from them validate a universe; *la clarté cartésienne* was the visual manifestation of what Foucault calls "the great utopia of a perfectly transparent language." Barthes had already written, in *Mythologies,* of that "blissful clarity," how it "abolishes the complexity of human acts," giving them "the simplicity of essences," organizing "a world without contradictions because it is without depth, a word . . . wallowing in the evident." The myth was powerful enough, even in America, that an American graduate student could be told to read Kant in a French translation, because (*bien sûr,* this was forty years ago) it was impossible to be obscure in French. Clarity was the glory of that class monopoly, "the great French language," whose "lexicon and euphony," Barthes notes in "Authors and Writers," could be "respectfully preserved" even through that "greatest paroxysm of French history," the Revolution. Though nineteenth-century authors might broaden, even transform that language, they were still its "acknowledged owners." Let us reactivate our English-speaking incredulity: it is quite simply inconceivable to us that authors, of all people, could even in imagination own a language. We speak and write a language that from its beginnings has been the product not of authority but of receptivity, of foreign influence and invasion, that from the time of its greatest poet, and in his person, has been defined by its rich intransigence, its falls into obscurity, its resistance to purity or purification. For us as for Shakespeare, language has been the product not of Authors, but of people talking.

But Barthes, with Derrida and Foucault and fifty million other Frenchmen, grew up within the secure structures of the great French language. There were forty Immortals in their youth, and there are forty Immortals today, three hundred and fifty years after Richelieu and two hundred years after that revolutionary paroxysm which nevertheless scarcely interrupted the Academy's guardianship over the integrity of French. Americans from time to time are made aware of the Immortals, as during the flap over the admission of the late Marguerite Yourcenar, and we are reminded that this is something that seems to matter—to matter less, presumably, than when three brilliant French minds were being formed by an educational system whose director was said to have claimed that he knew what page in what book every French schoolchild was turning on a given day, but still far more than we can readily imagine. The Quarante Immortels are still at work on their Dictionary. A centralized educational system still guarantees that a whole nation invests its emotions in the idea of an authoritative language. Summering in a country village, the astonished foreigner is lectured on what is and is not permissible French by the man who retails fish from door to door. Someone encountered in a train, asked to explain a word he has probably known all his life, defines it, then quickly adds, "But that's not French." It is, of course, *argot*—what we'd call slang, rich and self-renewing like any popular speech. When Victor Hugo introduced a few phrases of thieves' argot into *Les Misérables,* he appended thousands of words of justification. Authority is defined by power, and power is defined by its ability to forbid. That the vocabulary of classic French drama is confined to some 2,500 words (2,000, says Barthes, for Racine) as against Shakespeare's 25,000 is not just a quirk of literary history, still less of national character. It is the product of conscious decision. Though the vocabulary of permissible French is of course very much larger today, it is still defined by exclusion.

Helen Vendler has described the "intellectual formation of a French child attracted to literature"—the *cahier* (the obligatory blot-free notebook), the *dictée,* the *manuel littéraire* enshrining every received idea of literary history—and has noted Barthes's own awareness of "how little he could escape from this training." Barthes, in *S/Z,* describes it considerably more abstractly: "a predetermination of messages, as in secondary-school education." But the structures of French civilization are formed long before its elite attends the *lycée,* which is what Barthes understands by secondary education. The certitudes and imperatives of French are encountered much earlier. Few of the children whose education Lawrence Wylie describes in his *Village in the Vaucluse* would ever reach secondary school. Yet in their elementary classroom the Cartesian light still shone, clear and sharp, mandating a dedication to abstract formulation, to structural analysis, to classification, that readers of contemporary French theory will find eerily familiar. American amateurs of the School of Paris may compare Wylie's description with their own grade-school experience and ponder how it applies to their favorite authors—or texts—as these exemplify it at once in conformity and rebellion.

> In teaching morals, grammar, arithmetic, and science the teacher always follows the same method. She first introduces a principle or rule that each pupil is supposed to memorize so thoroughly that it can be repeated on any occasion without the slightest faltering. Then a concrete illustration or problem is presented and studied or solved in the light of the principle. More problems or examples are given until the children can recognize the abstract principle implicit in the concrete circumstance. . . . The principle itself is not questioned and is hardly discussed.

"Children," Wylie observes, "are not encouraged to formulate principles independently on the basis of an examination of concrete cases. They are given the impression that principles exist autono-mously . . . always there: immutable and constant. One can only learn to recognize . . . and accept them." French education is not Baconian; its motion is not inductive but deductive. English-speak-ing readers may recall a flicker of surprise upon discovering that "empirical" is not, for French theorists, a word of praise.

In approaching a subject, "the children are first presented with a general framework which they are asked to memorize. . . . An iso-lated fact is unimportant in itself. It assumes importance only when one recognizes [the] relationship . . . of the part to the whole." Applied to literature, this ensures that "no attempt is made to un-derstand or to appreciate the text which is presented to the class until it has been thoroughly . . . analyzed, . . . broken down into its logical divisions, and the author's purpose in each division . . . ex-plained. . . . Thus a child comes to believe that every fact, every phenomenon . . . is an integral part of a larger unit," intelligible "only if their proper relationship is recognized." "To approach problems with these assumptions is to approach them sensibly, rea-sonably, logically, and therefore . . . correctly."

French, of course, "is recognized as the most important subject taught. . . . Any other subject may be slighted or sacrificed in order to increase the time for drill" in the proper use of *la langue mater-nelle*. Wylie notes how hard it is for an Anglo-Saxon "to com-prehend how essential this language study is to the French." Yet this is what we must comprehend if we are to appreciate the sense of free air breathed at last that pervades Barthes's *écriture*. Though so diffi-cult a writing must severely, if regretfully, limit Equality and Frater-nity, Liberty's banner floats triumphant, celebrating freedom from the Author/Father/God, from his "predetermined messages," his tyrannical intentions; from the imposed interpretation that wallows in the evident; from consistency; from logic. To rebel against the Author is to challenge Authority in a way neither imaginable nor necessary in an educational culture which valorizes the wayward and the polyphonic; which begs reluctant students to question prin-ciples they would much rather accept; and where no author (just ask one) has authority over language or anything else.

Barthes opens *Le Plaisir du texte,* his celebration of the delight of reading, with imagining

> an individual . . . who would abolish within himself all barri-
> ers, all classes, all exclusions, not by syncretism but by simply
> getting rid of that old specter: *logical contradiction;* who would
> mix up all kinds of languages, even those thought incompati-
> ble; who would mutely endure all the accusations of il-
> logicality, of infidelity; who would remain impassive in the face
> of Socratic irony (which works by leading the other to the
> supreme opprobrium: *to contradict oneself*) and of legal ter-
> rorism (how much penal evidence is founded on a psychology
> of consistency!). That man would be in our society the lowest
> of the low; the courts, the school, the asylum, ordinary conver-
> sation would make him a stranger: who endures contradiction
> without shame?

Any reader whose pleasure has been taken largely in texts written in English will recognize an accent, even in translation. From Chaucer to Sterne to Salman Rushdie, the glory of English has been the mixing up of languages thought incompatible. And only in French could "illogicality" be associated with "infidelity." The translator of the American edition was forced to render *infidélité* as "in-congruity" lest he stymie the English-speaking reader in mid-sentence. *Infidelity?* To whom? To whom but the Author-God, with his "hierarchical sentence," his tyrannical meanings; with his hypostases of law, science, reason; with his fixation on logical consistency. God is *French*. That great rebel against the Rules, Victor Hugo, could still write with perfect naturalness in *Les Misérables* that "artistic peoples are logical peoples," since "the ideal is nothing but the culmination of logic, just as beauty is the apex of truth." No wonder Barthes complained, defending *Sur Racine,* that the *classes supér-ieures,* universalizing their own ideal of language, put forward "la 'logique' française" as "une logique absolue." The disclaiming quotes are, of course, Barthes's own.

Who endures contradiction without shame? Barthes's language vac-illates here, as he likes it to do, with its initial suggestion that it's the representatives of school, court, and asylum who can't bear to be contradicted by Barthes's "counter-hero," the reader-writer taking his free pleasure. But "shame" takes us back to that *abjection* which I have translated as "the lowest of the low," to the shame of a Frenchman who has been caught out in a logical contradiction. *C'n'est pas logique!* Even the superficial tourist has heard it, in the racket of a train station or screamed on a playground: the continuing battle cry of Cartesian clarity.

Who, then, can endure the shame of logical contradiction? English shouts its answer. Emerson can endure it ("A foolish consistency is the hobgoblin of little minds"); Whitman can endure it ("Do I contradict myself? Very well then I contradict myself"); Blake can endure it; the Metaphysicals can endure it. Shakespeare can endure it. Sir Philip Sidney, cosmopolite and aristocrat, his own French almost accentless, rejected a "mungrell Tragy-comedie" that mingled kings and clowns. Shakespeare went right ahead, befouling the purity of tragedy with comic gravediggers who spoke the people's prose. Voltaire hated the gravediggers, though there were a lot of things he admired in Shakespeare; you don't come across such barbarities in Racine.

French intellectuals, of course, do not read Emerson or Whitman; they read Poe, who is *plus logique*. And they generally read in French. Barthes refers to "The Purloined Letter" in Mallarmé's translation. Though he does quote Blake (a single Proverb of Hell) he quotes in French, and his reference is not to *The Marriage of Heaven and Hell* but to a book (in translation) by Norman O. Brown. He seems unaware of the literature of modernism in English; there is an extraordinary passage in *Plaisir* in which he describes the experience of sitting in a bar, amusing himself by enumerating its "whole stereophony" of "music, conversations, noises of chairs, of glasses," the "little voices" which dissolve the hierarchical sentence into the "non-sentence."

It is as if Joyce's "Sirens" had never been written—or translated. "Why," he asks, in his autobiography, "so little talent for foreign languages?" English at the lycée was "boring (*Queen Mab, David Copperfield, She Stoops to Conquer*)." The candor is characteristic and disarming; still, so comfortable an admission is unexpected from someone who feels so intensely the difference between one word and another, and emphasizes the distinction between denotation and connotation as if he had discovered it. Although he excoriated the "narcissisme linguistique" of the guardians of the "idiome sacré," French is for him "nothing more or less than the umbilical language." It is in French he writes, in French he reads (with occasional hints of German and Italian); it is to the readers and writers of *la langue maternelle* that he addresses his *écriture*.

So it is curious that it is not in France that his work has acquired its maximum power. There the liberation of the text from the structures of decorum, of consistency, of logic could be felt as an exhilarating duty. Let its false and deceptive unity dissolve, its meanings float free, in "a paradise of words" a "happy Babel" in which "one may hear the grain of the gullet, the patina of consonants, the voluptuousness of vowels," and exult in the amorous perversity (his word) of an *écriture* that "granulates, . . . crackles, . . . caresses, . . . grates, . . . cuts," and at last, joyously, "*comes*." But how perverse is that perversity for readers whose experience of literature has been formed by the happy Babel of Chaucer, of Shakespeare, of Carroll and Lear and Joyce? What needs exploring is why these quintessentially French linguistic preoccupations have found so warm a welcome in an educational culture so different from, even antithetic to, that of France.

After all, it's been fifty years and more that English and American criticism has been preoccupied with language; with metaphors and metaphorical systems (Caroline Spurgeon got us started in 1930); with the referentiality of poetic statement (I. A. Richards and T. S. Eliot in the 1920s); with the layered suggestiveness that makes words rejoice as they fend off all attempts at paraphrase. French students learn that their greatest playwright wrote the speeches out in prose to cast into alexandrines; in classical French "no word," wrote Barthes in *Writing Degree Zero*, "has a density by itself." Here few students who undergo Introduction to Literature escape an exercise expressly designed to raise their consciousness of verbal densities. The distinction between denotation and connotation has been a staple of freshman writing texts ever since this year's retirees can remember. The inseparability of content and form is a truism: as Cleanth Brooks wrote in 1938, in words destined to inform introductory literature courses in colleges, then high schools, all over America, "the experience that [the poet] 'communicates' is itself created by the organization of the symbols he uses," so that "the total poem is therefore the communication, and indistinguishable from it." The sentence, including its suspicion of communication, could be Barthes's own. As he would put it twenty-one years later, with characteristic abstraction, "signification [is] the union of what signifies and what is signified . . . neither form nor content, but the proceedings between them."

Barthes's Author-God emitted "messages" in 1968: Brooks and Warren had warned American teenagers to stop hunting them thirty years before. Barthes put the Author's intentionality in question; "the intentional fallacy" hit American criticism in 1946. Did New Critics direct us away from the poet to The Poem Itself? In 1963, so did Barthes, rejecting traditional criticism's interest in "coordinating the details of a work with the details of a life" in favor of an "immanent analysis" functioning "in a realm purely internal to the work," "a criticism which establishes itself within the work and posits its relation to the world only after having entirely described it from within."

Nor could it have surprised an English-speaker to have read that "the Word in poetry can never be untrue," shining as it does "with an infinite freedom," "preparing to radiate toward innumerable and uncertain connections." For how many years have we been telling each other that poetic language is inexhaustible? In French, however, ambiguity is not a positive value: my *Larousse de poche* defines it as "a defect of that which is equivocal." We may cheer, then, as Barthes in 1963 converts defect to virtue and tells the French establishment that "each time we write ambiguously enough to suspend meaning . . . writing releases a question . . . gives the world an energy . . . permits us to breathe." Indeed, breathing wasn't all that easy; Barthes would soon have to defend against professional attack his "right" (imagine it!) to read in Racine's "literal discourse" "other senses which [he was still stepping gingerly] do not contradict it." But though his valorization of ambiguity might be news to the French Academy, the American academy had started amusing itself with seven types of ambiguity in 1930. Thrilling as it is to read of language as "an immense halo of implications" making "knowledge

festive" with words "flung out as projections, explosions, vibra-
tions, devices, flavors," readers whose language long before
Hopkins embraced "all things counter, original, spare, strange,"
must take it as confirmation rather than battle cry.

Even deconstruction has a familiar ring. Excise the word *personal* from the following; guess the writer; guess the date: "That radical mode of romantic polysemism in which the latent personal significance of a narrative poem is found not merely to underlie, but to
contradict and cancel the surface intention." In 1966, confronting
Picard, Barthes was still leery of contradiction. In 1953, M. H.
Abrams was as much at home with it as Blake had been in 1790.

Nor can Barthes's amorous embrace of the concrete, of the
physical object seem radical, though it may surprise us as we per-
severe through aridities of abstraction which, while less extensive
than those in Foucault and Derrida, are equally uninviting to the
Anglo-American explorer. Empiricism informs English-speaking
style as well as English-speaking epistemology. Freshman composition texts are as one in discouraging abstraction and enjoining specificity; like McGuffey before them, they do their best to get American
students, in Wylie's words, "to formulate principles independently
on the basis of an examination of concrete cases." Helen Vendler's
examples of "compositional subjects of the sort set for French students—'Arrogance,' 'Ease,' 'Coincidence'"—would appear, if at all,
only to illustrate the kind of subject to avoid. Barthes, too, believes
in concreteness. Outraged when Picard accuses him of "an inhuman
abstraction," he insists that "the works of *la nouvelle critique* are very
rarely abstract, because they treat of substances and objects." Revers-
ing the deductive method taught the French pupil, he "starts," he
says "from a sensuous object, and then hopes to meet in his work
with the possibility of finding an *abstraction* for it" (italics his). He
complains of the classic taste that considers objects "trivial," in-
congruous when introduced "into a rational discourse"; he commits
himself to the object in the full physicality he likes to call erotic; his
"body," he says, "cannot accommodate itself to *generality*, the generality that is in language." The language is a bit warm for a freshman
text, but the message (you should excuse the expression) is wholly
familiar.

American critics, intellectual historians, and pedagogues, how-
ever, are not among the prior traces that constitute the text called
Roland Barthes, which is entirely truthful in saying in 1963 ("What
Is Criticism?") that French criticism "owes little or nothing to An-
glo-American criticism." (The Anglo-American texts Barthes does
refer to address very different preoccupations: Bruno Bettelheim,
D. W. Winnicott, Alan Watts, Norman O. Brown.) The relation of
La Nouvelle Critique to The New Criticism is *post,* not *propter.*

What, then, explains our fascination? There is, of course, a peculiar pleasure in reencountering one's own *idées reçues,* especially
when expressed with an elegant difficulty that lends them the dark
glow of revelation. From New to Nouvelle was an easy transition, as
the case of Hillis Miller shows. The transatlantic breezes started
blowing just as the New began to seem old hat. Barthes was affirm-
ing, with supremely French intelligence, the pieties of English 101.

But of course there's more to it. In retrospect, the New Critics
seem surprisingly modest. They might distrust "messages," but they
were comfortable enough with meanings. They left epistemology
alone; they had no aspirations to philosophy or psychology. Though
they discouraged biographical approaches, though they directed
attention from poet to speaker and novelist to narrator, though they
might (some of them) bracket authorial intentions, they didn't meddle with the idea of the self. But if authorial selves are (in the words
of Vincent Leitch) "fabrications . . . interpretations . . . effects of
language, not causes," why should our own selves be any different?
As Frank Lentricchia puts it, "the self is an intersubjective construct
formed by cultural systems over which the individual person has no
control." A heady idea, the dissolution of the self; if personal responsibility dissolves along with it, it's a well-known revolutionary
maxim that you can't make an omelet without breaking eggs.

Because there *is* more to it than old wine in new bottles. There is
true exhilaration in the dissolving of certainties, the breaking of
tablets. "Damn braces: bless relaxes," said Blake, in the book he
began in 1789. The New Critics had scarcely been revolutionaries,
literary or philosophical, least of all political. Yet the familiarity of
their ideas could pave the way to the Paris of '68. Though the
shadow of the Author-God did not reach across the sea, though the

guardians and structures of English possessed minimal power either
to preserve or coerce, though these were French texts speaking to
the French, still they had their message for American intellectuals
living in a country whose imperial impositions were increasingly
difficult to ignore or justify. They aimed at the Author, but their
target was Power. We could imagine with them a grand international democracy of power-free language—or if that were an impossible dream, we could at least proclaim our awareness of the invisibly
tyrannical habits of our discourse. In the disillusioned seventies and
the shameful eighties, there were new, progressive uses for our old
New Critical techniques. They could be applied to any writing.
"Literature" was only a category, as artificial as any of those frozen
seventeenth-century genres. Guilt of nationality, class, and gender
could revivify a tired scrutiny. For there is a politics of language.
Orwell had told us that in 1946, in his blunt, concrete, English way;
thirty years later, we could examine the matter with new French
subtlety.

And somewhere in that last paragraph irony gives way to appreciation. Barthes would have recognized the movement: of reversal,
of the statement no sooner made than put in question, of contradiction not merely acknowledged but embraced. One may—I do—
question the cost-free radicalism, so much easier than actual political engagement, of our American warriors of theory, called to no
undertaking more heroic than the reading of these admittedly ex-
igent texts and the acquisition of a *parole* which now, in universities
all over the country, itself exerts the power to require, insist, and
exclude. For academics who have joined the club, the return of
grand theory has brought not risk but a bonanza of renewal, liberating them into a hermeneutic paradise of publication where the professional reader (not the hapless freshman, who retains the privilege
of getting things wrong) is Adam, forever encountering beasts that
invite him to name them anew. Critical theory, I'm told, is a game;
you don't have to play it unless you enjoy it. But power games are
rarely optional. Barthes, like Foucault, like Derrida, had something
more radical in mind than the substitution of one linguistic tyranny
for another.

For they were French. A true radicalism goes to the root; theirs

attacked the root assumptions of an unusually restrictive socio-po-
litico-linguistic culture. There was a heroism in their assault on
clarté, their determination to validate a darkness all the richer by
contrast with that vaunted *éclaircissement,* to honor the category of
what Foucault called "the unthought." It's even explicable, though it
would have surprised, then appalled Orwell, that stylistic obscurity
should join the other insignia of liberation, the *étandards sanglants*
of the good fight they were fighting.

Their status as revolutionaries was helped, of course, by the
unique history of the French seventeenth century, which permit-
ted such a ready association of oppressive structures of literature
with oppressive structures of economics and of class. A phrase like
Barthes's "the entire classical capitalist period" won't work in England or America, neither of which has a classical tradition you
could put in your eye. In France it is at least intelligible. With "capitalist" functioning as negative shorthand in literature as well as economics, Barthes could claim a radicalism just as genuine as Sartre's,
and a lot more subtle. Though Susan Sontag admires Barthes, she
calls him a dandy. That's not wholly fair. When he rejects political
engagement for a different responsibility, the responsibility to his
umbilical language, it is more than mere aestheticism. The radicalism was genuine, the status as outsider absolutely real. In his
fragmentary autobiography, Barthes defines himself as his culture
had defined him: religiously, sexually, and academically marginal.
"Who does not feel how *natural* it is, in France, to be Catholic,
married, and properly accredited with the right degrees?" He wasn't,
he tells us, even right-handed. We should not forget that the game
American insiders now play was originally an enterprise of risk.

Barthes meant it about power. His essays were *essais* in Montaigne's original sense, tentative, trials of ideas. In his last decade
even these came to seem too domineering, too insistently coherent,
too "classical"; better to relax, to group paragraphs under topic
headings, in alphabetical order, open to the aleatory air. Thus *The
Pleasure of the Text, Roland Barthes by Roland Barthes, A Lover's
Discourse. Aleatory* was a favorite word. Perhaps, to do him justice,
that's the way this essay should end, miming his progress from the
impersonal to the personal, from the essay's assertive form—thesis,

argument, conclusion—to something more wavering, more faithful to the moods of thought, its tenuous demands, how it's always escaping, from reader, from writer, yet can't escape its paradoxical consistency, its message, its loyalty to the values of a lifetime. The older you get, the more everything you write and do connects—yes, into a self. What Keats, who didn't get old, called soul-making. So:

Abstraction: How could he escape it? And though we may grumble for a more fraternal ratio of specific to general, we had better appreciate it. Abstraction, analysis, is just so much *harder* than concrete specificity, not just to read but to do. Anybody can learn to be specific, and most of our freshmen will. But try setting them to write on Arrogance, Coincidence, or Ease. To discuss an abstraction and produce anything but truisms you have to really think. In *A Lover's Discourse* Barthes produces eight pages (in ten short takes) of analysis of the "holophrase" I-love-you. Here's just a bit of it:

> *I-love-you* is active. It affirms itself as force—against . . . the thousand forces of the world, which are, all of them, disparaging forces (science, *doxa,* reality, reason, etc.). Or again: against language. Just as the *amen* is at the limit of language, without collusion with its system . . . so the proffering of love (*I-love-you*) stands at the limit of syntax, welcomes tautology (*I-love-you* means *I-love-you*), rejects the servility of the Sentence . . . is not a sign, but plays against the signs.

No wonder we're impressed. As Dr. Faustus said, "Sweet Analytics, 'tis thou hast ravish'd me." As well they might. But they don't always. "The actantial model" may "stand the test of a large number of narratives," but it's hard to keep our attention on "the regulated transformations (replacements, confusions, duplications, substitutions) . . . of an actantial typology" through page after page when the ratio of generalization to example is about 50 to 1.

Assertion: How nicely RB tries to avoid it, sure that it can't be done. "The work is always dogmatic"; the author's (his word) "silences, his regrets, his naïvetés, his scruples, his fears, everything that would make the work fraternal—none of this can pass into the written object." The sentence is by nature assertive; "writing *de-clares;* "there is no such thing as a generous language." Perhaps not. But that's what he tried for.

Author: In *RB by RB,* RB reproduces without comment a secondary-school exam question on a passage he had written twenty-four years and hundreds of thousands of words ago. He knows, who better, that he has become the Author. Style, he wrote then, is "a way of speaking, a lexicon . . . born of the body and the past of the writer . . . an autarchic language . . . its depths in the personal and secret mythology of the author." Do I contradict myself? Very well, I contain multitudes.

Boredom: has an entry to itself in *The Pleasure of the Text,* pervades his writing about literature/life. Who, he asks, reads a classic text without skipping? The word *nausea,* too, recurs, as in this from *S/Z:* "The referential codes have a kind of emetic virtue, they bring on nausea by the boredom, conformism, and disgust that establishes them." Master of a tradition that bores him, he sticks with it; he doesn't go foraging abroad, or open a backward window on Villon or Rabelais. What are you going to *do* with a story like "Sarrasine"? Forget it, we might say, but Barthes is *French;* the myth of the great French language is *his* myth, however he demythicizes; Balzac is *his* Author. Skipping is one solution; another is to read into, read around, read under—having already dissolved the Author, so the question of whether to credit him with all these new pluralizing riches needn't arise. Here's a technique that can work with any text one's read so many times one can no longer imagine what it might be to encounter it, freshly. RB liberated, alas, not so much the reader as the professor.

Bourgeois: show them no mercy. Functions, like "capitalist," as a simple pejorative. Nobody is nicer, more generous than RB, yet he depersonalizes with a word. For him, Marx joins with Flaubert to evoke in mid-twentieth century M. Homais and the boredom of Yonville. The domain of the bourgeois is the domain of the "self-evident," of the "violence" of unexamined conventions, of those who are "content to utter *what is self-evident, what follows of itself:* the 'natural' is, in short, *the ultimate outrage.*" Emphasis, of course, his.

Though he rejected stereotypes, including those of the left, he held on to this one.

Dilettante: what he was. In its fine, original sense. He did read skippingly, skim over the flowers, take what he could use, leave it behind when it came to bore him, committed not to philosophy but to pleasure. Unlike ourselves, who now take him so seriously.

Fragments: RB on himself, in his not very impersonal third-person: "His first, or nearly first text (1942) consists of fragments, . . . 'because incoherence is preferable to a distorting order.' Since then . . . he has never stopped writing in brief bursts. . . ." As in "Fragments d'un discours amoureux," which precisely does not equal "A lover's discourse."

Freedom: the primary, pervasive value. From the self-evident, from the classic, from the bourgeois, from what he called the *Doxa;* from Nature which is not nature but nurture; from the "binary prison" of conventional sexuality; text and sexuality released together. Released from what? Ah, there's the rub. "From meaning." To "achieve a state of infinite expansion." In a text of enjoyment, of *jouissance,* a text which "comes."

Grammar: Abstract by its very nature, who in English can write like this about it?

> Obsolete in spoken French, the preterite, which is the cornerstone of Narration, always signifies the presence of Art. . . . Its function is no longer that of a tense [but] to reduce reality to a point of time, and to abstract, from the depth of a multiplicity of experiences, a pure verbal act. . . . It presupposes a world which is constructed, elaborated, self-sufficient, reduced to significant lines, and not one which has been sent sprawling before us, for us to take or leave. Behind the preterite there always lurks a demiurge, a God, or a reciter.

Can you get any more intelligent than this?

Logic: The mind can't entertain two ideas at once, wrote Descartes, because the pineal gland can't be in two places at the same time. *C'n'est pas logique.* Boileau's Twelfth Satire equated ambiguity and equivocation long before Larousse. Reason was the Goddess the Revolution installed in Notre Dame. In the French words of the *Internationale,* it's Reason that announces the final conflict. It's Justice in the English version. Experiential versus cognitive, empirical versus rational.

Neologism: Professor Picard accused him of jargon. He loved neologisms: they too were insignia of liberty. Against *Doxa,* paradox; against stereotypes, "novation": escape from the limits of authorized French. Playing with roots. With Greek ("holophrase," "semiophysis," "semioclasty"). The petty bourgeois can't do it; their Larousse, unlike English dictionaries, gives no derivations. You have to go to Littré, Robert; derivations are the privilege of the educated, the signifiers of (don't say it) power.

Object: He believes in it, repudiates abstraction. Yet *il n'y a pas de hors-texte.* There being no outside to the text, the object is hard to get at. The text is our universe, and we live inside it like the Shropshire Lad, in a world we never made. But what for Derrida is a philosophical position is for Barthes the actuality of experience. He really does live in a universe of signs. It's not surprising that he wants us to join him there; language, he says somewhere, was his Nature. He likes to quote vivid descriptions; it's the physicality of objects that he admires in Michelet. Yet his own language rarely evokes direct physical experience. The scarf the lover of *A Lover's Discourse* selects for his beloved is merely a sign; we are not told its texture or color. What RB describes, so well that we examine them as never before, are not objects but texts, written but also visual, stills from *Ivan the Terrible,* the plates of the *Grande Encyclopédie:* signifying phrases of the world's language. Texts were for him Nature, took the place of the conventional Nature which excluded him and which he repudiated as one more of the masks of *clarté.* Language he can describe incomparably, the nuance of its structures, the susurrus of its words. It is the rustle of language that he hears, not the rustle of Julia's silks, or anybody else's. Vendler doubts, in the course of her fine appreciation, that he was interested enough in people to write the novel he intended; and indeed, even in the clearly personal *A Lover's Discourse* the beloved X seems as abstract as his designation. Through abstraction the brilliant intelligence can at once confess its pain and hold it at an ironic distance. So the examples are far more often taken from literature than from life: Proust, Goethe. When we do get a signifying object, the blue coat and yellow vest belong to Werther.

Obscurity: RB by RB: "He realizes then how obscure such statements, clear as they are to him, must be for many others." Language obscure enough, elliptical enough, must in its "dreadful freedom" sacrifice fraternity and equality to liberty. The reader is continually being tested: are you intelligent enough? Industrious enough? Not what RB envisaged in 1963 when he rejected an academic ideology "articulated around a technique difficult enough to constitute an instrument of selection," in favor of an "immanent criticism" that required, "in the work's presence, only a power of astonishment." Obscurity becomes protective clothing, thick enough, all too often, to convert what might otherwise be productive challenge into dismissible peevishness: that wasn't Barthes's intention, who claimed, growing older, "no power, a little knowledge, a little wisdom, and as much flavor as possible." The author's work escapes him; he told us that. And the academy does not deal in astonishment; he told us that too.

Plural: Central to his lexicon, the word evokes the consistency of a life. Invoking *La Déesse Homosexualité* ("all she permits to say, to do, to understand, to know"), he would speak of "cruising," in reading too. That too was liberty.

Power: Why so much when he claimed none? The young thrill, perhaps, of putting everything at risk, safe in the suspicion that everything deconstructed will come together again through pure bourgeois inertia?

Received ideas: He had his own. Marxism afforded them; so did psychoanalysis. *Self-evident,* they *followed of themselves.*

Responsibility: "What we can ask of a writer is that he be responsible"—but not for his opinions, and not to truth, to which he "loses all claim." Yet Barthes continues: a writer's "true responsibility" is to "literature . . . as a Mosaic glance at the Promised Land of the real." For him, as for Orwell, writing was an ethical enterprise. But where Orwell warred against the abstraction that obfuscates the appalling cruelty of the actualities it is our duty to see feelingly, Barthes felt the characteristic French responsibility, not first to the real, but to language. Still, though you can desire the escape from meaning, try for it, you can't accomplish it. Language foils you, stubbornly referential. The reader foils you, always looking for a meaning, not really satisfied to think he's free to find his own, wanting at least to approximate yours. And saying the same thing over a lifetime's *écriture*, you foil yourself. You thought it was true, and necessary to be said. Which brings us back to responsibility— the old-fashioned kind.

Truth: "Literature has an effect of truth much more violent for me than that of religion." A sentence from his journal, his last published work; he had been reading of the death of old Prince Bolkonsky in *War and Peace* while his own mother was dying. Cagey still: an *effect*. Yet somehow *truth* made its way into the sentence. When push comes to shove, it's the Promised Land that seems real.

(Hand) Writing: Introducing *RB by RB:* "All this must be considered as if spoken by a character in a novel." Cagey again; hide and seek, RB's discreet charm. Yet he arranged for the words to appear not in print but in his own fine rapid cursive, most personal of signatures. On another page, notes made in bed show handwriting loosened but still his own. Of course he didn't type.

Zed: He called it "the letter of deviance" and made it his own. First the straight line of assertion, then the zigzag of "reversal, contradiction, reactive energy"; *but, on the other hand, yet.* In the end of *Mythologies,* for instance: one deciphers the bourgeois myth of "good French wine"—but thereby regretfully "cut[s] oneself off from those who are . . . warmed" by what is in fact good, condemned, however progressive one's politics, to a sociality one's intelligence renders merely theoretical. So too the Author zigzags back in *The Pleasure of the Text;* though "as an institution" he's dead, yet "lost in the midst of the text (not *behind* it, like a god from the machine) there's always the other, the author." For (emphasis again his) "*I desire* the author"—"*d'une certaine façon.*"

When the Author died in France in 1968 it seemed a local matter. But as the report spread and discipline after discipline faced the demands of grand theory, the game turns serious. The insouciant critic gives way to the sober philosopher; people get nervous. In 1989 the lead article in the journal of the American Historical Association called "authorial presence" a "dream"; invoked Barthes, and after him Foucault and Derrida; worried whether, the author absent, intellectual history could be written at all. The simplicity of the answer may perhaps startle; the writer confessed that "it is beginning to look as if *belief* in the author may be our best response" (italics his). "Writers from a variety of disciplines are now suggesting that, if we hope to make sense of any text, we must first attribute to it an author." He had to read an awful lot to get to that point; my grandmother called it going round your elbow to get to your thumb. Perhaps, after the years in the wilderness, the professors are again turning their eyes toward the Promised Land, rejoining the Common Reader, to whose common sense Dr. Johnson trusted because it was "uncorrupted with literary prejudice," "the refinements of subtilty," or "the dogmatism of learning."

"Of all the intellectual notables who have emerged since World War II in France," writes Susan Sontag, "Roland Barthes is the one whose work I am most certain will endure." If so, it is because he is the one whose writing can be read, at least intermittently, for pleasure. Pleasure of the text and pleasure of the author, no god and no authority, but a human being to be enjoyed, for his commitment to freedom, to multiplicity, and to enjoyment, for his intelligence, and for the generosity of his intentions. He desired the author. So do we.

From *The Hudson Review*, Autumn 1990.

Afterword: Mortal Stakes

Criticism and teaching: if that's the subject and this is the space,* there's no room to argue principles. Representation, expression; Mirror or Lamp, Mirror *and* Lamp; truth, reality, "truth," "reality"—I can, shall we say, bracket them in good conscience. Instead, three anecdotes. I like anecdotes better than dialectic anyway— anecdote, story, myth; that's why I teach literature and not philosophy. In the *Phaedo,* Plato makes Socrates at last stop arguing the soul's immortality and tell a story instead, one of his three great myths of where the soul goes after death. It's easy to forget the arguments, especially since they're not very good ones (though they may be the best there are); it is the myth that speaks, and the life story that surrounds it, for Socrates tells it as he is about to die. My stories are anecdotes, however, not myths or parables. I was never good at making things up; that's why I teach literature and don't write fiction. These are teachers' anecdotes, of things that happened. Subject to interpretation, of course; still, they did happen this way. They concern three students, two smart ones and a dumb one.

Some years ago I had in my introductory lit course a bright-eyed and responsive freshman, the kind you're grateful for because as you say things and read aloud and ask questions, you can tell by his expression he's *there.* And he stayed there, over the years; though he didn't take any more of my courses, he was the type who spent a lot of time in teachers' offices, mine included, worrying about what he was reading, about himself, about his particular problem (how much of a Jew he was or ought to be), about the common undergraduate problem (what he should do with his life). After a while he

---

*The editor, getting together an issue on directions in literary criticism and teaching, had specified both subject and length: one thousand words.

229

was reading Derrida, as yet only a name to me. I was beginning to know that it was a name of power, though, so I kept my ears open to see what I could learn. One phrase entered my mind word for word, engraved there by his intensity and excitement: "The exhilaration of nihilism." I think it must have been his own; I have never seen it in Derrida.

He graduated. Six months later, I got a call: he was just back from Israel, he hadn't even been home yet, there were people he wanted to talk to, could he have a bed? He arrived at the door weighed down with two huge grips, though his blue jeans suggested the simple backpack of the international student. It wasn't until I asked him to dinner that I learned what was in them: food. He could no longer eat mine. And with all his old passion, he told me that he was in a yeshiva studying Torah; all his life wouldn't be enough for it. There was a prayer shawl in the grip too, and phylacteries; he prayed four times a day. I couldn't not ask it: "What about the exhilaration of nihilism?" "Oh," he said, "you can't *live* by that."

The second anecdote I'll tell in the present tense, because it just happened. I have before me an undergraduate thesis. The student argues that *Ulysses* wrote itself, that the Circe episode (on which he has produced fifty pages) is an insoluble puzzle, the identity of the "play master" behind it "an unplumbable mystery"; that Circe "is simply playing games with itself," a set of frisky signifiers in endless, open free play. Although the game is "unwinnable," not to worry. Gleefully, in full *jouissance,* he gives the "positive side": "the game can go on forever."

The thesis is dazzling; I love reading it. So I can hardly credit what I gradually perceive, that this student's brilliance has enabled him to overlook the obvious: that there are occurrences in Circe as well as dreams, that both are crafted to contribute to our understanding of the characters and their story, that a man named James Joyce is visible behind the play of the text, that the play is (Frost's line) play for mortal stakes.

And so I return to that third student. He is often in my mind, though it is twenty-five years since I taught him and I have heard nothing of him since—a country boy not at all smart, who read our

Great Books slowly and with difficulty, sat quiet in the back row, did the best he could, and just once asked a question. "We've read what Homer says about the afterlife, and what Plato says, and now we're reading what Dante says, and they're all different. Mrs. Park. *Which of them is true?*"

I could hear the smart kids rustle, and see their ironic smiles. My own was about to join them, but I stopped it in time. I might not have the answer, but he certainly had the question. The stakes are mortal, or if they are not, our work and our play, however absorbing, are vain. Vain in its root meaning. Empty.

I teach for that student, for inside every smart student there is, fortunately, a dumb one waiting to be liberated. As Dostoevsky wrote, most people are "much more naive and simplehearted than we suppose. And we ourselves are too."

From the *Voice Literary Supplement,* October 1988.